WOMEN'S HUMAN RIGHTS IN INDIA

This book focusses on women's human rights in India. Drawing on case studies, it provides a clear overview of the key sources on gender and rights in the country. Further, it contextualises women's rights at the critical intersection of caste, religion and class, and analyses barriers to the realization of women's human rights in practice. It also develops strategies for moving forward towards greater recognition, protection, promotion and fulfilment of women's human rights in India.

Drawing on critical pedagogical tools to analyse groundbreaking court cases, this book will be a key text in human rights studies. It will be indispensable to students, scholars and researchers of gender studies, sociology, law and human rights.

Christine Forster is Associate Professor in Law, University of New South Wales, Australia, where she teaches torts, health and medical law and women's human rights. Her areas of research include women's human rights, *CEDAW*, gender equality laws and violence against women (particularly in the Asia Pacific).

Jaya Sagade is Director of the Women's Studies Centre at ILS Law College, Pune, where she was the vice-principal and taught Women and the Law and Family Law for 32 years. Her areas of research are violence against women, gender equality, women's human rights and *CEDAW*. She has a range of publications in these areas.

WOMEN'S HUMAN RIGHTS IN INDIA

Christine Forster and Jaya Sagade

Routledge
Taylor & Francis Group
LONDON AND NEW YORK

First published 2020
by Routledge
2 Park Square, Milton Park, Abingdon, Oxon OX14 4RN

and by Routledge
52 Vanderbilt Avenue, New York, NY 10017

Routledge is an imprint of the Taylor & Francis Group, an informa business

British Library Cataloguing-in-Publication Data
A catalogue record for this book is available from the British Library

Library of Congress Cataloging-in-Publication Data
Names: Forster, Christine, author. | Sagade, Jaya, author.
Title: Women's human rights in India / Christine Forster and Jaya Sagade.
Description: Abingdon, Oxon ; New York, NY : Routledge, 2020. | Includes bibliographical references and index.
Identifiers: LCCN 2019019131
Subjects: LCSH: Women's rights—India. | Human rights—India. | Women—Legal status, laws, etc.—India.
Classification: LCC HQ1236.5.I4 F67 2020 | DDC 305.420954—dc23
LC record available at https://lccn.loc.gov/2019019131

ISBN: 978-1-138-06799-8 (hbk)
ISBN: 978-0-367-33497-0 (pbk)
ISBN: 978-0-429-32020-0 (ebk)

Typeset in Bembo
by Apex CoVantage, LLC

MIX
Paper from responsible sources
FSC™ C013985
FSC
www.fsc.org

Printed in the United Kingdom
by Henry Ling Limited

CONTENTS

BOXES

FOREWORD

Women in India, rural and urban, of all castes, classes and religions, face inequality, marginalisation and subordination throughout their life-cycle. It begins before conception with the practice of preconception selection, where prospective parents preselect chromosomes to ensure a boy child. It continues after conception with sex-selection practices that determine the sex of the foetus for the purpose of aborting female foetuses. During pregnancy and birthing, many women are not provided with adequate maternity facilities and services and suffer death or serious morbidity issues and other harms in childbirth. (After birth, foeticide [where female children are killed in favour of sons] is still widespread.) The girl child many times experiences discrimination in the provision of healthcare, access to education and basic nutrition and also in social issues. Within marriage (and live-in relationships), domestic and family violence (including dowry violence) are widespread. At educational facilities and at places of employment, she may be a victim of sexual harassment and earns less than men. In the public sphere, she is under-represented at all levels of decision-making. As a female senior citizen, she experiences neglect and abuse.

Women's human rights principles and theories can, however, assist us to advance women's rights in India by providing standards through which to examine domestic legal frameworks from a critical, feminist standpoint. Writing on women's experiences in India has a long and rich history and is rapidly expanding. This book contributes to that body of work. It represents the first comprehensive overview of women's human rights in India approached primarily through the lens of the *Convention on the Elimination of All Forms of Discrimination against Women* 1979, an international human rights convention focussing on women's rights, acceded to by India in 1983. I think it is a unique feature of the book.

The book introduces the reader to women's human rights principles and theories in simple, understandable language. It links women's human rights theories with transformative practice; provides a valuable resource for those working, teaching and researching within and outside the legal discipline and uses rich examples from many areas of women's lives to illustrate how theory and women's human rights principles can foster and support positive change.

The book will develop skills of analysis critique in the reader and equip the reader to use the law as a tool of change, rather than a mechanism of subordination, and stimulate the reader to evaluate the international human rights framework and its applicability to the Indian context and the specific subcultures within Indian society in all areas of women's lives. It will be invaluable to academics, students, the judiciary, non-government organisations, policy-makers and the regular citizen.

Thus, the authors are successful in placing sufficient material before the readers which will give different insight, develop vision and lead attitudinal change in them.

Best wishes,

16-4-2019

Justice Mridula Bhatkar
Bombay High Court

ACKNOWLEDGEMENTS

We would like to acknowledge and thank our three research assistants, who provided invaluable and tireless contributions at various stages of the production of this book. Justin Forster, who conducted a thorough literature review on women's human rights at the start of the project; Ruby Langton-Batty who gathered and organised a vast array of cases, academic articles and reports and Phoebe Port, who, in the final stages of the manuscript, read, footnoted and made numerous, thoughtful and novel suggestions.

We would also like to thank our institutions, the ILS Law College, Pune, India, and the Law Faculty at the University of New South Wales, Sydney, Australia, for their support during the process of writing this book.

1

INTRODUCTION

Background context

This book focusses on women's human rights in India. In particular, the book focusses on human rights in significant areas of women's lives, including a right to equality and non-discrimination, a right to a life free from violence, a right to equality in marriage and family relations, a right to equal political representation and participation and a right to economic empowerment. Women face discrimination and inequality in the enjoyment of each of these rights.

The book represents the first comprehensive overview of women's human rights in India approached primarily through the lens of the *Convention on the Elimination of All Forms of Discrimination against Women* 1979 (*CEDAW*).[1] *CEDAW*, adopted in 1979 and acceded to by India in 1983, is an international human rights convention focussing on women's rights. The full and equal participation of women in political, civil, economic, social and cultural life at the national, regional and international levels and the eradication of all forms of discrimination on the grounds of sex and gender are priority objectives of the women's human rights framework.

Indeed, *CEDAW* establishes a woman's human rights framework that can be utilised to define, analyse and articulate women's experiences of violence, subordination, discrimination and marginality. It influences domestic legal systems by providing a standard for courts to use in judicial decision-making in cases that involve women's rights, it creates a benchmark for government and civil society to critique and assess domestic laws and legislative amendments, it can be utilised as a tool for gender advocates to argue for the strengthening of local laws and for the introduction of gender equality mechanisms and initiatives and provides a framework for government and civil society to run public-awareness campaigns.[2] It provides a means for making the state accountable for violations of its international obligation to respect and fulfil women's human rights.[3] Finally, it provides a forum (at both the international and national levels) to discuss women's human rights issues.[4] As such, *CEDAW* has become an increasingly important normative framework in India.[5]

The Indian women's movement has a long and rich herstory, beginning with linkages to the social reform movements of the nineteenth century and the political challenge to British colonialism in the twentieth century.[6] Sarala Devi for example, born in 1872, was a political leader in the Freedom Struggle Movement and the leader of the Anti-British Movement.[7] She founded the first woman's organisation in India, known as *Bharat Stree Mahamandal* in Allahabad in 1910. The main goal of *Bharat Stree Mahamandal* was to promote and improve female education by bringing together all Indian women.[8] Membership was obtained through an entry fee of one rupee and was open to all women, regardless of caste, race or class.[9] The beginnings of the contemporary Indian women's movement can be traced to the early 1970s, when women were active in radical protests against the Indian state.[10] The influence of the international human rights framework on that movement as it emerged, particularly *CEDAW*, is evident in its tactical use by women's organisations and in the responses and actions of the state to their demands for law reform.[11] Indeed, significant law reform changes were achieved in the 1980s, including criminalising dowry deaths, reform of discriminatory citizenship provisions and amendments to some of the personal laws.[12] From the 1990s through to 2019, the women's movement has grown, expanded and diversified. It comprises numerous groups and organisations, which vary in location, form and type. They are urban, rural, small, large, informal, formal, localized, national, internationally affiliated and combinations of all these forms.[13] Debates within the women's movement have focussed on reservations for women in state legislatures and the Union Parliament, the personal laws, women's economic empowerment, reproductive and sexual rights including alternate sexualities and violence against women.[14]

The women's movement's engagement with international human rights law occurs at multiple levels. As petitioners, women are challenging the legal system to recognise their rights by appealing to norms of equality and non-discrimination in both international and national law.[15] At the level of the judiciary, the Supreme Court of India now explicitly incorporates the rules and principles of *CEDAW* where gaps exist in national legislation.[16] At the law-making level, the legislature has begun to initiate laws that are consistent with women's human rights.[17] Despite such promising developments, the material reality of women's lives in India does not reflect significant improvement, nor has the gap between formal rights and the actual status of women been narrowed sufficiently as a result of the legalisation of women's human rights.[18]

The birth of a girl in India, according to a popular Hindu saying, is like the arrival of Lakshmi, the four-armed goddess of wealth, often depicted holding lotus flowers and an overflowing pot of gold.[19] However, discrimination against women in India occurs throughout her life-cycle in a range of forms, in every aspect of her life in both public and private spheres.[20] Indeed, in 2018 India ranked a dismal 108 overall out of countries in the Global Gender Gap Report (Report) produced by the World Economic Forum.[21] The Report ranks 144 countries on the progress they have made towards gender parity in four areas – health, education, economics and politics.

India ranked 142 for economic participation and opportunities. The Report noted a number of marked inequalities between women and men. For example, 66 percent of women's work is unpaid, compared to 12 percent of men's; only 1.8 percent of women are employed in skilled work, compared to 8.1 percent of men and only 42.6 percent of women have a bank account, compared to 62.5 percent of men.[22] In addition, the Report noted a significant gender gap among legislators, senior officials and managers, as well as professional and technical workers. In other economic figures, on average women earn 25 percent of what men earn,[23] women do 65 percent of the daily unpaid work[24] and the employment of women in the workforce has declined from 36 percent employed in 2005–2006 to 24 percent in 2015–2016.[25]

On the health and survival pillar, India ranked a very low 147, with disturbingly poor statistics on women's health.[26] According to the Report, one in five women, many who are child mothers, die during pregnancy or childbirth.[27] Many women are not provided with adequate maternity facilities and services and suffer death or serious morbidity issues and other harms in childbirth, and infants are born with preventable conditions.[28] Lastly, there is a high prevalence of gender-based violence which significantly lowered India's ranking on this pillar.[29]

India ranked 114 on educational attainment. India has succeeded in fully closing its primary education enrolment gender gaps with an enrolment of 92.9 percent; however, enrolment drops to 62.2 percent at secondary school.[30] Indeed, the 2011 census reveals that 82 percent of boys are literate while only 65 percent of girls can read and write.[31] In many schools, there are no separate toilet facilities for girls. The lack of privacy means many girls drop out of school at menstruation.[32] Additionally, the lack of girls-only schools in rural areas, the cultural bias in favour of boys, early marriage, the heavier domestic and subsistence duties of girls and the lack of female primary teachers in rural areas all combine to discourage girls from participating in education.[33] Further, many families do not want to lose a helping hand at home and on the land by sending their daughters to school.[34] Poverty and malnutrition, coupled with the preferential feeding of boys, also ensure that girls are more likely to be undernourished.[35] This adversely affects their school performance and their retention rate. Although the tertiary education gender gap is almost closed, with the 26.6 percent of women attending almost equal to men at 27 percent, many women do not continue to work in the professions in which they have trained after marriage.[36]

The most successful ranking was on political empowerment, where India ranked 19. This is in part, however, a reflection of the low political participation of women globally,[37] rather than an outstanding performance by India. India has

11.8 percent women in the national parliament, and 18.5 percent of ministerial positions are held by women.[38] Women have a low rate of participation in local government; however in the panchayat system, since the introduction of reservations, women's representation has soared.[39]

Defining women's human rights

A standard definition of human rights is those rights a person has because they are human. They are, according to this definition, universal, inalienable and indivisible – they cannot be transferred, forfeited or waived.[40] Although human rights may be understood in an abstract, philosophical or moral sense, in this book, women's human rights are explored in their legal context. In a legal sense, human rights are expressed and guaranteed by international law in the form of charters, treaties, conventions, declarations and various statements made by treaty-bodies.[41] Civil and political rights include the right to equality and non-discrimination; the right to privacy and the freedoms of thought, speech, religion, press, assembly and movement; the right to a fair trial; due process; the right to seek redress or a legal remedy; freedom of association; the right to assemble; the right to petition and the right to vote.[42] Economic, social and cultural rights include rights to work, social security, education, an adequate standard of living, housing, the highest attainable standard of physical and mental health including freedom from violence, a healthy environment and a cultural life.[43]

A country that becomes a party to an international human rights instrument is obligated to act in certain ways or to refrain from certain acts, in order to respect, protect and fulfil the human rights and fundamental freedoms of individuals or groups. The obligation to respect requires the state and its representatives to abstain from violating the integrity of the individual or infringing on her or his freedom. The obligation to protect requires the state and its representatives to take measures necessary to prevent other individuals or groups from violating the integrity, freedom of action or other human rights of the individual. The obligation to fulfil requires the state to take the measures necessary to ensure for each individual within its jurisdiction opportunities to obtain satisfaction of those needs, recognised in the human rights instruments, which cannot be secured by personal efforts.[44]

While women's human rights can be simply defined as the concept that human rights apply to women, more aptly, the concept describes the process of embedding women's perspectives, experiences and lives into human rights standards and practice.[45] Once embedded, women's human rights establish a unifying set of standards that must be translated into domestic law and subsequently realised and enjoyed by women in all aspects of their lives.[46]

International legal instruments that were initially drafted and enacted to promote, fulfil and protect the rights of all were developed primarily by men in a male-focussed world.[47] Within this structure, women's voices were often in the periphery: ignored, undermined, unheard. The concept of women's human rights has emerged, therefore, to specifically highlight and promote women's experiences of discrimination and inequality.[48] Indeed, a women's human rights framework equips women and their advocates with a way to define, analyse and articulate their experiences of discrimination, inequality, violence, subordination and marginality.[49]

Aims of book

This book focusses, in large part, on the human rights framework and the domestic legal framework of India, including the Constitution, legislation, judicial decisions and customary law. It assesses the extent to which the constitutional and domestic law framework of India has integrated international human rights standards, in particular *CEDAW*. Once integrated, the ability of constitutional and domestic law frameworks to deliver to women the enjoyment of their human rights rests on many additional factors. Factors beyond law include the political will to respect international obligations and to implement the law, community knowledge of the law, effective mechanisms to enable the implementation of law and the strength of traditional practices and cultural norms which are not in accord with the principles of equality and non-discrimination.[50] While these factors are significant, they are not the focus of this book. The translation of women's human rights into domestic law, while only characterising a first step in delivering to women the enjoyment of their human rights, is in our view a crucial step in women's enjoyment of their human rights. As Swapna Mukhopadhyay has emphasised, and we agree, law has an important role to play in bringing positive change to the women of India.[51] Approaching women's human rights from a legal perspective enables us to scrutinise government action and to evaluate legal mechanisms and remedies and marks the location of our inquiry: the point at which idealistic rights are codified in law and applied by decision-makers. Despite the primary focus on law this book does include case studies that illustrate women's enjoyment of human rights where available and relevant.

The book is not exhaustive. It does not purport to comprehensively cover all the experiences of women in India that form the subject matter of each chapter. Instead, examples of cases, policies and legislation are selected as illustrations, enabling us to deconstruct and understand the multifaceted character of women's rights, experiences and personhood in India.

The specific aims of the book are as follows:

First, the book aims to introduce the reader to women's human rights principles through a clear overview of the key sources of women's human rights in India, international and domestic, formal and informal, and to explore the linkages between international law, constitutional law, domestic law and customary practices.

Second, the book aims to introduce the reader to women's human rights theories and to understand their role in critiquing the human rights framework and their capacity to support solutions and positive reform.

Third, the book aims to link women's human rights theories with transformative practice. Theory, which provides a tentative explanation of facts or events, contributes to the development of knowledge.[52] Theories of law provide explanatory frameworks for the existence of law, the purpose of law and the impact of law, particularly as it relates to the larger political, cultural and social contexts in which it exists.[53] Feminist legal theory focusses on explaining the role of law in reinforcing and perpetuating women's subordination and inequality.[54] Women's human rights theories, informed, driven and derived by and from feminist legal theories, focus on both inserting women into the human rights framework and utilising women's human rights principles to end discrimination and inequality.[55] The book utilises women's human rights theories and local Indian feminist discourses in order to provide relevant global and local perspectives on the inequalities and discrimination faced by Indian women.[56] Women's human rights theories identify a gap between the women's human rights ideal (the promise that every woman enjoys fundamental rights) and the practice (a world where women are often excluded from the enjoyment of human rights).

Fourth, using the language of women's human rights principles, the book aims to advance understanding of how discriminatory structures embedded within law, society and culture perpetuate and entrench women's subordinate position throughout all layers of Indian society. Using the language of women's human rights principles as a powerful voice for change, we aim also to illustrate how to develop arguments in litigation; how to lobby for legislative and policy changes at local, national and international levels and how to inform and strengthen grassroots mobilisation and organisation by women's groups, civil society and non-government organisations to foster collaborative strategies. Finally, we aim to provide guidance for governments in policy-making.

Fifth, the book aims to provide a practical guide to applying women's human rights principles and theoretical perspectives to concrete problems. We apply women's human rights theories and principles to selected examples to illustrate how they can assist us to strategise to end discrimination and inequality. The factors influencing the application of rights include many political, religious, economic and social understandings of womanhood, almost always from the male perspective. The human rights framework creates a space in which the possibility for a different account of women's lives can be developed and provides a vocabulary for women to share the experiences of other women around the world and work collaboratively for change. As Nussbaum has stated in reference to *CEDAW*, the very existence of a document ratified by most of the nations of the world provides a language to use, particularly in combination with pressure from domestic interest groups.[57]

Sixth, the book aims to illustrate how women's human rights engage the state in ways that other approaches cannot. The conceptualisation of an inequality as a breach of a human right immediately involves the recognition of state and international responsibility if that claim is denied or violated. Women's human rights not only create entitlements for rights holders, but they also create duties for states – legislative, administrative, policy and programmatic.[53] States are required to ensure the fulfilment of women's human rights by acting in a way that enables rights holders to enjoy the rights to which they are entitled.[59]

Finally, the book aims to foster skills of analysis and critique in the reader to equip her or him to use the law as a tool of change. It also aims to stimulate the reader to question the tensions between different interpretations of women's rights and to evaluate the international human rights framework and its applicability to the Indian context and the specific subcultures within Indian society in all areas of women's lives.

Organisation of book

Chapter 2 sets out, critically and analytically, the primary sources of women's human rights, international and domestic, in India. After tracing the emergence of the human rights framework, the chapter considers international sources of women's human rights, including conventions (binding agreements between states) and declarations and charters (non-binding statements of intent and aspiration). It maps the process by which women's human rights, as a gender-specific body of rights, were inserted into the human rights framework particularly focussing on *CEDAW* and the Beijing Declaration (BD) and Beijing Platform for Action (BPA).[60] To be meaningful, the women's human rights identified in international instruments must be translated into domestic legal systems, and this chapter considers the state legal system (consisting of the constitution, legislation, judicial decisions including public interest litigation and state-recognised customary law) and the non-state legal system (consisting of customs and practices not recognised as law by the state and administered by both informal bodies, such as caste panchayats, tribal councils and government recognised bodies such as the *nari adalats*) evaluating them as sources of women's human rights.[61]

Chapter 3 sets out, critically, the key theories of women's human rights which are utilised throughout the book to understand the role of the human rights framework in addressing the inequality and subordination experienced by women across India. The theories overviewed in this chapter are not exhaustive. The chapter begins by tracing the emergence of key feminist legal theories – liberal, cultural and radical – and overviews the critique of those theories by postmodern feminist theorists. The chapter then documents how women's human rights theories emerged within and alongside feminist legal theory to critique the conceptualisation of human rights in international instruments. It focusses on three central theoretical themes in women's human rights theories. The first is the framing and interpretation of the concept of equality and non-discrimination in human rights law and its failure to achieve real substantive equality for women.[62] The second theme is the debate between universalism and cultural relativism and the intervention of feminist perspectives into that debate.[63] The third theme explores the argument that human rights violations of women perpetrated in the private domestic sphere are invisible and deemed to be beyond the purview of the state.[64]

Additionally, the prioritisation of public sphere 'political and civil rights' over private sphere 'economic, social and cultural rights' marginalises women further, perpetuating their inequality and subordination.[65] Finally, this chapter collates core principles of the different women's human right's theories and blends them to provide a theoretical framework for the book.

Chapter 4 focusses on the role of the right to equality and non-discrimination guaranteed in the *Constitution of India* 1950 in article 14 and article 15 in the advancement of women's human rights. Equality and non-discrimination provisions, particularly if embedded in a constitution, have important symbolic and practical dimensions. They provide a standard of conduct to guide the state in its law and policy decision-making and to hold it accountable to that standard.[66] If a guarantee of equality and non-discrimination places a positive obligation on the state to achieve equality and prevent discrimination, this represents an active mandate for the state.[67] The chapter explains how *CEDAW* expanded human rights understandings of equality to include substantive equality; how it expanded human rights understandings of non-discrimination to include both direct and indirect discrimination, positing sex and gender as alternate sources of discrimination and inequality and, finally, how it identified the compounding effect of multiple discriminations.[68] It then examines the context in which articles 14 and 15 were drafted and explores their interpretation in the courts and the extent to which those articles comply, both in their plain language and their interpretation, with the obligations created by the human rights framework, in particular *CEDAW*. Finally, it evaluates, with the use of case and legislative examples, the extent to which women's human rights principles and theories have been or could be utilised to broaden the scope and impact of articles 14 and 15.

Chapter 5 focusses on women's right to a life free from violence. Violence against women is widespread in India, and although its impact differs across disparities in location and across divisions of caste, religion and class, all women are vulnerable to violence.[69] The chapter assesses the extent to which women's human rights principles and theories have been or could be utilised to advance women's right to a life free from violence. We use, for example, the *Protection of Women from Domestic Violence Act* 2005 to illustrate how principles and theories of women's human rights can lead to positive law reform. We examine violence against women through selected (representative) forms of violence – domestic and family violence, including dowry violence; sexual violence and honour crimes. In each of these areas, using examples of feminist-driven law reform, policy and judicial reasoning, we illustrate how principles and theories of women's human rights can be used to understand and strengthen the state's response to violence against women and to develop strategies for reducing and ultimately ending violence against women.

Chapter 6 focusses on women's right to equality in marriage and family relations. Marriage and family are powerful social institutions in Indian society where women experience subordination and discrimination.[70] Although article

44 of the Constitution requires the state to 'endeavour to secure for the citizens a uniform civil code throughout the territory of India', India has no universal family law. Rather, there are different personal laws for each religious community – Muslim, Hindu, Buddhist, Jain and Sikh, Lingayat, followers of Prarthana and Brahmo and Arya Samaj – and a secular personal law. Each offers differing levels of human rights protections for women. The chapter assesses the extent to which women's human rights principles (particularly those detailed in article 16 of *CEDAW* (Marriage and Family Relations), General Recommendation (GR) 21 (Equality in Marriage and Family Relations)[71] and GR 29 (Economic Consequences of Marriage, Family Relations and their Dissolution)[72] and how women's human rights theories have been or could be utilised to advance the rights of women in key illustrative areas. We argue that equality in marriage and family relations is a universal value and therefore support the introduction of a secular uniform family law code that meets international norms. We also argue, however, that cultural and religious practices that do not erode or infringe upon women's human rights should be retained in each community's family law framework.

Chapter 7 focusses on the political representation and participation of women. India is a bicameral parliamentary democracy, with a strong multiparty political system. Women have become increasingly active and influential in the political life of India, marked by increased participation in voting since 2012, greater political representation at the panchayat levels and an increased input into decision-making and policy formulation.[73] The chapter assesses the extent to which women's human rights principles, particularly those outlined in article 7 of *CEDAW*, and women's human rights theories have been or could be utilised to advance the political representation and participation of women in key areas. Those areas include women's participation as voters; women's representation in elected public office at all levels of governance, extending from the national government to local panchayats where day-to-day administration occurs and, finally, women's participation in decision-making, policy formulation and lawmaking once elected to public office. All components are central to the full political representation and participation of women, which is a fundamental prerequisite for gender equality and genuine democracy.

Chapter 8 focusses on the economic empowerment of women in both the organised and unorganised economic sectors. The organised sector includes employment that is subject to income taxes and formal business structures. The unorganised sector includes all forms of informal employment that is not subject to taxes and informal businesses (small and large) that are not licenced, registered or incorporated. India's gender balance in economic participation and entrepreneurship is among the lowest in the world, and we argue that increasing the economic empowerment of women will, as well as improving women's lives and meeting India's international obligations, also result in a significant contribution to the Indian economy.[74] It will fuel poverty reduction, improve health outcomes and increase the level of education and welfare of the whole community.[75] The chapter assesses the extent to which women's human rights principles have been or could be utilised to advance the economic empowerment of women in key economic sectors. Those sectors include women's employment in the organised economic sector, with a focus on equal pay, maternity, paternity and parental leave; sexual harassment and (discriminatory) protective legislation; women's participation in formal business structures, with a focus on the licensing and incorporation of businesses and access to finance and credit and, finally, women's participation in the unorganised economic sector, overwhelmingly the most significant site of women's economic participation.[76] We examine the challenges faced by women in all three sectors as workers and entrepreneurs and identify ways for women to generate and maintain their own income streams. Utilising women's human rights theories of the public and the private and principles of equality and non-discrimination, we conclude that the unorganised sector is the most fruitful location for the economic empowerment of women.

Chapter 9, the conclusion, links the themes of Chapters 3 through 8 to the theoretical framework laid out in Chapter 2. It summarises the small and ambitious reforms, initiatives and measures recommended throughout the book, navigating an increasingly complex international legal framework and utilising both Western and Indian discourses. It concludes with support for women's human rights as universal but argues that the implementation of those rights can and must be modified by the cultural context of India. Gender equality inevitably resists, rather than accommodating, relativist approaches to the interpretation of human rights. We use language as our instrument and law as our most powerful mechanism to effect change.

Notes

1 UN General Assembly, *Convention on the Elimination of All Forms of Discrimination against Women*, 18 December 1979, United Nations, Treaty Series, vol. 1249.
2 Hilkka Pietila and Jeanne Vickers, *Making Women Matter: The Role of the United Nations* (Zed Books, 1996) 123; Christopher McCrudden, 'Why Do National Court Judges Refer to Human Rights Treaties? A Comparative International Law Analysis of *CEDAW*' (2015) 109(3) *American Journal of International Law* 534–550.
3 Neil Englehart and Melissa K. Miller, 'The *CEDAW* Effect: International Law's Impact on Women's Rights' (2014) 13(1) *Journal of Human Rights* 22–47, 39, 40.
4 Susanne Zwingel, *Translating International Women's Rights* (Palgrave MacMillan, 2016) 219–226, 148, 152.
5 Madhu Mehra, 'India's *CEDAW* Story' in Anne Hellum and Henrietta Aasen (eds.) *Women's Human Rights: CEDAW in International, Regional and National Law* (Cambridge University Press, 2013) 385–409, 391–394.
6 Raka Ray, *Fields of Protest: Women's Movements in India* (University of Minnesota Press, 1999) 3; Padma Anagol, *The Emergence of Feminism in India, 1850–1920* (Routledge, 2017).
7 Sukhendu Ray, Malavika Karlekar and Bharati Ray, *The Many Worlds of Sarala Devi: A Diary and the Tagores and Sartorial Style: A Photo Essay* (Routledge, 2017); Manraj Singh, 'Role of Women in India's Struggle for Freedom' (2014) 1(2) *International Journal of Research* 37–56; Saroj Singh, *Role of Women in India* (RedShine Publication, 2017). See generally Anagol n 6 for an overview of the early rise of feminism in India.

8 Vijaya Lakshmi, 'Women's Movement in Coastal Andhra' (2017) 4(6)(1) *International Journal of Academic Research* 91–94, 92.
9 Madhumita Mondol, 'Swarnakumari Devi: A Trend Setter in Colonial Bengal' in Bipasha Raha and Subhayu Chattopadhyay (eds.) *Mapping the Path to Maturity* (Routledge, 2017) 181–206.
10 Radha Kumar, 'From Chipko to Sati: The Contemporary Indian Women's Movement' in Amrita Basu (ed.) *The Challenge of Local Feminisms* (Routledge, 2018) 58–86.
11 Madhu n 5, 388.
12 Srimati Basu, *The Trouble with Marriage: Feminists Confront Law and Violence in India*, Vol. 1 (University of California Press, 2015).
13 Mangala Subramaniam, 'The Indian Women's Movement' (2004) 33(6) *Contemporary Sociology* 635–639, 635; Maitrayee Chaudhuri, 'Feminism in India: The Tale and Its Telling' (2012) 209 *Revue Tiers Monde* 19–36, 33.
14 Ibid Subramaniam 635–639, 637.
15 See *Githa Hariharan v. Reserve Bank of India* AIR 1999 1149 where the Reserve Bank of India refused to accept Githa Hariharan as guardian of investments made on behalf of her and her husband's son. The Bank drew on the *Hindu Minority and Guardianship Act* 1956, which provides that a father is the natural guardian of their children, while Githa drew on the equality provisions of the *Constitution of India* 1950. Although the court upheld Githa's claim, it did not declare the legislation unconstitutional.
16 See *Vishaka v. State of Rajhasthan* 1997 6 SCC 241, where the Supreme Court cited *CEDAW* in holding the Indian state responsible for preventing the sexual harassment of women in their place of employment.
17 See *Sexual Harassment of Women at Work Place (Prevention, Prohibition & Redressal) Act* 2013 prohibiting sexual harassment and establishing a complaints process for victims; *Protection of Women from Domestic Violence Act* 2005 providing protection orders and other remedies for victims of domestic violence; *Hindu Succession (Amendment) Act* 2005, extending equal succession rights to daughters; *Criminal Law (Amendment) Act* 2013, introducing a contemporary sexual assault offences framework.
18 Diva Dhar, Tarun Jain and Seema Jayachandran, 'Intergenerational Transmission of Gender Attitudes: Evidence from India' (2018) *Journal of Development Studies* 1–21, 1, 3.
19 Nita Bhalla, 'India Advances, but Many Women Still Trapped in Dark Ages' *World New Reuters*, 13 June 2012. www.reuters.com/article/us-g20-women-india/india-advances-but-many-women-still-trapped-in-dark-ages-idUSBRE85C00A20120613 Accessed 17/4/19.
20 Sanjukta Chaudhuri, 'A Life Course Model of Human Rights Realisation, Female Empowerment and Gender Inequality in India' (2013) 52 *World Development* 55–70; Silvia Barcellos, Leandro S. Carvalho and Adriana Lleras-Muney, 'Child Gender and Parental Investments in India: Are Boys and Girls Treated Differently?' (2014) 6(1) *American Economic Journal: Applied Economics* 157–189, 158.
21 World Economic Forum, *Global Gender Gap Report*, 2018. www.weforum.org/reports/the-global-gender-gap-report-2018 Accessed 17/4/19.
22 Ibid.
23 Ibid.
24 Ibid.
25 Ibid.
26 Ibid.
27 Ibid.
28 Ana Flávia Pires, Lucas d'Oliveira, Simone Grilo Diniz and Lilia Blima Schraiber, 'Violence against Women in Health-Care Institutions: An Emerging Problem' (2002) 359 *The Lancet* 1681–1685.
29 Priya Banerjee, 'Dowry in 21st Century India: The Sociocultural Face of Exploitation' (2014) 15(1) *Trauma, Violence and Abuse* 34–40; Luojia Hu and Analía Schlosser, 'Prenatal Sex Selection and Girls' Well-Being: Evidence from India' (2015) 125(587) *Economic Journal* 1227–1261.

30 World Economic Forum, n 21.
31 Census 2011, 'Literacy in India'. www.census2011.co.in/literacy.php Accessed 17/4/19.
32 Anna van Eijk, Muthusamy Sivakami, Mamita Bora Thakkar, Ashley Bauman, Kayla Laserson, Susanne Coates and Penelope Phillips-Howard, 'Menstrual Hygiene Management among Adolescent Girls in India: A Systematic Review and Meta-Analysis' (2016) 6(3) *BMJ Open* 1–12, 1, 6; Suman Bodat, Mrunalini M. Ghate and Jyoti R. Majumdar, 'School Absenteeism during Menstruation among Rural Adolescent Girls in Pune' (2013) 4(2) *National Journal of Community Medicine* 212–216, 214.
33 Rohini Sahni and V. Kalyan Shankar, 'Girls' Higher Education in India on the Road to Inclusiveness: On Track but Heading Where?' (2012) 63(2) *Higher Education* 237–256, 239, 248; Shahidul Islam and Zehadul Karim, 'Factors Contributing to School Dropout among the Girls: A Review of Literature' (2015) 3(2) *European Journal of Research and Reflection in Educational Sciences* 25–36, 26–31.
34 Gaurav Siddhu, 'Can Families in Rural India Bear the Additional Burden of Secondary Education? Investigating the Determinants of Transition' Research Monograph Number 50. (Department of International Justice, UK Government 2010). www.gov.uk/dfid-research-outputs/can-families-in-rural-india-bear-the-additional-burden-of-secondary-education-investigating-the-determinants-of-transition Accessed 17/4/19; Lalitha Bhagavatheeswaran, Sapna Nair, Hollie Stone and Tara Beattie, 'The Barriers and Enablers to Education among Scheduled Caste and Scheduled Tribe Adolescent Girls in Northern Karnataka, South India: A Qualitative Study' (2016) 49 *International Journal of Educational Development* 262–270, 263, 266.
35 Srinivas Goli, Anu Rammohan and Deepti Singh, 'The Effect of Early Marriages and Early Childbearing on Women's Nutritional Status in India' (2015) 19(8) *Maternal and Child Health Journal* 1864–1880.
36 Varun Kap and Kanika Dhingra, 'Sexual Harassment against Women in India' (2013) 6(10) *OIDA International Journal of Sustainable Development* 85–92.
37 Inter-Parliamentary Union, *Women in National Parliaments*. The global average at 1 January 2019 is 24.3 percent. India is ranked 150 out of 193 countries. http://archive.ipu.org/wmn-e/classif.htm Accessed 17/4/19.
38 Ibid.
39 Ashok Kumar, 'Elected Tribal Women Representatives in Panchayati Raj Institutions in Karnataka: A Study of Mysore District' (2018) 2(7) *International Journal in Advances in Social Sciences and Humanities* 7–11.
40 Janusz Symonides, *Human Rights: Concept and Standards* (Routledge, 2017) 17.
41 Michael Freeman, *Human Rights* (John Wiley and Sons, 2017) 10.
42 *International Covenant on Civil and Political Rights* 1966 (*ICCPR*).
43 *International Covenant on Economic, Social and Cultural Rights* 1966 (*ICESCR*).
44 Gerard Quinn and Philip Alston, 'The Nature and Scope of States Parties' Obligations under the International Covenant on Economic, Social and Cultural Rights' in Manisuli Ssenyonjo (ed.) *Economic, Social and Cultural Rights* (Routledge, 2017) 3–76; Jack Donnelly and Daniel J. Whelan, *International Human Rights* (Hachette, 2017).
45 Charlotte Bunch, 'Transforming Human Rights from a Feminist Perspective' in *Women's Rights, Human Rights* (Routledge, 2018) 11–17.
46 Anne Hellum and Henrietta Aasen (eds.) 'Introduction' in *Women's Human Rights: CEDAW in International, Regional and National Law*, n 5, 1–23, 2, 3, 5.
47 Hilary Charlesworth, Christine Chinkin and Shelley Wright, 'Feminist Approaches to International Law' (1991) 85(4) *American Journal of International Law* 613–645, 621.
48 Eileen Botting, *Wollstonecraft, Mill and Women's Human Rights* (Yale University Press, 2016) 3, 6.
49 Christine Chinkin, 'Feminist Interventions into International Law' (1997) 19 *Adelaide Law Review* 1–25, 13, 24.
50 Upendra Baxi, 'Voices of Suffering, Fragmented Universality, and the Future of Human Rights' in Robert McCorquodale (ed.) *Human Rights* (Routledge, 2003) 159–214.

51 Swapna Mukhopadhyay, *In the Name of Justice: Women and Law in Society* (Manohar Publishers, New Delhi, 1998) 9; Gita Sen and Avanti Mukherjee, 'No Empowerment Without Rights, No Rights without Politics: Gender-Equality, MDGs and the Post-2015 Development Agenda' (2014) 15(2) *Journal of Human Development and Capabilities* 188–202.
52 Barney Glaserand and Anselm L. Strauss, *Discovery of Grounded Theory: Strategies for Qualitative Research* (Routledge, 2017) 3.
53 Hans Kelsen (Translated by Bonnie Litchewski Paulson and Stanley L. Paulson), *Introduction to the Problems of Legal Theory* (Clarendon Press, 1992); Kim Scheppele, 'Legal Theory and Social Theory' in *Legal Theory and the Social Sciences* (Routledge, 2017) 29–52.
54 Nancy Levit, Robert R. M. Verchick and Martha Minow, *Feminist Legal Theory: A Primer* (New York University Press, 2016); Vanessa E. Munro, *The Ashgate Research Companion to Feminist Legal Theory* (Routledge, 2013); Ratna Kapur and Brenda Cossman, *Subversive Sites: Feminist Engagements with Law in India* (Sage Publications, 1996) 31, 35, 39.
55 Niamh Reilly, *Women's Human Rights: Seeking Justice in a Globalizing Age* (Polity Press, 2009) 28, 45, 51.
56 Amrita Basu, *The Challenge of Local Feminisms: Women's Movements in Global Perspective* (Routledge, 1995).
57 Martha Nussbaum, 'Women's Progress and Women's Human Rights' (2016) 38(3) *Human Rights Quarterly* 589–622.
58 Rebecca Cook, 'State Responsibility for Violations of Women's Human Rights' (1994) 7 *Harvard Journal of Human Rights* 125–175; Elisabeth Friedman, 'Women's Human Rights: The Emergence of a Movement' *Women's Rights, Human Rights* (Routledge, 1994) 18–35.
59 Ibid Cook, 127, 138.
60 Beijing Declaration and Platform for Action, Fourth World Conference on Women, 15 September 1995 (A/CONF.177/20).
61 Sesha Kethineni, Murugesan Srinivasan and Suman Kakar, 'Combating Violence against Women in India: Nari Adalats and Gender-Based Justice' (2016) 26(4) *Women & Criminal Justice* 281–300; Sylvia Vatuk, 'The "Women's Court" in India: An Alternative Dispute Resolution Body for Women in Distress' (2013) 45(1) *The Journal of Legal Pluralism and Unofficial Law* 76–103.
62 Simone Cusack and Lisa Pusey, '*CEDAW* and the Right to Non-Discrimination and Equality' (2013) 14 *Melbourne Journal of International Law* 54–92.
63 Cyra Choudhury, 'Beyond Culture: Human Rights Universalism versus Religious and Cultural Relativism in the Activism for Gender Justice' (2015) 30(2) *Berkeley Journal of Gender, Law and Justice* 226–267.
64 Christine Chinkin, 'A Critique of the Public/Private Dimension' (1999) 10 *European Journal of International Law* 387–395.
65 Ibid.
66 Adele Cassola, Amy Raub, Danielle Foley and Jody Heymann, 'Where Do Women Stand? New Evidence on the Presence and Absence of Gender Equality in the World's Constitutions' (2014) 10(2) *Politics and Gender* 200–235, 201.
67 Cusack and Pusey, n 62.
68 Ibid.
69 Bina Srinivasan, *Negotiating Complexities: A Collection of Feminist Essays* (Promilla and Co, 2007) 188.
70 Kapur and Cossman, n 54, 88.
71 *CEDAW* Committee, General Recommendation 21, *Equality in Marriage and Family Relations*, 1994 (UN Doc A/49/38).
72 *CEDAW* Committee, General Recommendation 29, *Economic Consequences of Marriage, Family Relations and their Dissolution*, 2013 (UN Doc CEDAW/C/GC/29).
73 Esther Duflo, 'Women Empowerment and Economic Development' (2012) 50(4) *Journal of Economic Literature* 1051–1079.

74 Amit Singh Khokhar and Bharat Singh, 'Status of Women Entrepreneurship in India' (2016) 4(5) *Asian Journal of Multidisciplinary Studies* 199–204, 199.

75 Sylvia Chant and Caroline Sweetman, 'Fixing Women or Fixing the World? "Smart Economics", Efficiency Approaches, and Gender Equality in Development' (2012) 20(3) *Gender & Development* 517–529, 523.

76 Diptirekha Mohapatra, 'Female Workers in the Unorganised Sector in India' International Conference on Studies in Humanities and Social Sciences, 2015 1–4. http://icehm.org/upload/6334ED715042.pdf Accessed 17/4/19.

2

SOURCES OF WOMEN'S HUMAN RIGHTS

Introduction

This chapter sets out, critically and analytically, the primary sources of women's human rights, international and domestic, in India. Identifying the sources of women's human rights, their limitations and their utility assists us in understanding the role and capacity of the human rights framework in advancing women's human rights and achieving gender equality. The gradual insertion of women's human rights into the human rights framework illustrates that human rights are not a static concept but instead are fluid and have capacity to evolve as social contexts change.[1] In the international arena, this chapter illustrates that *CEDAW*[2] and the BD and BPA[3] are living documents which have increasingly become rich sources of women's human rights. In the domestic arena, women's human rights must be translated into law. With the application of women's human rights principles and theories, legislation and constitutions can be and are amended, judicial decisions become more cognisant of changing social contexts and customary law evolves to better reflect the principles of equality and non-discrimination.

In 2.2, the chapter traces the emergence of the human rights framework. It sets out the key components of that framework, including the obligation that ratification places on state parties to respect, protect and fulfil the rights contained in each human rights convention. In 2.3, the chapter considers international sources of women's human rights including conventions (binding agreements between states) and declarations and charters (non-binding statements of intent and aspiration). It maps the process by which women's human rights, as a gender-specific body of rights, were inserted into the human rights framework, particularly focussing on *CEDAW* and the BD and BPA.

To be meaningful, the women's human rights identified in international instruments must be translated into domestic legal systems.[4] Therefore, in section 2.4, we consider the state legal system (consisting of the *Constitution of India* 1950 (Constitution), legislation, judicial decisions including public interest litigation and state recognised customary law) and the non-state legal system (consisting of customs and practices not recognised as law by the state and administered by both informal bodies such as caste panchayats, tribal councils and government-recognised bodies such as the *nari adalats*), evaluating them as sources of women's human rights. While we argue the state legal system is limited in various ways, the non-state legal system has no oversight by the human rights system and is the weakest source of women's human rights.[5]

BOX 2.1 KEY CONCEPTS IN THE HUMAN RIGHTS FRAMEWORK

International instruments

Conventions, charters, declarations and other international documents that together form international law.

Conventions and/or treaties

Agreements under international law entered into by sovereign states.

Declarations

Declare certain aspirations but are not legally binding.

Signature

Country provides preliminary endorsement by signing instruments indicating agreement in principle but does not create a binding legal obligation.

Ratification

Country agrees to be party to a convention, which is legally binding.

Accession

Country agrees to become a party to a convention already negotiated and signed by other countries. It has the same legal effect as ratification.

State party

Country which has ratified or acceded to a binding legal instrument.

Reservation

State parties declare themselves not bound by parts of a convention.

Treaty body

A committee of international experts responsible for monitoring a convention/treaty.

General Recommendation/General Comment

A statement by a treaty body that elaborates, explains and expands on the general principles of a convention.

Optional Protocol

An additional legal instrument that adds to a convention.

Domestic law

Law established within a state to govern events, transactions and persons within a state.

International law

Law that governs the *legal* relations between or among states or nations.

Source: Authors

Human rights framework

This section overviews the human rights framework. After two world wars that included persecution of minorities and in particular the atrocities against the Jewish people by the Nazi regime, a number of world powers came together to establish a human rights framework to restrain governments and to map out commonly agreed standards of rights for all people.[6] A number of international instruments including legally binding treaties, charters and conventions (hard law) as well as commitments expressed in declarations, resolutions, guiding principles and codes of conduct (soft law) were drafted and adopted.

The Charter of the United Nations (UN) 1945 and the *Universal Declaration of Human Rights* 1948 (UDHR) set out, for the first time, fundamental human rights to be universally protected. The nine conventions known collectively as the 'core' human rights conventions followed, including *CEDAW*, the *International Covenant on Civil and Political Rights* 1966 (*ICCPR*), the *International Covenant on Economic, Social and Cultural Rights* 1966 (*ICESCR*), the *Convention on the Elimination of All Forms of Racial Discrimination* 1969 (*CERD*), the *Convention on the Rights of the Child 1990* (*CRC*), the *International Convention on the Protection of the Rights of All Migrant Workers and Members of Their Families* 2003 (*ICRMW*), the *Convention on the Rights of Persons with Disabilities* 2008 (*CRPD*) and the *International Convention for the Protection of All Persons from Enforced Disappearances* 2008 (*ICPPED*). Conventions are ratified or acceded to by states on a voluntary basis. India has ratified or acceded to seven of the nine 'core' human rights conventions.

TABLE 2.1 Human Rights Conventions to Which India Is Party

	ICCPR	*ICESCR*	*CEDAW*	*CERD*	*CRC*	*CRPD*	*ICERD*
Signature Date	**x**	**x**	**30 July 1980**	**2 March 1967**	**x**	**30 March 2007**	**x**
Ratification Accession Date	**10 April 1979**	**10 April 1979**	**9 July 1993**	**3 December 1968**	**11 December 1992**	**1 October 2007**	**3 December 1968**

Source: Authors

Two types of monitoring organs emerged. The first, charter-based organs (for example, the General Assembly, the Human Rights Council, the Security Council and the Economic and Social Council), draw their authority from the UN Charter. They have broad mandates, focussing on a wide range of issues including promoting awareness and responding to violations of human rights standards. They have a constantly expanding mandate to respond to crises as they emerge.

The second, treaty-based organs (for example the Human Rights Committee and the *CEDAW* Committee), draw their authority from particular human rights conventions. They have a narrower but crucial objective to develop the content and jurisprudence of the rights and obligations in the convention to which they are anchored.

Obligations of ratification or accession

Once a country has ratified or acceded to a convention, they are obligated to respect, protect and fulfil the rights contained within it.[7] A country complies with the obligation to 'respect' the rights by not violating them.[8] Protection and fulfilment of those rights is achieved first by a country ensuring that the domestic legal framework accords with the fundamental rights created by the convention so that persons can enforce their rights and second by ensuring that the obligations are not just recorded in law but implemented in practice with the intended results.[9]

International law, including conventions, is incorporated into a domestic legal framework in two ways. In some countries, international law is self-executing, meaning that it becomes automatically part of the domestic law when a state ratifies or accedes to a convention. This is known as a monist system.[10] It enables international law to be directly applied in the courts, both to enforce rights in areas where there is no domestic law and to assist in interpreting existing law in line with the international standards. In other countries, international law must be specifically incorporated into the domestic legal system through either the constitution or other legislation. This is known as a dualist system.[11] In a dualist system, an important and certain way of ensuring that international law, including conventions, is incorporated into national legal frameworks is to include a provision in the constitution that clearly declares that international law is part of the domestic law.[12] Otherwise, compliance requires a lengthy process of amending domestic laws to accord with each ratified international convention.[13]

India has a dualist system. Although the Constitution does not expressly make international law part of domestic law, the Constitution in article 51(c) directs the state 'to foster respect for international law and treaty obligations'.[14] Additionally, article 253 of it confers on Parliament the power to initiate legislation to implement international agreements, treaties and conventions entered into with other countries, which include any decision made at an international conference or convention. The Indian judiciary has interpreted these provisions to mean that it must 'interpret the language of the Constitution . . . in the light of the United Nations Charter and solemn declarations subscribed to by India' and 'construe our legislation so as to be in conformity with international law and not in conflict with it'.[15] More recently, the courts have expanded that position with a finding that if there is an ambiguity in domestic law, 'the national rule is to be interpreted in accordance with the state's international obligations'.[16] The Supreme Court has further stated that international laws that 'elucidate and go to effectuate the fundamental rights guaranteed by our Constitution can certainly be relied upon by courts as facets of those fundamental rights and hence are enforceable as such.'[17]

The Indian courts have utilised international conventions as a persuasive tool in many important judgments.[18] In *Vishaka v. State of Rajasthan*, for example, the Supreme Court used *CEDAW* as authority for developing guidelines prohibiting sexual harassment in the workplace.[19] Similarly, in *Sakshi v. Union of India and Ors*,[20] the Supreme Court accepted the use of international conventions, including *CEDAW*, by a women's organisation that argued the lack of targeted provisions around child sexual assault was contrary to India's international obligations. The Supreme Court created preliminary guidelines for conducting trials in child sexual assault cases.[21]

Reservations and declarations

A reservation to a convention means that, although accepting other aspects of the convention, the country will not implement a particular provision or aspect of the convention, thus limiting acceptance of the convention.[22] The rationale behind the concept of reservations is to encourage a greater number of countries to ratify conventions so as to maximize their force and effect.[23] Historically, all state parties had to approve any reservation to an international convention proposed by another country before ratification or accession would be approved.[24] However, to ameliorate the rigidity of that system and to encourage more parties to ratify and accede to conventions, in 1980 the *Vienna Convention on the Law of Treaties* implemented a new regime to govern the reservations system.[25] The Vienna Convention states that a reservation is permissible so long as it is not contrary to the object and purpose of the convention.[26] A declaration to a convention, in contrast to a reservation, is a statement about the state party's understanding of a matter contained in or the interpretation of a particular provision in a convention.[27] It does not purport to exclude or modify the legal effects of a convention; rather, it explains or interprets what the state party deems unclear.[28] Reservations and declarations can be withdrawn completely or partially at any time.[29]

Monitoring

Each convention has a committee known as a treaty body that monitors compliance by state parties, typically made up of independent experts elected from the countries which are party to it.[30] Usually there are ten to twenty-three members who are nominated and elected for fixed, renewable terms of four years by state parties from among their nationals.[31] Elections are staggered every two years so that only half the membership changes after any one election.[32] Each treaty body has the capacity to make General Comments or General Recommendations. These are detailed statements on broadly worded articles or principles of a convention to provide greater detail of the meaning or the standards expected of state parties, to provide clear guidance on the application of a convention in particular situations and to provide guidance on reporting requirements.[33]

Four distinct types of monitoring procedures have been established by the human rights system.

The first is the reporting procedures, the main monitoring mechanism, which requires state parties to report periodically to the treaty body on the steps they have taken to implement their obligations under the convention and to identify difficulties in implementation.[34] As part of the reporting procedure, a country's non-governmental organisations often submit 'shadow reports' to the treaty body. The reports provide their own account of the country's compliance and may dispute a country's official report or provide information on unreported violations. Concluding observations are issued by a treaty body after it has considered a state party's report and the shadow report. Concluding observations refer both to the positive aspects of a country's implementation of the convention and to areas of concern, where the treaty body recommends that further action needs to be taken. The treaty bodies are committed to issuing concluding observations that are concrete, focussed and implementable and are paying increasing attention to measures to ensure effective follow-up.[35]

The second is the individual communications procedures adopted by five of the core conventions, enabling treaty bodies to receive and consider communications from individuals alleging violations of their rights under the convention by countries which have accepted the individual communication procedure.[36]

The third is the inquiry procedure adopted by only two conventions, enabling treaty bodies to initiate inquiries on their own initiative if they have received reliable information about serious or systematic violations of the rights protected by their conventions.[37]

Finally, most conventions have an interstate communications procedure which enables one state party to lodge a complaint with the relevant treaty body about another state party alleging that the latter has not carried out its obligations under the convention.[38] Interstate communications are often optional and will only apply if both countries have opted in.

As well as providing remedies to individual victims, the treaty bodies, through the complaints and inquiry procedures, can elaborate on the meaning of the rights contained in a convention and contribute to the development of international jurisprudence.[39]

Optional Protocols

An Optional Protocol is an optional addition to an existing convention. A country that is party to the original convention can choose to sign, accede to or ratify the Optional Protocol. There are two kinds of Optional Protocols amongst human rights conventions. First, those that address a new substantive area that was not included in the original text of a convention. For example, the Second Optional Protocol to the *ICCPR* commits state parties that ratify or accede to it to abolish the death penalty within their borders. Second, those that strengthen procedural aspects of the original convention, changing how that convention operates and is enforced. For example, by creating new compliance mechanisms as in the case of the Optional Protocol to *CEDAW*, which establishes both an individual communications procedure not included in *CEDAW* and an inquiry procedure to be administered by the *CEDAW* Committee.[40]

UN-sponsored international conferences

Another mechanism for achieving a consensus for the advancement of human rights, developed by the UN, is sponsoring international conferences focussed on the achievement of human rights through goal setting. The World Conference on Human Rights held in Vienna in 1993, for example, focussed on a range of human rights issues, including the rights of women. The main outcome of the conference was the Vienna Declaration and Programme of Action. The International Conference on Population and Development held in Cairo in 1994 focussed on women's right to sexual and reproductive health, and the Fourth World Conference on Women held in Beijing in 1995 focussed on a range of issues affecting women. These two significant conferences specifically developed the standards for the promotion of the human rights of women.

International sources of women's human rights

Formal equality between men and women was central to human rights conventions from their emergence. However, women's experiences, perspectives, disadvantages and harms were largely absent from the mainstream human rights discourse during its first two decades.[41] Although the UN Commission on the Status of Women (CSW), a charter-based body, was established by the UN in 1946 to address discrimination against women and to promote their advancement, progress was slow.[42] Between 1949 and 1965, the CSW focussed on the political rights of women, the nationality of married women, consent to marriage, minimum age for marriage and registration of marriages and drafted instruments focussed on these specific topics.[43] However, by the mid-1960s, discrimination against women worldwide became a serious concern for the CSW,[44] and it was clear the existing instruments were weak on gender inequalities and had 'failed to deal with discrimination against women in a comprehensive way.'[45] The CSW drafted the Declaration on the Elimination of Discrimination against Women, which was adopted by the General Assembly on 7 November 1967.[46] The declaration is non-binding and was merely a 'statement of moral and political intent'.[47] The CSW proposed that the UN consider the creation of a binding convention.[48]

Convention on the Elimination of All Forms of Discrimination against Women

The CSW began drafting *CEDAW* in 1976.[49] It was adopted by the UN General Assembly in 1979 by 130 votes by UN member states in favour and 10 abstentions and it entered into force on 3 September 1981.[50] It was a decade after its adoption before India acceded to *CEDAW* in 1993, only two years before the Fourth World Conference on Women in Beijing, which gave rise to the Beijing Platform and Declaration. The timing is likely related as there was a growth of alliance building and networking amongst women's organisations and activists across India in the lead up to Beijing Conference with many groups utilising *CEDAW* as an effective tool to pursue women's rights.[51] There was also growing pressure on India from international funders (such as the World Bank and the International Monetary Fund) to improve governance, including advancing gender equality, and India was positioning itself to become a significant member of the international community.[52]

CEDAW is an important and rich source of women's human rights in India. It has been described as an international Bill of Rights for women[53] and is considered the 'most important of the conventions on the status of women'.[54] It develops human rights norms from a woman's perspective, superseding the earlier human rights conventions by specifically addressing the pervasive and systemic nature of discrimination against women.[55] *CEDAW* is a living document and therefore the following articles must be understood in the context of the 37 General Recommendations and the concluding observations which have expanded the meanings of the convention. Those expansions will be discussed in the chapters that follow in relation to each topic area covered in this book.

The number of countries that have ratified or acceded to *CEDAW* has increased from 20 in 1981 to 189 in 2019, including India in 1993, comprising over 95 percent of the members of the UN.[56] *CEDAW* consists of a preamble and 30 articles, which are divided into six parts. In the preamble, state parties declare that they are 'determined to adopt the measures required for the elimination of discrimination in all its forms and manifestations'.

Articles 1 through 4 set out the basic principles underscoring *CEDAW*, specifically equality, non-discrimination and state obligation. Article 1 provides a comprehensive definition of discrimination to include 'any distinction, exclusion or restriction made on the basis of sex which has the effect or purpose of impairing or nullifying the recognition, enjoyment or exercise by women, irrespective of their marital status, on a basis of equality of men and women, of human rights and fundamental freedoms in the political, economic, social, cultural, civil or any other field.'

Article 2 establishes the framework for the subsequent substantive articles (articles 6 through 16). Article 2 is central to the obligations of state parties under *CEDAW*.[57] Article 2 requires state parties to condemn discrimination against women in all its forms (covering all discrimination even if not specifically identified in the convention)[58] and pursue by all appropriate means and without delay (no justification for delay is permissible, including lack of financial and technical resources) a policy of eliminating discrimination against women.[59] Uniquely, while other international human rights conventions are typically limited to the conduct of state parties and their agencies, article 2 requires state parties to eliminate discrimination against women by any person, organisation or enterprise. The extension of anti-discrimination protection to non-state actors is indicative of the recognition that to effectively combat discrimination in all areas of women's lives, the regulation of both state and non-state actors throughout the public and private spheres of women's lives is required.[60]

Article 3 requires state parties to take all appropriate measures, including legislation, in the political, social, economic and cultural fields, to ensure the full development and advancement of women, for the purpose of guaranteeing them the exercise and enjoyment of human rights and fundamental freedoms on the basis of equality with men.

Article 4 requires state parties to introduce temporary special measures aimed at accelerating substantive equality between men and women. Temporary special measures are not to be considered discrimination. They 'shall in no way entail as a consequence the maintenance of unequal or separate standards' and must be discontinued 'when the objectives of equality of opportunity and treatment have been achieved.'[61]

Article 5 requires state parties to take all appropriate measures to modify the social and cultural patterns of conduct of men and women in order to eliminate practices based on the inferiority of either of the sexes or based on stereotyped roles.

Article 6 requires state parties to take all appropriate measures, including legislation to, suppress all forms of traffic in women and exploitation of prostitution of women.

Articles 7 through 9 are primarily concerned with discrimination against women in the public sphere. State parties are obliged to ensure equal voting rights, equal opportunities to enable women to represent their governments and equal opportunities to participate in the work of international organisations. The rights of women to full and equal citizenship and the rights of women to pass on their nationality to their children are also identified in these articles.

Articles 10 through 14 envisage broader social reform in relation to access to education, equality in employment, access to health care, access to financial services and equal participation in social and cultural life. In addition, article 14 addresses the specific needs of rural women.

Article 15 and 16 cover the rights of women to equality before the law and within the family.

Articles 17 through 22 contain the provisions governing the operation and international enforcement of *CEDAW*, including the creation of the *CEDAW* Committee to oversee the implementation of *CEDAW*.[62] Although there is an interstate procedure allowing state parties to initiate proceedings against another state for alleged breaches of *CEDAW*, no country has utilised it to date. Instead, the primary means provided to the *CEDAW* Committee (in accord with all major human rights conventions) to monitor the domestic implementation of *CEDAW* is a periodic reports system established by Article 18.[63] All state parties to *CEDAW* are required to provide a national report within one year of ratification or accession, followed by periodic reports at least once every four years.[64] There is no particular standard for the procedure that state parties should adhere to in collecting the relevant data and compiling the report.[65] The *CEDAW* Committee has, however, issued guidelines on the information that reports should contain.[66] The *CEDAW* Committee meets twice per year to review initial and periodic reports and to scrutinise state parties' progress in implementing the Convention.[67] During the review process, the *CEDAW* Committee adopts a dialogue approach, questioning the state's representatives on specific portions of the report and about deficiencies and discrepancies between the report and information received from other sources.[68] The *CEDAW* Committee can request 'specialized agencies', which can include NGOs and UN organisations, to submit shadow reports on the performance of government and general implementation of the convention in areas falling within the scope of their activities.[69] After considering the country report and other information that has been gathered, including any shadow report submitted by non-government organisations which may highlight issues not raised by their governments or point out where the government may be misleading the committee about the real situation, the *CEDAW* Committee compiles its concluding observations and submits them to the UN General Assembly through the Economic and Social Council.[70] India provided its initial report to the *CEDAW* Committee in 2000, its combined second and third periodic report in 2007, and its fourth report in 2014.[71] Relevant aspects of the *CEDAW* Committee's concluding observations to India will be referred to in the chapters that follow, where relevant.

Article 21 empowers the *CEDAW* Committee to formulate General Recommendations to provide interpretation of the meaning of *CEDAW*'s articles. General Recommendation 19 of the *CEDAW* Committee, for example, identifies gender-based violence as a form of discrimination which seriously inhibits women's ability to enjoy rights and freedoms on a basis of equality with men. As of 2019 the committee has made 37 General Recommendations.[72]

Articles 23 through 30 cover administration and procedural processes.

Article 28 enables reservations. However, according to article 28(2), reservations 'incompatible with the object and purpose of the present Convention shall not be permitted'. Thus, although reservations are permitted, those that are contrary to the object and purpose of *CEDAW* are not. *CEDAW* is nevertheless the most heavily reserved convention in the UN human rights system.[73] As of 2019, 58 state parties had entered reservations to *CEDAW*.[74] Most reservations on human rights conventions relate to dispute resolution provisions.[75] *CEDAW*, however, is most often reserved on the ground that national law, tradition, religion or culture is incongruent with some of its articles or principles.[76] Most of the reservations lodged relate to article 2 (elimination of discrimination against women), article 5 (modification or elimination of social and cultural patterns of conduct that lead to the inferiority of women) or article 16 (equality between men and women in all aspects of marriage and family life).[77] As many commentators have noted, however (and we agree), a convention is weakened by a system that allows parties to choose to adhere to some parts of the convention and not to others.[78] Additionally, reservations on *CEDAW* are often used by countries to maintain customary and traditional practices that discriminate against women, thereby stifling women's voices and debate.[79] Indeed, many of the key issues that women face and that require reform, for example family planning, reproductive rights, marriage and divorce rights, inheritance, succession and maintenance, are encapsulated in the very articles that are most heavily reserved.[80] We recommend that the *CEDAW* Committee establish a mechanism to evaluate reservations, to determine whether a state party has breached the compatibility requirement and, if it has, to require the country to amend or withdraw its reservation.[81]

Although other regions of the world where custom and culture continue to govern personal relations typically have reservations on article 5 and article 16, India has a reservation only on article 29(1) which provides that:

> Any dispute between two or more state parties concerning the interpretation or application of the present Convention which is not settled by negotiation shall, at the request of one of them, be submitted to arbitration. If within six months from the date of the request for arbitration the parties are unable to agree on the organization of the arbitration, any one of those parties may refer the dispute to the International Court of Justice by request in conformity with the Statute of the Court.

However, India has made two declarations. First, with regard to article 5(a), which requires state parties to take all appropriate measures 'to modify the social and cultural patterns of conduct of men and women, with a view to achieving the elimination of prejudices and customary and all other practices which are based on the idea of the inferiority or the superiority of either of the sexes or on stereotyped roles for men and women', India has declared 'its policy of non-interference in the personal affairs of any community without its initiative and consent'. Second, in relation to article 16(2), which requires state parties to ensure that the 'betrothal and the marriage of a child shall have no legal effect, and all necessary action, including legislation, shall be taken to specify a minimum age for marriage and to make the registration of marriages in an official registry compulsory', India has declared that although 'in principle it fully supports the principle of compulsory registration of marriage it is not practical in a vast country like India with its variety of customs, religions and levels of literacy'.[82] Both declarations have the appearance of reservations,[83] since both purport to exclude or modify the legal effect of *CEDAW* by naming obligations that they will not implement: first, that they will not modify the personal laws without the consent of the communities involved and second, that they cannot implement the compulsory registration of marriage. We recommend that the *CEDAW* Committee strongly challenge both declarations. The second declaration in particular has little foundation since the Supreme Court has called for mandatory registration of marriages.[84] Moreover, marriage registration does not require literacy, and in any case, India should be committed to achieving universal literacy and not utilising it as an excuse to avoid its human rights obligations under *CEDAW*.[85]

Optional Protocol to CEDAW

The *CEDAW* Committee's powers of enforcement were strengthened on 6 October 1999, when the Optional Protocol to *CEDAW* was adopted by the UN General Assembly.[86] It entered into force on 22 December 2000, and as of 2019, 110 countries have ratified or acceded to the protocol. India, however, has not done so to date. The Optional Protocol enables women who have not received justice in their domestic legal systems to have their claims heard at the international level through two enforcement procedures. The first is a communications procedure through which the *CEDAW* Committee can receive and consider complaints from individuals or groups of individuals who claim to be victims of violations of rights set out in *CEDAW* or by their designated representatives, or by others on behalf of an alleged victim where the alleged victim consents.[87] A communication must be in writing, cannot be anonymous and must concern a party to the Optional Protocol in order for it to be 'received' by the *CEDAW* Committee.[88] Once a communication is registered, the *CEDAW* Committee must decide by a simple majority whether it is admissible. To be admissible, all available domestic remedies must have been exhausted, it must not be a matter previously under examination by the *CEDAW* Committee or another procedure of international investigation or settlement, it must be compatible with the provisions of the convention, it must be sufficiently substantiated and the violation must have occurred after the state party acceded to or ratified the Optional Protocol. If the *CEDAW* Committee decides that a communication is admissible, it examines the merits of the allegations. The *CEDAW* Committee decides whether the state party has met its legal obligations under *CEDAW* and publishes 'views', in which it identifies whether the state party violated rights in *CEDAW*. If a violation is found, the *CEDAW* Committee makes recommendations on how the state party should redress those violations. Although views are not legally binding, the state party must provide a formal written response to the *CEDAW* Committee within six months, which includes information about steps it has taken to address the *CEDAW* Committee's views and implement its recommendations.

The second is the inquiry procedure, which is a mechanism enabling the *CEDAW* Committee to investigate grave or systematic violations of *CEDAW* by a state party.[89] Upon receipt of reliable information, the *CEDAW* Committee invites the state party to submit observations. Select members of the *CEDAW* Committee, who may visit the country to gather information, then conduct a confidential inquiry and report back to the *CEDAW* Committee. The *CEDAW* Committee considers the report and then provides recommendations, if appropriate, to the country, which has six months to respond.

Unlike *CEDAW*, no reservations to the Optional Protocol are permitted,[90] although article 10 permits state parties to opt out of the inquiry procedure. While the Optional Protocol places *CEDAW* on a more equal footing with other international instruments,[91] India has not ratified or acceded to the protocol, and therefore, the reports process continues to be the main method of international monitoring of India's progress.

Beijing Declaration and Platform for Action

The BD and the BPA,[92] the outcome documents of the UN Fourth World Conference on Women held in Beijing on 15 September 1995, provide a source of women's human rights despite not having the force and effect of a convention. The Beijing Declaration is a resolution promulgating a set of principles for achieving the equality of men and women. The Platform for Action is a progressive blueprint for advancing women's rights. Both can be utilised as advocacy tools to support law and policy reform. The following 12 areas were identified as the most critical areas for action.[93]

BOX 2.2 PLATFORM FOR ACTION: 12 CRITICAL AREAS OF CONCERN

1 Persistent and increasing burden of poverty on women.
2 Inequalities and inadequacies in and unequal access to education and training.
3 Inequalities and inadequacies in and unequal access to health care and related services.
4 Violence against women.
5 Effects of armed or other kinds of conflict on women, including those living under foreign occupation.
6 Inequality in economic structures and policies, in all forms of productive activities and in access to resources.
7 Inequality between men and women in the sharing of power and decision-making at all levels.
8 Insufficient mechanisms at all levels to promote the advancement of women.
9 Lack of respect for and inadequate promotion and protection of the human rights of women.
10 Stereotyping of women and inequality in women's access to and participation in all communication systems, especially in the media.
11 Gender inequalities in the management of natural resources and in the safeguarding of the environment.
12 Persistent discrimination against and violation of the rights of the girl child.

Source: Authors

The BPA requires governments and the international community and civil society, including non-governmental organisations and the private sector, to take strategic action in those 12 areas of concern.[94] The 189 governments, including India, that endorsed the BD and the BPA stated that they were determined to '[t]ake all necessary measures to eliminate all forms of discrimination against women and the girl child and remove all obstacles to gender equality and the advancement and empowerment of women'.[95]

The BPA was initially a five-year action plan for the period from 1995 through 2000. Women's organisations, however, reported at the end of the five years that '[g]overnments worldwide have displayed a lack of will in turning their commitments to women's rights into decisive action, instead adopting a piecemeal and incremental approach that cannot achieve the economic, social and political transformation underlying the promises of Beijing.'[96]

Ten years after Beijing, in March 2005, the CSW presided over an intergovernmental meeting in New York to review the progress achieved on the commitments made in the BD and the BPA. The 'Plus 10' event was not agenda setting but agenda confirming and not policy formulation but policy affirmation.[97] In 2015 the 'Plus 20' event was similarly a review of progress made since the adoption of the BD and BPA. Each country was requested to report to the review, including India, which reported on its progress in implementing numerous legislative and policy initiatives.[98] India acknowledged in its report that gender-based inequalities continue in education, income and employment and health. Despite the lack of action at the national level, the UN and its agencies still expect governments that endorsed the BD and BPA to continue to implement the objectives of the two instruments.[99] They continue, therefore, as sources of women's human rights in India.

Translating women's human rights into domestic law

The translation of women's human rights into domestic law, other than through the direct application of *CEDAW* and other international instruments in the courts, requires the active participation of the legislature and the judiciary.[100] There are two discernible legal systems in India through which women's human rights can be translated into domestic law.

The first is the state legal system, which draws its authority from the state.[101] The state legal system consists of a detailed federal structure in which legislative authority is divided between the Union Parliament and the state and territory legislatures. Within the states and territories, there is a state government and local government in urban areas (municipalities) and in rural areas (panchayats), which do not have legislative capacity. Sources of law in the state legal system consist of the Constitution, legislation enacted by Union and state legislatures; judicial decisions, particularly India's unique system of public interest litigation and, finally, customs recognised as law by the state, in both urban and rural communities, utilised by tribal peoples and Muslims (sharia law). Each source of law is shaped by India's history as a British colony.[102]

The state legal system has the potential to be an important source of women's human rights for the following reasons. First, the Union and the state parliaments have significant control over, and primary responsibility for, women's human rights through law and policy. The Union Parliament, for example, has power to make law and policy in the area of banking, many areas of taxation and for some natural resources while the state parliaments have power to make law and policy in relation to the police, public health, land, water and public services. Important concurrent powers shared by the Union and state parliaments include criminal law, marriage and divorce, economic and social planning and education. Since India is party to *CEDAW* and has a corresponding obligation to modify legislation and other laws to comply and accord with *CEDAW*, the state legal system could be a strong source of women's human rights.[103] Second, the state legal system is much more accessible to women than the international human rights system, which primarily monitors the state.[104] As India has not acceded to the Optional Protocol to *CEDAW*, there is no individual complaints process open to Indian citizens. Third, there are binding and effective remedies available in the state legal system that are absent from the international system, which relies in large part on voluntary compliance.[105] The extent to which the state legal system does provide powerful and important sources of women's human rights will be discussed in the chapters that follow.

The second legal system operating in India is a non-state legal system which consists of norms or institutions – viewed as having the force of law by those subject to them – that draw their moral authority from contemporary or traditional culture, customs and religious beliefs rather than from the political authority of the state.[106] The non-state legal system is a less reliable and unlikely source of women's human rights. It consists of customary rules over which the state has no oversight, administered primarily by caste panchayats and village councils and staffed almost exclusively by men.[107] However, for many women in rural areas, slum areas or poor urban areas, the non-state legal system is the most accessible and acceptable forum for resolving disputes.[108] The *nari adalats* provide an illustrative example, however, of how the non-state legal system can be utilised to uphold women's human rights, as discussed more fully next.

State legal system

Constitution of India 1950

A constitution provides the strongest legal mechanism for translating a country's international obligations into domestic law. Constitutional law is not only more legally powerful than ordinary legislation, but a constitution often acquires a legitimacy and moral force that legislation rarely acquires.[109] A constitution, therefore, provides the strongest legal means of protecting the fundamental rights and freedoms of women, including their right to equality and non-discrimination.[110]

The Constitution was drafted over a period of three years as part of the independence process as Great Britain withdrew from India.[111] It is supreme law, taking precedence over all domestic law. Women's human rights were not a primary concern of the Indian drafters, and although some protection of women's human rights was incorporated into the Constitution, it took the form of either a formal equality or a protectionist approach.[112] Subsequent amendments, however, did give women's human rights a greater space in the Constitution: for example, the introduction of a 33 percent quota for women in panchayats and municipalities, although this was not extended to state governments or the Union government.[113] The Constitution has 22 parts; the following are those that provide sources of women's human rights. The particular ways in which the Constitution, including its interpretation in the courts, advances, protects or fails to protect women's human rights will be discussed in the chapters that follow.

BOX 2.3 SIGNIFICANT SOURCES OF WOMEN'S HUMAN RIGHTS IN THE CONSTITUTION

- Part II sets out the rules for citizenship of India, an important source of rights for women.
- Part III sets out the Fundamental Rights and includes many of the civil and political fundamental rights and freedoms important to women, including the right to equality before the law, the right to be free from discrimination, the right against exploitation and cultural and educational rights.
- Part IV sets out the Directive Principles of State, which are largely premised on social, economic and cultural rights and include the right to work, the right to education, the obligation to develop a uniform civil code and the duty of the state to improve public health. They are not 'enforceable by any court' but are 'fundamental in the governance of the country'.
- Part IV-A sets out the Fundamental Duties of citizens, also not enforceable by any court, including renouncing practices derogatory to the dignity of women, abjuring violence and for a parent or guardian to provide opportunities for education to her or his child.
- Part V sets out the process for the election of the president and establishes the three major arms of the Union. The first arm is the executive, which is the part of government that has sole authority and responsibility for the daily administration of the state. The second arm is the legislature, which has the power to pass, amend and repeal laws and to accept, amend or reject budgets. The legislature is bicameral, with an upper house called the Rajya Sabha ('Council of States') and a lower house called the Lok Sabha ('House of the People'). The third arm is the

judiciary, the system of courts that interprets and applies the law in the name of the state. It is a three-tier and independent judiciary consisting of the Supreme Court, headed by the Chief Justice of India; 24 high courts and a large number of trial courts.

- Parts IX and IX-A establish the administration the panchayats and the municipalities (including a 33 percent quota for women).
- Part XV sets out the processes and ruled for elections, including the establishment of the electoral commission, which is charged with the organisation of elections, detailing the required qualifications of voters and candidates and other electoral procedures.

Source: Authors

Legislation

Legislation is law that has been made and enacted by a legislature, such as a parliament. A single piece of legislation is also known as an act of parliament or a statute, while legislation is broadly known as statutory law.[114] In India, legislation takes precedence over judicial decisions but is inferior to the Constitution. Formulating new legislation and reviewing and amending existing legislation are the main business of the Union, state and territory parliaments. The legislative procedure for the Union Parliament requires that proposed bills pass through the two legislative houses – the Lok Sabha (Lower House) and the Rajya Sabha (Upper House). The legislative procedure for states with bicameral legislatures[115] requires that proposed bills be passed in the Vidhan Sabha (Lower House), but they do not have to be passed in the Vidhan Parishad (Upper House). For states with unicameral legislatures,[116] laws and bills need to be passed only in the state's single house, the Vidhan Sabha.[117]

Legislation, including subordinate legislation in the form of rules, regulations and by-laws, is a primary source of law in India, including a vast body of legislation enacted before, during and after colonisation. There are three sources of legislation. First, legislation enacted in Great Britain during colonisation that extended to India by paramount operation and did not reflect local Indian norms. For example, the *Government of India Act* 1858, which provided that India was to be governed directly and in the name of the British Crown.[118] Second, legislation enacted by Great Britain for India during colonisation that consisted of both British legal standards and local norms. For example, on 1 January 1860, Great Britain enacted the *Indian Penal Code*, which had its basis in British law but also included norms relevant to the Indian context.[119] Third, legislation enacted after Independence based on local norms or a combination of local norms and British norms. For example, the *Hindu Marriage Act*, enacted in 1955, enables Hindu marriages to be solemnised 'in accordance with the customary rites and ceremonies of either party' but also includes actions for restitution of conjugal rights and judicial separation, which have their origins in the ecclesiastical law which informed British family law at the time.[120]

Legislation provides a major source of women's human rights in both public and private spheres. In the public sphere, legislation supporting women's human rights includes the *Equal Remuneration Act* 1976, which requires employers to pay equal remuneration to its male and female employees who are carrying out the same or similar work and prohibits employers from discriminating between men and women while recruiting, unless there is a restriction under law to employ women in certain industries; the *Sexual Harassment of Women at Workplace (Prevention, Prohibition and Redressal) Act* 2013, which provides a complaints process for women subject to sexual harassment in the workplace and the *Maternity Benefit (Amendment) Act* 2016, which increases maternity leave available to working women from 12 weeks to 26 weeks for the first two children. In the private sphere, the *Protection of Women from Domestic Violence Act* 2005 provides women with access to protection and residence orders, the *Prohibition of Child Marriage Act* 2005 makes underage marriages voidable and the *Pre-natal Diagnostic Techniques (Regulation and Prevention) Act* 1994 prohibits sex selection before and after conception to halt the rise in female foeticide.

Legislation, however, also denies women's human rights in some instances. For example, under the *Indian Succession Act* 1925, a non-Parsi woman who is a widow of a Parsi man cannot inherit;[121] under both the *Hindu Marriage Act* 1955 and the *Special Marriage Act* 1954, the minimum age for marriage for a male is 21, but it is 18 for a female[122] and the *Hindu Minority and Guardianship Act* 1956 designates fathers the 'natural guardian' of a child.[123]

Judicial decisions

Decisions made by judges in the courts, known collectively as the common law, are another important source of law in India.[124] Common law was first introduced in India by the British in 1727 with the establishment of courts in Madras, Bombay and Bengal initially applying only to citizens of Great Britain.[125] In 1858 India was declared a Crown colony, and the common law system was extended to the whole of India.[126] British common law was received to the extent that it was suitable to Indian conditions and continued to be received during the period of colonisation. At Independence, the Constitution 'saved' the common law, and it continues as part of the body of Indian common law unless overridden by legislation or subsequent cases.[127]

Courts form a strict hierarchy of importance, with the Supreme Court at the top, followed by high courts and district courts at the bottom. Article 141 of the Constitution states that the law declared by the Supreme Court shall be binding on all courts within the territory of India. This accords with the system of precedent and means that judges must follow the rulings and determinations of judges in higher courts where a case involves similar facts and issues. Therefore, the judicial decisions of Indian superior courts are binding on all courts below them. These decisions constitute the most significant body of judicial decisions in India. The common law continues to develop and grow as judges hear cases and make determinations and increasingly, as women's organisations and gender advocates bring cases utilising feminist approaches and women's human rights principles, case law becomes a source of women's human rights.

Within the common law, there are some notable cases where women's rights have been recognised and have subsequently become sources of women's human rights. For example, when Mary Roy did not receive an equal share of the familial property after her father's death due to discriminatory provisions in the *Travancore Succession Act* 1916 governing succession for Christians living in Kerala, which provided that daughters were eligible for one quarter of the sons' share or IR 5,000, which ever was less, if the father died intestate. Mary Roy sued her brothers, asking for an equal right and challenging the provisions of the legislation.[128] She argued that the legislation was contrary to article 14 of the Constitution and therefore unconstitutional. The court did not decide on this point but held that the *Indian Succession Act* 1925 (which does not discriminate) included the Christian community in Kerala, rendering the *Travancore Succession Act* 1916 invalid. The successful outcome entitled her and, in the future, other Christian women in Kerala to an equal share from their father's property.[129]

Unfavourable outcomes may, however, result in judicial decisions that deny women's human rights. For example, in *Smt. Sowmithri Vishnu v. Union of India & Anor*,[130] the plaintiff argued that section 497 of the *Penal Code* 1860, which creates an offence for adultery by a husband but not a wife, was contrary to the equality provision article 14 of the Constitution (the equality provision) because (amongst other things) it enables the prosecution of a male adulterer but does not enable prosecution of a female adulterer. It also excludes cases where the husband has sexual relations with an unmarried woman. The court held that section 497 is not contrary to article 14 of the Constitution on the basis that the offence of adultery, by its very definition, can only be committed by a man and not by a woman. The court held that the argument of the petitioner related to the policy of the law and that, in defining the offence of adultery so as to restrict the class of offenders to men who have affairs with married women, no constitutional provision is infringed. The court stated: 'It is commonly accepted that it is the man who is the seducer and not the woman' and 'the contemplation of the law, evidently, is that the wife, who is involved in an illicit relationship with another man, is a victim and not the author of the crime.'[131] The finding of the court treats men differently from women, it hierarchises marriage above *de facto* relationships and does not recognise the autonomy and agency of woman to choose to engage in sexual relations. This provision was, however, declared unconstitutional in 2017, the court stating 'A time has come when the society must realise that a woman is equal to a man in every field. This provision, prima facie, appears to be quite archaic.'[132] This provides an excellent illustration of the power of the principle of equality and non-discrimination to foster reform.

Women's human rights scholars argue that the judicial process has limitations as a source of women's human rights. Litigation requires a harmed individual who can only litigate in relation to an individual harm she has suffered. The remedy, should the litigation succeed, is afforded only to the injured individual. No benefits, therefore, are provided to others in a similar situation.[133] Unless a decision is broadcast in the media, the lower judiciary, other lawyers and most of the community will be unaware of the decision. Additionally and crucially, compensation to a harmed individual or an injunction that prohibits an isolated behaviour to protect an individual does little to change or address the structural underpinnings of gender inequality.[134] For example, providing a rape victim with compensation in a civil action, while recognising to some extent the victim's 'human rights', does not address the institutional cause of rape or facilitate the recognition that men as a class need to develop 'ethically appropriate' norms in relation to sexual conduct.

Although we agree that private rights litigation, therefore, is limited as a source of women's human rights, we argue that women do rely on the courts for justice. Further, if a case results in discriminatory legislation being declared invalid, such as in Mary Roy's case, the outcome can be much more wide-ranging. Judicial decisions can be a significant source of women's human rights, therefore, in some instances.[135]

Public interest litigation

Public interest litigation (PIL) provides, we suggest, a unique source of women's human rights in India. The major function of the courts in judicial decision-making is the protection of private individuals by declaring and enforcing their private rights; however, PIL is litigation that represents the collective interests of the community or groups such as workers, the unemployed and women and minorities as the subjects of litigation, rather than individuals.[136] It provides, therefore, a much greater capacity to further women's human rights than ordinary judicial decision-making by framing gender inequality within a broader 'public' interest framework.[137]

PIL had its origins in the 1960s in the socio-political context of the civil rights movement in the United States (US), where it was specifically utilised by civil organisations to assist the disadvantaged. In India, inspired by the emergence of the movement in the US, lawyers pursued 'public interest' cases in an attempt to remedy the failure of government, administrative bodies and institutions to adequately represent and address marginalised interests. While initially India closely followed the developments in the US, by the end of the 1970s, the Indian judiciary had begun to take a very different path, deriving its authority over PIL actions from article 32 of the Constitution, which guarantees persons the right 'to move the Court by appropriate proceedings.'[138] While the language of article 32 is very broad, the courts used the provision to expand litigation procedurally and substantively, with some positive results for the rights of women. PIL allows an individual who claims a violation of her or his fundamental rights as enshrined in the Constitution to approach a high court or the Supreme Court.[139] The right to life, article 21 of the Constitution, has proved to be the greatest source of women's human rights in PIL, leading to recognition of a right to education, a right to food and clothing, a right not to be married underage or to be coerced into a sterilisation. PIL has enabled challenges to structural inequalities faced by women much more effectively than ordinary litigation. It has achieved this through the adoption of relaxed standing and a flexible array of remedies.[140]

Standing requirements have been relaxed in PIL actions to authorise anyone acting in good faith to pursue an action without any requirement for a personal stake. This has enhanced access to the courts by enabling non-government organisations and other organisations to lodge and pursue claims on behalf of both individual women and women collectively.[141] For example, in *Dr Jaya Sagade v. State of Maharashtra*,[142] Jaya Sagade (a law professor), the Lawyers Collective, Tata Institute of Social Sciences and Stree Mukti succeeded in a PIL in the Bombay High Court, where they challenged a circular issued by the Maharashtra government, which stated that counselling and mediation in domestic violence cases could only be conducted with the permission of the courts.[143] Although the petitioners were all working in the domestic violence field, they were not users of counselling or mediation and may not have had standing in ordinary litigation.

The ability (and practice) of the courts in PIL to award a flexible array of remedies, including directions and orders which have the status of legislation, have resulted in outcomes with the capacity to address structural gender inequalities more effectively.[144] For example, *Vishaka v. Rajasthan*,[145] in which the Supreme Court developed a sexual harassment code and ordered its immediate implementation across the country. The remedy, given legislative status, was not limited to the individual victim of the litigation (a woman who was gang raped in her place of employment) but explicitly aimed at protecting all working women in India. A further example is *Centre for Enquiry into Health and Allied Themes v. Union of India*,[146] where the court, after accepting the arguments of the petitioners that a ban on sex selection abortions was ineffective, issued a series of directions to both the Union government and the state governments to educate the public about the law and why sex selective abortion should cease. The court ordered that a central supervisory committee be set up to meet every six months to monitor and review the implementation of the legislation and to ensure that states produced quarterly reports detailing the measures that were being taken to implement the act. A final example is *Forum for Fact Finding Documentation and Advocacy v. Union of India Child Marriages*,[147] where a human rights monitoring organisation filed a public interest litigation before the Supreme Court, seeking a ban on child marriages. The petition called for strict enforcement of the existing *Child Marriage Restraint Act* 1929, the punishment of officials who failed to stop such marriages from taking place, compensation for girls whose marriages were solemnised and the instigation of criminal prosecutions by the state. It also requested the court to order the national and state governments to launch official campaigns against child marriage and to make birth and marriage registration mandatory. The Supreme Court agreed and directed Parliament to draft a new law to replace the previous legislation. Subsequently, the *Prohibition of Child Marriage Act* 2006 was enacted, bringing India in line with its obligations under both the *Convention on the Rights of the Child* 1989 and article 16 of *CEDAW* and providing protection for all children in India although it continues to be discriminatory with different ages of marriage for males and females.

Some of these outcomes have not been fully implemented as there is no monitoring system in place, limiting the capacity of PIL to provide a source of women's human rights. Nevertheless, PIL showcases issues and provides a forum for advancing women's human rights unique to India.

Customary law

Customary law is a customary practice followed by a community for a long period which is recognised as law by that community. There are two main bodies of customary practices that have the status of customary law in India and are recognised by the state legal system. Neither provide strong sources of women's human rights.

The first are customary practices in particular areas of life, primarily marriage and family relationships, which are recognised as law by legislation. The *Hindu Marriage Act* 1955 sets out a range of rules governing marriage between Hindus; however, for some of those rules, there are exceptions enabling a person to apply custom instead of the law. For example, the legislation provides that marriage may be solemnized between any two Hindus provided the parties are not sapindas of each other,[148] 'unless the custom or usage governing each of them permits of a marriage between the two'. The legislation defines custom as 'any rule which, having been continuously and uniformly observed for a long time, has obtained the force of law among Hindus in any local area, tribe, community, group or family'.[149]

Much of customary law is uncodified and undocumented, so it is difficult to assess its capacity as a source of women's human rights.[150] However, custom has been developed primarily by men, it is interpreted by men and therefore it likely supports the rights of men. It is therefore an unlikely source of women's human rights.

The second is sharia law, the religious law forming part of the Islamic tradition derived from the religious precepts of Islam, particularly the Quran and the Hadith, which regulate the personal affairs of Muslims in terms of marriage, divorce and inheritance.[151] According to the *Muslim Personal Law (Shariat) Application Act* 1937, if the parties are Muslim intestate succession, special property of females, including personal property inherited or obtained under contract or gift or any other provision of personal law; marriage; dissolution of marriage, including *talaq*, *ila*, *zihar*, *lian*, *khula* and *mubaraat*; maintenance; dower; guardianship; gifts; trusts and trust properties and *waqfs* (other than charities and charitable institutions and charitable and religious endowments) are governed by sharia law.[152] Sharia law is not applicable in other areas of law, such as the criminal law, which are governed by the formal law.[153] There are some aspects of sharia law which do meet women's human rights standards, such as the requirement for consent before a marriage is valid, which is not replicated in Hindu law. However, this is not the result of feminist advocacy. Indeed, there are many other examples in sharia law where the rights of women are not recognised and which are not in accord with women's human rights standards. For example, women cannot be the natural guardians of their children,[154] women receive only half of the share of inheritance received by their male counterparts and through the practice of *halala*, if a man divorces his wife three times, then he cannot remarry her unless she marries another man and is either divorced by her new husband or becomes a widow.[155]

Neither body of customary law offers a viable source of women's human rights.[156] Indeed, both bodies of law contain clear violations of women's human rights. State parties have an obligation to remove any inconsistency between international human rights law binding on it and any religious or customary laws operating.[157] In particular, article 2(f) and article 5(a) of *CEDAW* require state parties to implement appropriate measures to eliminate discrimination against women in customary practices. Although the task of eliminating discriminatory customary law is considerable, India has a clear obligation under human rights law to develop mechanisms and strategies to fulfil its obligations.

Non-state legal system

There are many practices and customs in India that do not have the force of law and are not recognised by the state legal system. These customs have great strength and can be a source of women's human rights but are more likely to be contrary to women's human rights.[158] Customs and practices that are outside the state legal system are implemented by caste panchayats and tribal councils in both rural and urban areas. It is difficult to know the content of the customs and practices in different communities as most are not codified or documented.[159] In the following two subsections we examine first, caste panchayats and tribal councils, which are examples of non-state institutions enforcing local customs and practices and, second, the *nari adalats*, which are established (indirectly) by the state yet also enforce local customs and practices that do not have the status of law. Although the *nari adalats* have more potential than caste panchayats and tribal councils to be sources of women's human rights, none of these institutions has the oversight of the human rights system.[160]

Caste panchayats and tribal councils

Caste panchayats operate alongside and separate from the local courts established by the state legal system.[161] Each caste has a caste association, some more formal than others, and caste panchayats are caste-specific juries of elders operating as an informal court in both rural and urban areas primarily in the lower and middle classes.[162] They draw on local customs and practices to determine disputes and issues, decide what evidence is required and the quantum and mode of punishment.[163] Payment is often required, and disputants sometimes must also pay for alcohol and *beedis*. The caste panchayats often deliver outcomes that do not reflect women's human rights standards.[164] Although the formal law is technically available to all women, few approach lawyers or go directly to the state courts and the police.[165] Although they do not have any legal authority, caste panchayats exert significant social influence within the community they represent. It is primarily a men's assembly where women are not able to participate although there is some evidence of an increasing women's presence in some areas.[166] While customs and practices vary throughout India and are largely undocumented, research suggests that women often do not receive treatment in accord with their legal rights or international norms.[167]

Tribal councils operate in most tribal communities. They are exclusively populated by men and operate similarly to the caste panchayats.[168] In an exceptional example in a tribal community in Lamka, Manipur, in the Northeast of India visited by the authors, the Paite tribe have codified their customs. In the *Paite Customary Law and Practices*, there are a number of local customs which are contrary to women's human rights. For example, giving birth in another person's house is defilement, and if a wife divorces her husband, she has no authority over her children. The code also contains sexual assault provisions which reflect a contemporary approach to consent. Sexual intercourse with a woman without her consent is rape. Sexual intercourse with an underage girl is rape regardless of consent.[169] Although this is a positive inclusion in the code in line with women's human rights principles, it operates outside the oversight of the formal legal system and the human rights system and cannot be relied upon to deliver women's human rights.

Nari adalats

Nari adalats are 'women's courts' established in 2001 by the Mahila Samakhyas, a women's group created by the central government to give poor, rural, marginalized sections of society and minority women a voice and an identity.[170] Although they are established by the state, the customs and practices they enforce are not recognised by the state, an intriguing mixture of a state institution administering non-state law. As of November 2014, there were 481 *nari adalats* in 11 states. These courts have presided over 30,000 cases since their inception.[171] The *nari adalats* represent a new system of justice for rural women, operating as an informal, conciliatory, non-adversarial social network which creates a protected social space for women to raise their concerns and to be heard.[172] A *nari adalat* consists of selected women from the community, a facilitator from a local women's empowerment program and women from various community organisations. There are no obvious caste, class or religious hierarchies in the judicial process. Members attend Mahila Samakhya's awareness-building camps, paralegal training, *mahiti melas* (female gatherings) to discuss legal issues for knowledge enhancement, experiential learning, inter-district sharing of experiences and periodic orientations and updates on legal information, including new laws. Meetings may be held on the veranda of the village government office, at a school building or under a tree in the middle of a village square.[173] Although they are not established by law and have no legal authority, the *nari adalats* decide and mediate cases including divorce, disputes between women and their in-laws and the abuse of widows, children and the elderly.[174] The agreement of all parties is an integral part of the settlement agreements made typically on bond paper.[175]

The *nari adalats* have been hailed for their ability to provide timely justice and have been recognised by some for supporting women's human rights using a community-based, informal legal system.[176] The *nari adalats* are not, however, formalised in law, and although some may apply the formal law, there is no requirement that they do, and the remedies they offer lack consistency and may not accord with women's human rights.[177] Further, their decisions cannot ultimately be enforced if a party refuses to comply.[178] Additionally, research suggests they retain their emphasis on ensuring the rights of women within the framework of marriage, rather than outside it. Their priority is on finding a solution for the woman within the ambit of social justice, rather than applying universal women's human rights.[179] A low level of understanding of laws, legal provisions and procedures, coupled with patriarchal ways of judging may lead to decisions that do not uphold women's rights, falling short of what the courts may offer through legislation more progressive than customary practices.[180] While the *nari adalat* may not currently offer victims remedies in accord with good practice international norms, relying instead on compromise, reconciliation, settlement and forgiveness, they have potential as an important source of women's human rights with formalisation bringing them fully inside the state legal system with training and support.[181]

Conclusion

This chapter has overviewed international and domestic sources of women's human rights and concluded that they provide positive and rich opportunities for law and policy-makers, women's advocates, litigants, women's organisations and other members of civil society to advance women's rights and to further gender equality. While gender equality is a formidable goal in the Indian context, women's human rights provide a tool for in the rapidly changing social context throughout India. While *CEDAW* provides the strongest source of women's human rights in the international human rights system, it is India's domestic legal framework that provides the most promising and immediate source of women's human rights, including the Constitution, legislation and judicial decisions, including PIL. All these sources have potential for greater opportunities, and in the next chapter, we lay out the women's human rights theories which can be utilised to make greater use of women's human rights standards and principles.

Notes

1 Sally Engle Merry, *Human Rights and Gender Violence: Translating International Law into Local Justice* (University of Chicago Press, 2006) 2.
2 UN General Assembly, *Convention on the Elimination of All Forms of Discrimination against Women*, 18 December 1979, United Nations, Treaty Series, vol. 1249.
3 Beijing Declaration and Platform for Action, Fourth World Conference on Women, 15 September, 1995 (A/CONF.177/20).
4 Merry, above n 1, 104.
5 Vasudha Nagaraj, 'Local and Customary Forums: Adapting and Innovating Rules of Formal Law' in Flavia Agnes and Shoba Gosh (eds.) *Negotiating Spaces: Legal Domains, Gender Concerns and Community Constructs* (Oxford University Press, 2012) 201–220, 202.
6 Sue Farran, *Human Rights in the South Pacific: Challenges and Changes* (Routledge & Cavendish, 2009) 59; Stephan Johnson and Nathan Mack, 'The United Nations Institutions: A Critical Analysis of Their Ability to Promote and Protect International Human Rights' (2014) 15(2) *Nagoya University of Commerce and Business Administration Journal of Language Culture and Communication*, 5–13, 5.
7 A. Reis Monteiro, *Ethics of Human Rights* (Springer, 2014) 136.
8 Ibid 137.
9 See Neil Englehart and Melissa Miller, 'The CEDAW Effect: International Law's Impact on Women's Rights' (2014) 13(1) *Journal of Human Rights* 22–47, 25 who argue, based on cross-sectional data, that *CEDAW* has 'a significant, positive effect on human rights conditions for women'.
10 Virginia Leary, *International Labour Conventions and National Law* (Springer, 1982) 165.
11 Barry Fitzpatrick, 'A Dualist House of Lords in a Sea of Monist Community Law?' in Paul Carmichael and Brice Dickson (eds.) *The House of Lords: Its Parliamentary and Judicial Roles* (Hart Publishing, 1999) 171.
12 Wayne Sandholtz, 'How Domestic Courts Use International Law' (2015) 38(2) *Fordham International Law Journal* 595–636, 610.
13 Eilionóir Flynn, 'Ireland' in Lisa Waddington and Anna Lawson (eds.) *The UN Convention on the Rights of Persons with Disabilities in Practice: A Comparative Analysis of the Role of Courts* (Oxford University Press, 2018).
14 *Constitution of India* 1950, art 51(c).
15 *Kesavananda Bharati Sripadagalvaru v. Kerala* (1973) Supp SCR 1, 165.
16 Bimal N. Patel, *The State Practice of India and the Development of International Law: Dynamic Interplay between Foreign Policy and Jurisprudence* (Brill-Nijhoff, 2016) 144.
17 *Peoples Union for Civil Liberties v. Union of India AIR* (1997) SC 1203, 13, 15. Vishwanath G. Hegde, 'Indian Courts and International Law' (2010) 23(1) *Leiden Journal of International Law* 53–77; See Sunil Agarwal, 'Implementation of International Law in India: Role of the Judiciary' (2011) for further discussion on the use of international law by the Indian courts. https://papers.ssrn.com/sol3/papers.cfm?abstract_id=1864489 Accessed 17/4/19.
18 Andrew Byrnes and Marsha Freeman, *The Impact of the CEDAW Convention: Paths to Equality* (World Bank, 2012).
19 *Vishaka v. Rajasthan* (1997) Supp 3 SCR 404; *TN Godaram Thirumulpad v. Union of India* (2012) 4 SCC 362.
20 *Sakshi v. Union of India and Ors AIR* (2004) SC 3566.
21 See Madhu Mehra, 'India's CEDAW Story' in Anne Hellum and Henrietta Aasen (eds.) *Women's Human Rights: CEDAW in International, Regional and National Law* (Cambridge University Press, 2013) 385–409, who overviews a range of Indian cases in which international conventions were utilised by the courts.
22 Jennifer Riddle, 'Making *CEDAW* Universal: A Critique of *CEDAW*'s Reservation Regime under Article 28 and the Effectiveness of the Reporting Process' (2002) 34(3) *George Washington International Law Review* 605–638, 605.

23 Michael Buenger, 'Human Rights Conventions and Reservations: An Examination of a Critical Deficit in the *CEDAW*' (2013–2014) 20 *Buffalo Human Rights Law Review* 67–90, 83–84.
24 See the *Vienna Convention on the Law of Treaties* (1155 UNTS 331) (*entry into force* 27 January 1980) art 2(1)(d) for a definition of a reservation at international law.
25 Ibid arts 19–23.
26 Ibid art 18.
27 'Declaration' in United Nations Treaty Collection 'Glossary of Terms Relating to Treaty Action' (2018) https://treaties.un.org/pages/overview.aspx?path=overview/glossary/page1_en.xml Accessed 17/4/19.
28 Ibid.
29 Ibid.
30 Helen Keller and Geir Ulfstein, *UN Human Rights Treaty Bodies: Law and Legitimacy* (Cambridge University Press, 2012) 86.
31 United Nations Human Rights Office of the High Commissioner 'Elections of Treaty Body Members' (2018). www.ohchr.org/EN/HRBodies/Pages/ElectionsofTreatyBodiesMembers.aspx Accessed 17/4/19.
32 Ibid.
33 Helen Keller and Geir Ulfstein, n 30, 126.
34 Office of the High Commissioner for Human Rights, fifth session of the Ad Hoc Committee on a Comprehensive and Integral International Convention on Protection and Promotion of the Rights and Dignity of Persons with Disabilities, *Monitoring Implementation of the International Human Rights Instruments: An Overview of the Current Treaty Body System*, 24 January–4 February 2005, 5. www.un.org/esa/socdev/enable/rights/ahc5ohchr.doc Accessed 17/4/19.
35 Ibid 9.
36 Ibid 5, 12.
37 Ibid 5, 13.
38 Ibid 5. See Andrew Byrnes, 'The Committee on the Elimination of Discrimination against Women' in Anne Hellum and Henrietta Aasen, n 19, 27–61, 39.
39 Sarah Joseph, Katie Mitchell, Linda Gyorki and Carin Benninger-Budel, *Seeking Remedies for Torture Victims: A Handbook on the Individual Complaints Procedures of the UN Treaty Bodies* (World Organisation Against Torture, 2006) 15.
40 United Nations Economic and Social Commission for Asia and the Pacific, *Combating Human Trafficking in Asia: A Resource Guide to International and Regional Legal Instruments, Political Commitments and Recommended Practices* (United Nations Publications, 2003) 231.
41 Fionnuala Ní Aoláin, 'Advancing Feminist Positioning in the Field of Transitional Justice' (2012) 6(2) *International Journal of Transitional Justice* 205–228, 206; Hilary Charlesworth, 'Gender and International Law' in Jill Steans and Daniela Tepe-Belfrage (eds.) *Handbook on Gender in World Politics* (Elgar, 2016) 137–144, 137.
42 Felipe Isa, 'The Optional Protocol for the Convention on the Elimination of All Forms of Discrimination against Women: Strengthening the Protection Mechanisms of Women's Human Rights' (2003) 20 *Arizona Journal of International and Comparative Law* 291–321, 295.
43 CEDAW, *Progress Achieved in the Implementation of the Convention on the Elimination of all Forms of Discrimination Against Women* – Report by the Committee on the Elimination of Discrimination against Women (UN Doc A/CONF.177/7) (4 September 1995), at [9–10]. The other four instruments are: the *Convention on the Political Rights of Women*, opened for signature 31 March 1953 (*entry into force* 7 July 1954); the *Convention on the Nationality of Married Women*, opened for signature 29 January 1957 (*entry into force* 11: August 1958); the *Convention on Consent to Marriage, Minimum Age for Marriage and Registration of Marriages* opened for signature 7 November 1962 (*entry into force* 9 December 1964); and the *Recommendation on Consent to Marriage, Minimum Age for Marriage and Registration of Marriages* (adopted 1 November 1965).

44 Margaret E. Galey, 'Promoting Non-Discrimination against Women: The UN Commission on the Status of Women' 23(2) *International Studies Quarterly* 273–302, 276.
45 Hannah Elizabeth Kington, *Why Has the United States Never Ratified the UN Convention on the Elimination of All Forms of Discrimination against Women?* (Western Kentucky University, 2009) 5.
46 UN General Assembly, *Declaration on the Elimination of Discrimination against Women* 7 November 1967 (A/RES/2263(XXII)).
47 Noreen Burrows, 'The 1979 Convention on the Elimination of All Forms of Discrimination against Women' (1985) 32 *Netherlands International Law Review* 419–460.
48 Ibid.
49 Beth Simmons, *Mobilizing for Human Rights: International Law in Domestic Politics* (Harvard University Press, 2009) 206.
50 Ibid.
51 Mehra, n 21, 393.
52 Esteve-Volart, Berta, 'Sex Discrimination and Growth', Working Paper No 84 (International Monetary Fund, 2000).
53 Hilkka Pietila and Jeanne Vickers, *Making Women Matter: The Role of the United Nations* (Zed Books, 1996) 123.
54 Ibid.
55 Bobbie Khanna, '*CEDAW* and the Impact on Violence against Women in India' (2013) 17 *University of Washington Bothell Policy Journal* 31–41, 32.
56 State Parties to UN General Assembly, Convention on the Elimination of All Forms of Discrimination against Women, 18 December 1979, United Nations, Treaty Series, vol. 1249, 13 www.un.org/womenwatch/daw/cedaw/states.htm Accessed 17/4/19.
57 *CEDAW*, Committee, General Recommendation 28, *The Core Obligations of States Parties* 18 December 1979, United Nations, Treaty Series, vol. 1249, art 2, at [41]. www.ohchr.org/en/hrbodies/cedaw/pages/recommendations.aspx Accessed 18/4/19.
58 Ibid at [15].
59 Ibid.
60 Andrew Clapham, *Human Rights in the Private Sphere* (Oxford University Press, 1993) 100.
61 *CEDAW*, n 2, art 4(1).
62 Ibid art 17(1).
63 Ibid arts 18, 21–22.
64 Ibid art 18 (a)–(b).
65 Julia Ernst, 'US Ratification of the Convention on the Elimination of All Forms of Discrimination against Women' (1995) 3 *Michigan Journal of Gender and Law* 299–367, 341.
66 CEDAW Committee, *Results of the Fortieth Session of the Committee on the Elimination of Discrimination against Women*, Annex 1 (UN Doc E/CN6/2008/CRP/1) (11 February 2008).
67 *CEDAW*, n 2, arts 20–22.
68 Ernst, n 65, 341.
69 *CEDAW*, n 2, art 22.
70 Ibid art 21(1).
71 *CEDAW* Committee, *United Nations Committee on the Elimination of Discrimination against Women to Meet*, 30 June to 18 July, Geneva (UN Doc E/CN6/2014/CRP/4) (25 June 2018).
72 The most recent is General Recommendation No 37 on *Gender-Related Dimensions of Disaster Risk Reduction in the Context of Climate Change*, March 2018 (UN Doc CEDAW/C/GC/37). www.ohchr.org/en/hrbodies/cedaw/pages/recommendations.aspx Accessed 17/4/19.
73 Riddle, n 22, 606.
74 See generally, United Nations Treaty Collection. https://treaties.un.org/pages/viewdetails.aspx?src=treaty&mtdsg_no=iv-8&chapter=4&lang=en Accessed 17/4/19.

75 Belinda Clark, 'The Vienna Convention Reservations Regime and the Convention on Discrimination against Women' (1991) 85 *American Journal of International Law* 281–321, 316.
76 Marijke de Pauw, 'Women's Rights: From Bad to Worse? Assessing the Evolution of Incompatible Reservations to the *CEDAW* Convention' (2013) 29(77) *Merkourios* 51–65.
77 See, for specific reservations on Articles 2, 5 and 16 made by different countries, www.un.org/womenwatch/daw/cedaw/reservations.htm Accessed 18/4/19.
78 Eryn Krivansky, *The Reality of Reservations: A Quantitative Analysis of the Influence of CEDAW on Women's Holistic Rights* (Pennsylvania State University, 2016); Clark, n 75, 289; Linda Keller, 'The Impact of States Parties' Reservations to the Convention on the Elimination of All Forms of Discrimination against Women' (2014) 2014(2) *Michigan State Law Review* 309–326; Christine Chinkin, 'The Convention on the Elimination of Discrimination against Women' in *Handbook on Gender in World Politics*, n 41, 145–152, 147.
79 Rumana Islam, '*CEDAW*. The Pain and the Promise' (2017) *ELCOP Yearbook*, 21–38, 37.
80 Kasey McCall-Smith, 'Severing Reservation' (2014) 63(3) *International and Comparative Law Quarterly* 599–634; Radhika Coomaraswamy, 'Women and Children: The Cutting Edge of International Law' (2015) 1(7) *American University International Law Review* 1–41.
81 Islam, n 79, 32.
82 Peu Ghosh, *Indian Governments and Politics* (Prentice-Hall of India Pvt. Ltd, 2012) 418.
83 Dhrubajyoti Bhattacharya, *At the Intersection of Law, Human Rights, and Religion (November 12, 2012) Global Health Disputes and Disparities* (Routledge, 2012). http://ssrn.com/abstract=2328695 Accessed 17/4/19.
84 *Delhi (Compulsory Registration of Marriage)* Order (2014) F.1(12) DC/MC/2014/4392/dt 24.04.2014; *Smt Seema v. Aswini Kumar* in transfer petition (c) No 291 of 2005; Bedprakas SyamRoy, *India's Journey Towards Sustainable Population* (Springer International Publishing, 2017) 134.
85 See Asia Pacific, IWRAW, 'The Validity of Reservations and Declarations to CEDAW: The Indian Experience' (2005) 14, 18, where the authors argue the declarations are reservations and, as such, are severable and do not restrict India's obligations towards its citizens. http://ssrn.com/abstract=1146815 Accessed 17/4/19.
86 Optional Protocol to the Convention on the Elimination of All Forms of Discrimination against Women, opened for signature 6 October 1999, 2131 UNTS 83 (*entry into force* 22 December 2000) (the Optional Protocol).
87 Optional Protocol, n 86, art 2.
88 Ibid Optional Protocol, art 3; Kerri Ritz, 'Soft Enforcement: Inadequacies of Optional Protocol as a Remedy for the Convention on the Elimination of all Forms of Discrimination against Women' (2001) 25 *Suffolk Transnational Law Review* 191–226.
89 Ibid art 8(1).
90 Ibid art 17.
91 See Loveday Hodson, 'Women's Rights and the Periphery: CEDAW's Optional Protocol' (2014) 25(2) *European Journal of International Law* 561–578 for an overview of the global impact of the Optional Protocol.
92 Beijing Declaration and Platform for Action, n 2.
93 United Nations, *Report of the Fourth World Conference on Women Beijing*, 4–15 September 1995 (A/CONF.177/20/Rev.1) 188.
94 Ibid.
95 Beijing Declaration and Platform for Action, n 2, at [24].
96 June Zeitlin (ed.), *Beijing Betrayed: Women Worldwide Report That Governments Have Failed to Turn the Platform into Action* (Women's Environment and Development Organization, 2005).
97 Maxine Molyneux and Shahra Razavi, *Beijing Plus 10: An Ambivalent Record on Gender Justice Paper No 15* (United Nations Research Institute for Social Development, 2009).

www.unrisd.org/80256B3C005BCCF9/search/4EE168779E57E924C12571CA003C2295 Accessed 17/4/19.

98 India's Report on the Implementation of Beijing Declaration and Platform for Action in Context of the Twentieth Anniversary of the Fourth World Conference on Women and the Adoption of the Beijing Declaration and Platform for Action (2015). www.unwomen.org/~/media/headquarters/attachments/sections/csw/59/national_reviews/india_review_beijing20.pdf Accessed 17/4/19.

99 UN Women, 'The Beijing Platform for Action: Inspiration Then and Now' *Field Office Beijing Plus* (2015); Petra Debusscher, *Evaluation of the Beijing Platform for Action+ 20 and the Opportunities for Achieving Gender Equality and the Empowerment of Women in the post-2015 Development Agenda* (University of Antwerp, 2015) 1–55.

100 Sally Engle Merry, 'Legal Transplants and Cultural Translation: Making Human Rights in the Vernacular' and 'Localizing Human Rights and Rights Consciousness' in *Human Rights and Gender Violence: Translating International Law into Local Justice*, n 1, 134–218.

101 India is a federation composed of 29 states and 7 union territories. All states, and the union territories of Puducherry and the National Capital Territory of Delhi, have elected legislatures and governments, patterned on the Westminster model. Each state or union territory is further divided into administrative districts. The districts in turn are further divided into tehsils and then into villages.

102 Eleanor Newbigin, *Hindu Family and the Emergence of Modern India* (Cambridge University Press, 2013).

103 Mehra, n 21, 389–392.

104 Geetanjali Misra, Ajay Mahal and Rima Shah, 'Protecting the Rights of Sex Workers: The Indian Experience' in Geetanjali Misra and Radhika Chandiramani (eds.) *Sexuality, Gender and Rights: Exploring Theory and Practice in South and Southeast Asia* (Sage Publications, 2005).

105 Jana Von Stein, 'Making Promises, 'Keeping Promises: Democracy, Ratification and Compliance in International Human Rights Law' (2016) 46(3) *British Journal of Political Science* 655–679, 656, 661.

106 Mengia Hong Tschalaer, *Muslim Women's Quest for Justice: Gender, Law and Activism in India* (Cambridge University Press, 2017) 25–29.

107 Ibid 57, 134.

108 Aya Ikegame, 'Overlapping Sovereignties: Gurus and Citizenship' in Engin Isin (ed.) *Citizenship after Orientalism: Transforming Political Theory* (Palgrave MacMillan, 2015) 106.

109 Helen Irving, *Gender and the Constitution: Equity and Agency in Comparative Constitutional Law* (Cambridge University Press, 2008) 13.

110 Louise Chappell, *Gendering Government: Feminist Engagement with the State in Australia and Canada* (British Columbia Press, 2002) 126.

111 Arun Thiruvengadam, *The Constitution of India: A Contextual Analysis* (Bloomsbury, 2017) 2.

112 Sanjay Jain and Shirish Deshpande '"Fair Sex" and Unfair Treatment: Some Reflections on Constitutional Design and Institutional Response with Special Reference to India' in Jaya Sagade, Vedna Jivan and Christine Forster (eds.) *Feminism in the Subcontinent and Beyond: Challenging Laws, Changing Laws* (Eastern Book Company, 2014) 3–50. See Chapter 3 for definitions of formal equality and protectionism.

113 Tauffiqu Ahamad and Anil Kumar Mishra, 'Legal Status and Rights of Women in Indian Constitution' (2016) 1(1) *International Journal of Advanced Education and Research* 39–42. www.researchgate.net/publication/290691292_Legal_status_and_rights_of_women_in_Indian_constitution Accessed 17/4/19.

114 Jabez Gridley Sutherland, *Statutes and Statutory Construction* (Callaghan, 1904) 15.

115 Andhra Pradesh, Telangana, Bihar, Jammu-Kashmir, Karnataka, Maharashtra and Uttar Pradesh are bicameral. Puneet R. Gupta, *Soul of the Nation: Constitution of India* (Educreation Publishing, 2016) 198; Akhilesh Pal, *Federalism and Democratic Process in India* (Ashok Yakkaldevi, 2017) 10.

116 Gupta, n 115, 198.

117 Ibid.
118 David Skuy, 'Macaulay and the Indian Penal Code of 1862: The Myth of the Inherent Superiority and Modernity of the English Legal System Compared to India's Legal System in the Nineteenth Century' (1998) 32 *Modern Asian Studies* 513–557, 513.
119 Barry White, *Codification, Macaulay and the Indian Penal Code* (Routledge, 2011) 19.
120 Rochisha Narayan, 'Widows, Family, Community, and the Formation of Anglo-Hindu Law in Eighteenth-Century India' (2016) 50 *Modern Asian Studies Cambridge* 866–897, 869.
121 *Indian Succession Act* 1925, s 50(b).
122 *Hindu Marriage Act* 1955, s 5(iii); *Special Marriage Act* 1954, s 4(c).
123 *Hindu Minority and Guardianship Act* 1956, s 8.
124 If a similar case has been resolved in the past by a higher court, the court is bound to follow the reasoning used in the prior decision (this principle is known as stare decisis) to ensure consistent treatment. If the court finds that the current dispute is fundamentally distinct from all previous cases judges have the authority and duty to come to a different decision. The new decision becomes precedent and will bind future courts.
125 Sandra Fullerton Joireman, 'The Evolution of the Common Law: Legal Development in Kenya and India' (2006) 44(2) *Commonwealth & Comparative Politics* 190–210, 195.
126 *Government of India Act* 1858.
127 Art 372 of the Constitution provides that 'all the law in force in the territory of India immediately before the commencement of this Constitution shall continue in force therein until altered or repealed or amended by a competent legislature or other competent authority.'
128 *Mary Roy v. State of Kerala and Ors* (1986) AIR 1011; (1986) SCR (1) 371.
129 Susan Vellapally and Markos Vellapally, 'Repeal of the Travancore Christian Succession Act, 1916 and Its Aftermath' (Summer–Monsoon 1995) 22 *India International Centre Quarterly* 181–190.
130 *Smt. Sowmithri Vishnu v. Union of India & Anor* (1985) AIR 1618.
131 Ibid per Chief Justice Chandrachud.
132 *Joseph Shine vs* Union *of India* on 8 December (2017) Writ Petition (Criminal) No 194, 2017.
133 Ratna Kapur and Brenda Cossman, *Subversive Sites: Feminist Engagements with Law in India* (Sage Publications, 1996).
134 Ibid.
135 Kerry McBroom, 'Litigation as TB Rights Advocacy: A New Delhi Case Study' (2016) 18(1) *Health and Human Rights* 69–84.
136 Avani Mehta Sood, 'Gender Justice through Public Interest Litigation: Case Studies from India' (2008) 41 *Vanderbilt Journal of Transnational Law* 833–904, 835; Joshua Castellino, 'Public Interest Litigation as a Tool for Vulnerable Groups: Lessons from India' *FLAC Public Interest Law Seminar Series* Seminar 3 (16 June 2006) Structures for Public Interest Law and Litigation in Ireland. www.flac.ie/download/pdf/pil6_jcastellino_pilatool_16jun06.pdf Accessed 17/4/19.
137 Sara Hossain, 'Public Interest Litigation on Violence against Women in Bangladesh: Possibilities and Limits' in Amy Barrow and Joy L. Chia (eds.) *Gender, Violence and the State in Asia* (Routledge, 2016) 119–134.
138 *Constitution of India* 1950, art 32.
139 *Daryao v. State of UP* AIR (1961) SC 1457, 1461; Castellino, n 135, 5.
140 See Avani Mehta Sood, n 135, 839 for discussion on the expansion of standing in PIL cases from the traditional requirement of a person with a legal injury to any person representing disadvantaged classes of litigants. Judges have interpreted the remedy power in PIL cases as 'not only injunctive in ambit, that is, preventing the infringement of a fundamental right' but also 'remedial in scope and provides relief against a breach of the fundamental right already committed' in *M.C. Mehta v. Union of India* (1987) 1 SC R 819.

141 Zacharay Holladay, 'Public Interest Litigation in India as a Paradigm for Developing Nations' (2012) 19(2) *Indiana Journal of Global Legal Studies* 555–573, 561.
142 *Dr Jaya Sagade vs State of Maharashtra on 4 September* (2015) Public Interest Litigation No 104 of 2015.
143 See *Delhi Domestic Working Women's vs Union of India and Others 1994* (1995) SCC (1) 14, JT (1994) (7) 183 where the Delhi Domestic Workers Association represented four domestic servants who were subject to indecent sexual assault by seven army personnel.
144 Sood, n 136, 843.
145 *Vishaka v. Rajasthan* (1997) Supp 3 SCR 404.
146 *Centre for Enquiry into Health and Allied Themes v. Union of India* (2003) 8 SCC 398.
147 Petition 22, *Forum for Fact Finding Documentation and Advocacy v. Union of India*, W.P. (Civ.) No 212/2003 (India Apr. 25, 2003).
148 An offspring of any person within five generations (inclusive) on the groom's father's side and three generations (inclusive) on the mother's side, or vice versa, will be referred to as 'sapindas' of each other. Two persons are said to be sapindas of each other if one is a lineal ascendant of the other within the limits of sapinda relationship, or if they have a common lineal ascendant who is within the limits of sapinda relationship with reference to each of them.
149 *Hindu Marriage Act* 1955, s 3(a).
150 Jordan Paust, 'The Complex Nature, Sources and Evidences of Customary Human Rights' (1995/1996) 25 *Georgia Journal of International and Comparative Law* 147–164.
151 Aharon Layish, 'Marriage, Divorce and Succession in the Muslim Family' (1995) 2(3) *Islamic Law and Society* 215–218.
152 *Muslim Personal Law (Shariat) Application Act* 1937, s 2.
153 Narendra Subramanian, 'Legal Change and Gender Inequality: Changes in Muslim Family Law in India' (2008) 33(3) *Law & Social Inquiry* 631–672, 653.
154 Shahrzad Mojab, 'Theorizing the Politics of Islamic Feminism' (2001) 69 *Feminist Review* 124–146, 133.
155 Ibid. Subhro Bhattacharya and Akshay Shandilya, 'Arguing for a Uniform Civil Code in India in Light of Gender Discriminatory Practices under Muslim Personal Law' (2016) 10 *NUALS Law Journal* 1–30.
156 See Rebecca Cook, 'Women's International Human Rights Law: The Way Forward' (1993) 15 *Human Rights Quarterly* 230–261, 243 for a discussion on discriminatory personal law.
157 Abdullahi An-Na'im (ed.), *Islamic Family Law in a Changing World: A Global Resource Book* (Zed Books, 2002) 167.
158 Nava K. Das, 'Customary Law, Anthropological Jurisprudence and Gender Issues: Situating Women of North-East India in Feminist Discourse' in Melvil Pereira, R. Athparia, Sunumi Changmi and Jyotikona Chetia (eds.) *Gender Implications of Tribal Customary Law* (Rawat Publications, 2017) 27.
159 Vasudha Nagaraj, 'Local and Customary Forums: Adapting and Innovating Rules of Formal Law' in Flavia Agnes and Shoba Gosh (eds.) *Negotiating Spaces: Legal Domains, Gender Concerns and Community Constructs* (Oxford University Press, 2012) 201–220, 202.
160 Ibid 208.
161 Bina Agarwal, *Gender and Green Governance: The Political Economy of Women's Presence Within and Beyond Community Forestry* (Oxford University Press, 2010) 57. See generally, Robert M. Hayden 'A Note on Caste Panchayats and Government Courts in India' (1984) 16(22) *Journal of Legal Pluralism and Unofficial Law* 43–52.
162 Bina Agarwal, n 160, 57. See generally, Catherine Meschievitz and Marc Galanter, 'In Search of Nyaya Panchayats: The Politics of a Moribund Institution' (1982) in Richard Abel (ed.) *The Politics of Informal Justice* (Academic Press, 1982).
163 Ibid.
164 Vasudha Nagaraj, 'Local and Customary Forums: Adapting and Innovating Rules of Formal Law' (2010)17(3) *Indian Journal of Gender Studies* 429–450, 432.

165 Ibid 433.
166 Tushar Arora, 'Honour Killing: Belittling and Destructive Practices against Women by Khap Panchayat (Caste Panchayat and Its effect on Human Rights)' (2017) 7(10) *International Journal of Current Trends in Science and Technology* 20397–20401.
167 See Pereira, Athparia, Changmi and Chetia, n 157, who include a range of articles documenting the customary laws of tribal communities in North-East India.
168 Matthias Kötter, Tilmann. Röder; Folke Schuppert and Rudiger Wolfrum, *Non-State Justice Institutions and the Law: Decision-Making at the Interface of Tradition, Religion and the State* (Palgrave MacMillan, 2015).
169 *Paite Customary Law and Practices*, s 80.
170 Ravi J. Matthai Centre for Educational Innovation Indian Institute of Management Ahmedabad, 'Mahila Samakhya 2014: A National Review' (2014). http://mhrd.gov.in/sites/upload_files/mhrd/files/upload_document/Report-MSP.pdf Accessed 17/4/19.
171 Ibid 'Mahila Samakhya 2014: A National Review'.
172 Sarah Potthoff, 'Women within Family Disputes in Rural Northern Karnataka, India: Making and Negotiating a Claim at a Nari Adalat' (2016) 138 *ASIEN* 109–125,125.
173 Sesha Kethineni, Murugesan Srinivasan and Suman Kakar, 'Combating Violence against Women in India: Nari Adalats and Gender-Based Justice' (2016) 26(4) *Women and Criminal Justice* 281–300.
174 Radha Iyengar, 'Does the Certainty of Arrest Reduce Domestic Violence? Evidence from Mandatory and Recommended Arrest Laws' (2007) 93(1–2) *Journal of Public Economics* 85–98.
175 Nagaraj, n 163, 434.
176 Manju Agrawal and Hai Kakul, 'Women Courts: An Alternative Justice System for Women' (2016) 77(1) *Indian Journal of Social Work* 53–66, 64.
177 Sally Engle Merry, 'Transnational Human Rights and Local Activism: Mapping the Middle' (2006) 108(1) *American Anthropologist* 38–51, 47.
178 Sylvia Vatuk 'The "Women's Court" in India: An Alternative Dispute Resolution Body for Women in Distress' (2013) 45(1) *Journal of Legal Pluralism and Unofficial Law* 76–103.
179 Ibid.
180 Kethineni, Srinivasan and Kakar, n 172.
181 Nagaraj, n 163, 433–4, 441.

3

WOMEN'S HUMAN RIGHTS THEORIES

Introduction

This chapter sets out, critically, the key theories of women's human rights which we utilise in the chapters that follow to understand the role of the human rights framework in addressing the inequality and subordination experienced by women across India. The theories overviewed in this chapter are not exhaustive but represent a selection of women's human rights theories that support the development of strategies that can deliver real equality for women in major substantive areas of their lives.

The chapter has two main components. The first component overviews feminist legal theories. While theories of law provide explanatory frameworks for the existence of law, the purpose of law and the impact of law, particularly as it relates to the larger political, cultural and social context in which it exists,[1] feminist legal theory focusses on the role of law in reinforcing and perpetuating women's subordination and inequality.[2] The second component focusses on women's human rights theories which are a discrete body of scholarship within feminist legal theories that focusses on and critically examines the human rights framework from a feminist perspective.[3] Theories of women's human rights can and should be used to critically analyse both international and domestic sources of women's human rights, including constitutions, legislation and judicial decisions. They can be used to develop arguments in litigation; to develop proposals for law reform; to support advocacy by women's groups, civil society and non-government organisations and to guide governments in policy-making.

In 3.2 the chapter outlines the emergence of key feminist legal theories – liberal, cultural and radical – chronologically and overviews the critique of those theories by postmodern feminist theorists. The chapter then in 3.3 documents how women's human rights theories emerged within and alongside feminist legal theory

BOX 3.1 KEY CONCEPTS IN FEMINIST LEGAL THEORIES

Gender means socially constructed roles, behaviors, activities and attributes that a given society attributes to men and women.

Sex means women's biological differences from men.

Formal equality means the rights assigned to men as legal subjects are made available to women.

Substantive equality means equality in reality.

Direct discrimination means a law, act or measure that openly prevents or restricts a person from the exercise, enjoyment and fulfilment of a right.

Indirect discrimination means a law, act or measure that does not appear to prevent or restrict a person from the exercise, enjoyment and fulfilment of a right but disadvantages a person (often due to a pre-existing inequality) when it is put into effect.

Essentialism means that women have a given and universal essence because of biology and natural characteristics.

Anti-essentialism opposes the assumption that women have a given and universal essence because of biology and natural characteristics.

Intersections of discrimination mean sex and gender often intersect with other forms of discrimination, such as caste, class or age, heightening and magnifying the discrimination experienced by women and girls.

Source: Authors

to critique the conceptualisation of human rights. It focusses on three central theoretical themes in women's human rights theories. The three themes are first, the framing and interpretation of the concept of equality and non-discrimination in human rights law and its failure to achieve real substantive equality for women. The second theme is the debate between universalism and cultural relativism and the intervention of feminist perspectives into that debate. The third theme is the privileging of the public sphere of life while ignoring the (dangerous) lives of women in the private sphere. Human rights law does this by the privileging of 'public sphere' civil and political rights over 'private sphere' social, economic and cultural rights to the disadvantage of women and by focussing on the wrongs of states to the exclusion of wrongs committed by individuals and institutions within states. Finally, in section 3.4, we collate core principles of the different women's human right's theories and develop them to construct a women's human rights theoretical framework relevant to the Indian context that encompasses caste, class, gender, religion, ethnicity and geographical divide.

Feminist legal theories

This section overviews feminist legal theories chronologically as they emerged and developed from the 1970s to 2019, including liberal, radical, cultural and postmodern. We begin our discussion of feminist legal theories in the 1970s as they emerged in India and internationally; however, there is a lengthier and rich herstory of women's legal engagement in India on women's issues.[4] Feminist legal theories have two primary objectives. First, understanding and challenging the ways in which the law supports, reproduces and even creates the inequalities and discrimination faced by women.[5] Second, providing solutions that end the inequality and discrimination faced by women through reinterpretation of the law, the creation of new law or reworking of the law through a feminist lens.[6]

Each theoretical approach is diverse. The following subsections offer a summary of the key tenets of each body of theory.

Liberal feminist legal theory

Liberal feminist legal theory emerged first with a focus on achieving formal equality in law.[7] Modern liberalism emerged in the aftermath of two world wars to become the dominant political ethos in democratic society, endorsing a society characterised by individual freedom of thought, freedom of interference for individuals from others and the state, the rule of law, a focus on the welfare state and a transparent system of governance in which the rights of all citizens are protected and promoted.[8] Liberal feminist legal theory emerged alongside and out of liberalism, embracing its values but identifying the legal system, the main instrument by which the state enforces and protects liberal values,[9] as both a primary source of inequality for women and a platform for social transformation.[10] Liberal feminist legal theorists both in India and internationally focussed on achieving formal equality in law for women, arguing that women and men are alike and should receive equal and similar treatment. Specifically, this meant that the rights assigned to men as legal subjects should be made available to women whenever a comparison between the two revealed a disparity.[11] This could be achieved, according to proponents of the formal equality approach, by accommodating women within the existing paradigm of law.[12] The only relevant differences are women's biological differences, which are accommodated in this model with special provisions in instances where that difference leads to women's disadvantage.[13] For example, the child-bearing capacity of women can be accommodated in employment law with maternity leave provisions that ensure women do not lose pay or jobs during pregnancy, the birthing process and the immediate post delivery period.[14] Tarabai Shinde may have made the first claims for formal equality in India in 1882 when she stated, referring to law that prevented women, but not men, from remarrying after the death of their spouse: '[b]ut what if they laid down today that no man can remarry after his first wife has died?'.[15]

In India, some formal equality measures were introduced in the *Constitution of India* 1950 (Constitution), such as universal franchise, the equal right to stand for office and equality of opportunity for all citizens in matters relating to employment or appointment to any state office.[16] There continue to be many laws, however, that do not offer formal equality and exclude women from aspects of private and public life or treat women as subordinate. For example, Hindu women are not equal guardians of their children as the *Hindu Minority and Guardianship Act* 1956 designates a father as the 'natural guardian' of a child,[17] a Muslim mother can never be the natural guardian of her child,[18] employment law prohibits the employment of women, but not men, between 7:00 p.m. to 6:00 a.m. in mines and factories[19] or any *beedi* or cigar industrial premises,[20] the marriageable age for males is 21 but is 18 for females[21] and husbands enjoy a legal immunity for the rape of their wives who are over 18.[22] Some Indian feminists have embraced liberal feminism and challenged formal inequalities in law.[23] For example, pressure from women's groups resulted in the amendment of the *Hindu Succession Act* 1955 so as to give daughters equal rights with sons in joint family property in 2005.[24] Liberal feminist legal approaches continue to have purchase in the Indian context as formal equality has not yet been achieved in many areas of women's lives.

Cultural feminist legal theory

Cultural feminist legal theorists critique liberal feminist legal theory, arguing that rather than being the same as men, women are different.[25] Indeed, they argue, there are inherent differences between men and women – biological, psychological and social – and advocate for law to be modified to recognise and value those differences.[26] Although diverse, this body of theory challenges liberal feminist legal perspectives on the basis that formal equality requires women to become the same as men, rather than finding ways of valuing women's differences from men and incorporating those differences into law. Cultural feminists assert that women are 'essentially connected' rather than 'essentially separate' from the rest of human life, both materially through pregnancy, birth and breast-feeding and existentially, through their moral and practical lives.[27] Women therefore emphasize and value relationships and intimacy and have the capacity for nurturance and an ethic of care for the 'other'.[28] The cultural feminist explanation for women's heightened sense of connection is that women are more 'connected' to life through the umbilical cord because they are the primary caretakers of the newborn and because of the different relationships between daughters and sons and their mothers. There is a gender alignment between mothers and daughters, who 'fuse' their growing sense of identity with a sense of sameness with, and attachment to, their mothers. Conversely, because of the gender distinction between mothers and sons, young boys 'fuse' their growing sense of identity with a sense of difference and separation from their mothers.[29] Ultimately, the goal of cultural feminist legal theories is for law to provide equal recognition of women's differences. Law can achieve this, they argue, by delivering rights and resources and attaching worth to women's different contributions to human existence such as childbirth, child rearing and caring for the sick and elderly.[30]

Cultural feminist legal theory perspectives are represented in India. An example is provided through the arguments of some feminists for the introduction of a legislative community of property regime where all property and assets acquired during a marriage are equally divided at divorce. This model approaches all contributions to a marriage as equal, regardless of whether they are financial or non-financial, and therefore 'values' women's non-financial contributions such as domestic work, childcare and caring for the elderly equally with the financial contribution made by the earning spouse, typically the husband.[31] A second example is the *Family Courts Act* 1984, which states that when appointing family court judges, preference shall be given to women.[32] This is not a special measure; rather this provision is because women are viewed as better placed to understand the dynamics of family relationships and its complexities because of their inherently caring nature.

Radical feminist legal theory

Radical feminist legal theorists critique both liberal feminist legal theory and cultural feminist legal theory.[33] They reject cultural feminist legal theory, arguing that the female characteristics (the ethic of care) that are central to its thesis are the product of male domination.[34] Similarly, they criticise liberal feminist legal theorists and its aim of achieving formal equality on the basis that they ignore the reality of male power and domination.[35]

Indian feminists have utilised the seminal work of Catherine MacKinnon, who provides a compelling explanation of why formal equality does not, and cannot, lead to real equality for women from a radical feminist legal theory perspective.[36] MacKinnon's critique goes as follows. In the formal equality model, apart from their biological differences, women are conceptualised as the same as men with the same abilities and attributes. The formal equality model presumes that if women are treated as men, presented with the same opportunities as men and not discriminated against on the basis of their sex, they will exist equally and similarly to men.[37] Thus, equality can be achieved, and discrimination precluded, by extending to women all the formal rights previously afforded only to men. For example, the right to be educated, the right to hold public office and the right to receive the same pay as men.

However, the formal equality model fails, MacKinnon argues, because it adopts male experience and male perspective as the benchmark against which women are measured.[38] Women are given access to what men have to the extent that they can 'show themselves to be the same as men'.[39] However, men and women have not been historically treated in identical ways, and therefore, there are 'differences' between them that are not based on biological difference but rather the socially constructed roles, behaviours, activities and attributes that a given society assigns to men and women – their 'gender'.[40] By treating men and women the same, those 'gender differences' are ignored, reinforcing and reproducing that disadvantage and not resulting in equality. MacKinnon's solution is to focus on the power imbalance between men and women and those societal structures that support the domination of men and the subordination of women.[41]

Indian radical feminist legal theorists have applied the logic of MacKinnon's argument in the Indian context. They have also argued that both the liberal feminist theories (which endorse the formal equality approach) and cultural feminist theories (which accept differences between men and women as inherent) do not allow for any questioning about how law, public and social institutions, culture and religious systems maintain and construct the disadvantage of women.[42] For example, Goel argues, women in India are, through the institutions of marriage and family, solely or largely responsible for raising children and caring for the sick and elderly.[43] Giving women formal equality in pay and conditions of work has not led to their economic equality because the expectation that they must care for children and the elderly continued and hindered their ability to generate paid income in comparison to men.[44] Indian radical feminist legal theorists have also focussed on violence against women and the ways in which the police,[45] the courts[46] and the family[47] operate to maintain men's domination of women. They have lobbied successfully for domestic violence and sexual harassment legislation which specifically protects women from harms which do not have a male referent as they are perpetrated by men against women.[48]

Postmodern feminist legal theory

Postmodern feminist legal theorists critique liberal, radical and cultural feminist legal theories, arguing that no single all-encompassing 'essentialist' framework can explain inequality and discrimination because women themselves have many differences amongst them based on class, caste, religion, ethnicity, race, age and other factors.[49] Indeed, liberal, cultural and radical feminist legal theorists imagine, according to postmodern feminist legal feminists, an essential female whom they use to understand women's diverse experiences and problems, putting forth the solutions to her problems as the solutions to the problems of all women. Postmodern feminist legal theories call these theories 'grand' or 'essentialist' and reject them.[50] Essentialist feminist legal theories, by attributing a fixed essence to women,[51] make universalising and normalising claims for and about women, which are only true of white, Western, heterosexual, middle- or upper-class women.[52] Liberal feminist legal theory is essentialist because it assumes that women are the same as men. Radical feminist legal theory is essentialist because it assumes that all women are subordinate to all men. Both fail to account for the variety of differences and positions amongst women themselves based on other important intersections such as religion, class, caste, ethnicity and age and that men are also subordinate to others (including women) in certain circumstances, based on class, caste, religion and ethnicity.[53] Likewise, cultural feminist legal theory is essentialist because it assumes that all women are 'essentially connected' and all men are 'essentially unconnected', again failing to account for the differences amongst women and amongst men. Essentialism, they argue, limits the possibilities of change and thus of social reorganisation.[54]

Instead, postmodern feminist legal perspective posits that there is no single, universal truth that can be identified and usefully applied that takes account of the diversity of women in different cultural and geographic settings. An example of a postmodern feminist legal perspective approach in the Indian context can be provided by the mandate in the Constitution to introduce a uniform civil code to replace the different religious-based personal laws which currently regulate family relationships. From a postmodern feminist legal perspective, a uniform civil code cannot meet the diverse needs of the different religious communities as some perspectives must be subsumed into other perspectives.[55] The postmodern feminist legal perspective approach to the analysis of law has proven difficult to navigate because it renders concepts such as patriarchy and gender and the public and the private obsolete and weakens their explanatory strength. The result is that there is no shared platform from which women can collectively argue regarding their subordination, oppression and inequality.[56]

Women's human rights theories

This section overviews theories of women's human rights. By the 1990s, theories of women's human rights began to emerge to critique the human rights framework. Women's human rights theories are directed towards the following objectives. First, to analyse from a feminist perspective how human rights law supports, reproduces and, in some instances, creates the inequalities and discrimination faced by women. Second, to provide tools to define, analyse and articulate experiences of violence, discrimination, inequality and marginality within the human rights framework. Finally, and very importantly, to provide a framework for developing concrete strategies for legislative and policy changes at local, national and international levels. Three core theoretical themes can be identified in the women's human rights literature. These are first, theories of equality and non-discrimination, second, theories of universalism and cultural relativism and third, theories of representations of public and private. There are clear connections between each of the three themes and themes in feminist legal theory as discussed in the following subsections.

Equality and non-discrimination

The concepts of equality and non-discrimination have developed in human rights law over time. The *UDHR*, the *ICCPR* and the *ICESCR* all contain guarantees of formal equality and prohibit discrimination on the ground of sex. Women participated actively in the drafting process of these early conventions to establish formal equality rights provisions which would advance women's rights. This included, within a model of liberal feminist legal theory, formal rights to equality in all areas of women's political, economic, social, cultural and civil lives and an understanding of biological difference as the key source of discrimination against women.[57] Many world constitutions replicated these guarantees and incorporated formal rights to equality and non-discrimination on the basis of sex, including the Constitution. Article 14 of the Constitution prohibits the state from denying 'any person equality before the law or the equal protection of the laws within the territory of India' and article 15 prohibits the state from discriminating on the ground of sex.

After the adoption of these three general instruments, women's advocates identified the need for a convention focussed on women's specific inequality. *CEDAW*, adopted 30 years after the Indian Constitution, introduced into the human rights system a broader concept of equality and non-discrimination.[58] *CEDAW* requires that state parties achieve substantive ('true', 'effective', 'real', 'genuine')[59] equality between men and women and that they ensure that all forms of discrimination against women are prohibited and prevented.[60] In contrast to the preceding human rights instruments, this offered a different model of equality and non-discrimination. *CEDAW* offered deeper understanding of equality beyond formal equality, giving rise to the concept of substantive equality. The concept of substantive equality provided space to view formal equality, while important and necessary, as insufficient to achieve genuine equality. It also extended the understanding of discrimination on the ground of sex.

The requirement to ensure all forms of discrimination are prohibited and prevented offers the opportunity to differentiate between sex and gender and to consider both as sources of inequality impacting harshly on women. Women do experience discrimination because of their sex (their biological differences with men) but also, and more insidiously, because of their gender (the socially constructed roles, behaviors, activities and attributes that a given society assigns to men and women). For example, sex difference does not make men incapable of raising children or women incapable of driving trucks or auto-rickshaws; however, gender difference makes both difficult.

The requirement to ensure all forms of discrimination are prohibited and prevented also offered the opportunity to consider the compounding effect of other sources of disadvantage, such as race, caste, class, marital status, health and more. When sex and gender intersect with other forms of discrimination, the discrimination may be heightened, resulting in new or magnified forms of discrimination.[61] The requirement to ensure all forms of discrimination are prohibited and prevented also created space to extend a prohibition on direct discrimination (when law or measure openly prevents or restricts a person from the exercise, enjoyment and fulfilment of a right) to encompass indirect discrimination. An example of direct discrimination is the failure to provide toilet facilities for women in public spaces in most Indian cities. Indirect discrimination is when a law or measure does not appear to prevent or restrict a person from the exercise, enjoyment and fulfilment of a right but disadvantages a person (often due to pre-existing inequalities) when it is put into effect. For example, the Indian state regularly advertises for drivers to drive trucks, and there is no overt discrimination on the ground of sex; both men and women can apply. However, the trucks are physically designed for men to drive them.

Achieving substantive equality and non-discrimination

The concept of substantive equality and the broader understanding of discrimination set out in *CEDAW*, which identified more clearly the goals of equality and non-discrimination in human rights law (although not the means of achieving them), gave rise to a substantial body of theory advancing strategies for the advancement of women's human rights.

Some women's human rights theorists propose a guarantee of equality of opportunity as a means of setting a standard that could achieve substantive equality.[62] Providing men and women with the same starting point, however, is insufficient unless it considers the historical context and different lives of men and women. As Kapur and Cossman argue, this approach fails to analyse the 'underlying structures of oppression.'[63] Genuine equality of opportunity must account for and redress the disadvantages women face. For example, the provision of a 33 percent quota for women in panchayat raj institutions in 1993 appeared to provide a much greater opportunity for women to be represented in local public office.[64] Although a positive measure, which increased dramatically the numbers of women in panchayats, no support was provided to enable women to gain the experience, knowledge and self-confidence to actively and meaningfully participate. Research has indicated that women, particularly women from the scheduled tribes, do not fully participate in meetings, and male members with better education and economic positions continue to dominate.[65] Women are disadvantaged in their active participation in the panchayats by patriarchal social systems, social and cultural prejudices, financial dependence, lack of media support and exposure to political processes, limited training opportunities and family and child care responsibilities.[66]

Other women's human rights theorists propose placing on the state an obligation to achieve equality of results requiring that the outcomes of equality measures are judged to see whether they have resulted in change and equality on the ground.[67] While this is a useful goal, it does not explain how the state can achieve equality of results: for example, how to achieve proportionate or equal representation of women in particular jobs, in political representation and in education or how to break down the gendered division of labour which leaves women responsible for household chores and raising children.

The concepts of equality and non-discrimination, as they are framed and understood in the Indian legal system, are in part tethered to a limited (formal) understanding of equality. In expanding equality to embrace genuine substantive equality and in proposing strategies for moving towards that goal, the impact of culture and religion, class, caste and poverty on the lives of women combined with understanding the institutional structures that support these divisions must be navigated. The meaning of substantive equality must be determined within each cultural context.[68] For example, equal numbers of men and women in office may not constitute substantive equality if the women are relegated to less-powerful positions without decision-making powers or are not representative of Dalit women, women with disabilities or lesbian women. Substantive equality might be achieved instead if there are fewer women than men in public office but more women than men (and of diverse representation) who hold powerful, decision-making positions.

Sandra Fredman has proposed a four-part approach which, in combination, she argues can bring a society closer to substantive equality.[69] The first is breaking the cycle of disadvantage associated with disadvantaged or minority groups. She calls this the redistributive dimension of equality.[70] This approach requires focussing on the disadvantaged group – for example, women – and targeting their disadvantage.[71] For example, legislation could require that municipal political parties recruit more women and, once elected, that women are provided with exposure to and education on the responsibilities of office. Additionally, support for domestic responsibilities to support women in public office could be achieved through state support for a community kitchen where persons cook for the entire village and a community facility that provides care for children, those who are disabled and the elderly.

The second part of Fredman's four-part approach is promoting respect for dignity and worth, thereby redressing stigma, stereotyping, humiliation and violence because a person is female, lesbian or disabled.[72] She calls this the recognition dimension of equality.[73] This could be achieved by finding ways of countering son preference on conception, which is reflected in the sex ratio and which has not been resolved through sex-selection legislation in India. Programs could be launched by the state to welcome the birth of a girl child. In a Rajasthan village (Piplantri), for example, locals have instituted a ritual of planting 111 trees every time a girl is born. Such a program could be instituted at a state or national level and might constitute a recognition strategy.[74]

The third part of Fredman's four-part approach is to accommodate difference and achieve structural change.[75] She calls this the transformative dimension.[76] Structural change is difficult to achieve. It requires law reform, policy change and special measures. For example, the concept of illegitimacy, which marks children born out of wedlock, could be abolished so that children are not labelled and denied full property rights; personal laws could be reformed to prohibit discrimination against women; the state could implement special measures in employment and education.

The final part of Fredman's four-part approach is to facilitate full participation in society, both socially and politically.[77] She calls this the participative dimension.[78] In India, full social participation is difficult and complex to achieve. For example, participation for women in many religious ceremonies is restricted.[79] For example, in Maharashtra, there is an annual 15-day pilgrimage from Alandi to Pandharpur, which is the seat of the Hindu god Vithoba in state of Maharashtra, in honour of the deity carrying the footprints of various saints.[80] The tradition is more than 700 years old; however, women's place in that tradition is greatly restricted. The footprints of the saints represented by slippers in a box are bathed at every river but only by the men who lead the procession. Women, who are at the back of the procession, have no role in the significant, meaningful components of the pilgrimage. Supporting women pilgrims to demand equal participation at every stage in the ceremony, to walk beside the men and not behind and to share the bathing of the slippers in the river would be a participative strategy. Additionally, it is a 'bottom-up' strategy that respects religious practice but conceptualises religious tradition as fluid and adaptable and fully able to respect and incorporate the dignity and equality of women.

Fredman's approach is instructive in marking the limits of domestic law in achieving substantive equality but also acknowledges legal rights as an important 'first step' towards real equality.

Replacing equality with well-being

Some women's human rights theorists have moved away from equality and non-discrimination as the organising principles on which to strategise for and around and have recommended other approaches. Some focus on well-being, for example, as an alternative to equality, either analysing subjective categories (such as happiness)[81] or the material means to well-being (such as resources like income or wealth).[82] Martha Nussbaum focusses on well-being in her capability approach purporting that freedom to achieve well-being is determined by what people are able to do and to be and thus the kind of life they are effectively able to lead. Her conceptual approach envisages, first, the assessment of individual well-being; second, the evaluation and assessment of social arrangements and, finally, the design of policies and proposals that prioritise people's capabilities and their opportunities to realise them (such as their genuine opportunities to be educated and to move around or to enjoy supportive social relationships). Nussbaum specifies a list of capabilities that governments in all nations should guarantee to their citizens.[83]

Martha Fineman replaces the goals of liberty, dignity and equality with what she names the vulnerability approach as a more effective way of improving the lives of women.[84] She argues liberty and dignity are abstract and inevitably contested legal principles, while equality is an inherently comparative or relative measure. Vulnerability, she argues, is a more cogent principle of analysis to draw on to advocate for reform. She identifies two sources of vulnerability. The first source, which she names embodied difference are those 'universal' dependencies that all human beings do or can experience – being young, being aged, being sick and being disabled – and that are not contingent on individual attributes such as sex, race and sexuality.[85] The second source, which she names embedded differences, are those that arise because we are social beings embedded in social relationships.[86] The social roles defined by and through these relationships and institutions are not universally experienced, however, nor are their functions inevitable or inherent in the human condition. Rather, they are socially constructed and contingent, built and maintained within institutions such as the family, the school and the workplace.[87] Historically, both forms of vulnerability have taken a specifically gendered form because the caretaking of those unable to care for themselves was assigned to women in their roles as wives, mothers and daughters within the family. However, the disadvantages associated with vulnerability are not based on personal identity characteristics. Rather, they are burdens attached to the roles themselves that disadvantage the individuals who occupy them. For example, if men become carers, they also suffer economically and professionally. It is the social role not the sex of the caretaker that brings disadvantage.[88] The realities of our universal, constant and inescapable vulnerabilities in the past, present and future require a responsive state that recognises vulnerability and structures society's institutions accordingly.[89] Fineman is arguing, therefore, that rather than focussing on compelling the state to achieve gender equality, the focus should shift to compelling the state to respond to embodied and embedded differences or vulnerabilities. Presumably, if the state were to recognise the inevitability and the very real material needs that result from embodied differences, it would shift resources to meet those material needs, not specifically to women, but rather in the form of child-care centres and facilities for the elderly, the sick, and the disabled or, alternately, payments and resources for anyone who provides care. Once the state responds appropriately to embodied differences and embedded differences, then social roles will also change, according to Fineman, improving women's lives.

Universalism and cultural relativism

Universalism and cultural relativism provide opposing perspectives in the human rights system, and women's human rights theorists are situated on both sides of the debate. The United Nations Charter in 1945, in accord with the rise of modern liberalism, committed all state parties to promote 'universal respect for, and observance of, human rights and fundamental freedoms for all without distinction as to race, sex, language, or religion'.[90] After the ratification of the charter, the Commission on Human Rights was established to draft the *UDHR* with a membership broadly representative of the global community, including Australia, Belgium, Byelorussian Soviet Socialist Republic, Chile, Republic of China, Egypt, France, India, Iran, Lebanon, Panama, Philippines, United Kingdom, United States, Union of Soviet Socialist Republics, Uruguay and Yugoslavia.[91] The declaration and the series of conventions that followed were couched in 'universal' terms, underscored by a view that there should be a set of 'core' principles that governed all state parties in order to protect against totalitarianism and the destruction caused by World War II.[92] Adopting law and rights as a valid means of remedying the sharp inequities of post-colonial India with its divisions of class, caste, gender and religion, the Indian Constitution embodies the notion of the universality of human rights. Article 52(c) of the Constitution directs the state to fulfil its obligations under international law, and article 253 confers on Parliament the power to initiate legislation to implement international agreements, treaties or conventions entered into with other countries. In addition to these constitutional provisions, the *Protection of Human Rights Act* 1993 was enacted by Parliament, pursuant to the directive under article 51 of the Constitution, establishing national and state national human rights commissions tasked with protecting and promoting the human rights of all.

The language of universalism contained within human rights instruments, including *CEDAW*, has led to an (often) polarised debate about the application of human rights by women's human rights theorists.

Universalists and cultural relativists see the implications of 'universal' rights in their application to women's human rights in the following terms. Universalists argue there are 'core' standards that apply to all persons, regardless of their cultural traditions and religious beliefs.[93] Hence, the provisions of *CEDAW* must apply to women of all cultures and religions and throughout all state parties.[94] *CEDAW* embodies a collective response of 'vital human interests' by the international community to the oppression of women superseding the culture, tradition, custom and religious practices in both Western and non-Western countries alike.[95] Universalists deny that the universal standards are themselves culturally specific and allied to dominant regimes of power.[96] Indeed, they argue that any dilution of universal principles will permit renegade states to discard women's human rights provisions on the basis that they are contrary to the cultural and religious practices of the region.[97] In particular, universalists challenge cultural and religious practices which they argue are harmful to women, such as dowry, violence, honour killing, child marriage and polygamy, as well as those that lead to the economic disempowerment of women, such as the denial of nationality and domicile, unequal educational opportunities and discriminatory inheritance rules.[98]

From its inception, however, the human rights framework has been contested by cultural relativists. Cultural relativists argue that cultural and religious practices must be preserved despite universal norms.[99] Specifically, in relation to women's human rights, cultural relativists argue that 'core' human rights should not supersede cultural, religious and traditional norms.[100] Although cultural relativism, as it relates to *CEDAW*, incorporates a range of positions and arguments, the most common contention is that *CEDAW* was framed by a select group of women in line with Western norms, reflecting the concerns of Western women and then imposed on other nations.[101] The imposition of those norms, cultural relativists argue, is inappropriate for several reasons.

First, notions of right and wrong differ throughout the world due to diverse indigenous traditions, political and religious ideologies and institutional structures. Duties and moral standards should, therefore, be determined according to local standards rather than any external measurements.[102] Otherwise the imposition of universal norms may result in the erasure of cultural norms. For example, giving women equal inheritance rights over property could erase traditional norms, customs and hierarchies related to succession rights and harm important existing social structures.[103]

Second, for many women, cultural and religious practices are an important source of identity. The individual rights of women, particularly in many non-Western countries including India, are secondary to the family's and community's needs.[104] Indeed, human dignity is earned and preserved not through individual rights but through membership in a community.[105] The imposition of Western norms, which favour individual rights, fails to accommodate this alternate approach to identity. Indian feminists have explained, for example, that the family, not the self-interested individual of human rights, is the fundamental unit of Indian society, and duty is the primary basis for respect, value and dignity rather than rights.[106]

Such contrapositions in women's human rights theories in the debate between cultural relativism and universalism have led Shefali Desai and other theorists to argue that a path that reconciles the different viewpoints must be sought.[107] Desai argues that women's human rights theory which focusses on the preservation of cultural diversity does so because of a desire to value the voices and experiences of different women.[108] Accordingly, she argues that supporting women who oppose certain aspects of their culture is in accord with women's human rights objectives, and those perspectives must be included in defining universal human rights.[109] She calls for the adoption of strategies that 'listen to the voices of women' and argues that ignoring the voices of women who advocate for the abolition of certain cultural practices would amount to a failure to respect cultural diversity.[110]

Another approach that moderates the contrapositions of women's human rights theory in regard to the debate between universalism and cultural relativism is what Radhika Coomaraswamy has named the 'minimum core' rights approach.[111] Coomaraswamy argues we should separate those cultural and religious practices that reduce women's autonomy and prevent them from making decisions about their lives from those that do not. Any cultural or religious practice that prevents women from being able to make decisions about their lives should be abolished or modified, but those cultural practices which do not interfere with women's autonomy should be retained.[112] Coomaraswamy's framework can be usefully applied in the Indian context. Cultural differences which do not impact on women's autonomy might include the different food eaten by different communities (for example, cows are sacred in the Hindu religion, and pork is forbidden in the Muslim religion), different dress styles (states, regions and tribes have their own dress traditions) and the capacity of Muslims to marry their cousins, which is forbidden in Hindu marriage law. Other cultural practices such as child marriage, unequal inheritance laws and practices and son preference impact the autonomy of women and should be prohibited.

Public and private

Human rights law, some women's human rights theorists have argued, privileges the public sphere of business, economics, politics and law, representing it as the sphere of rationality and intellectual endeavour.[113] At the same time, it does not interfere in and regulate many aspects of the private sphere of marriage and family, hence supporting and obscuring the subordination of women in the private sphere.[114] Women's human rights theorists argue this is reflected in the human rights framework in two ways. First, it regulates violations by the state but not violations by individuals, enabling states to ignore discrimination and violence against women in the private sphere of home and family.[115] Second, it favours the regulation, protection and enhancement of civil and political rights (which operate in the public sphere) over social, cultural and economic rights (which operate in the private sphere) to the disadvantage of women.[116] Women live in both public and private spheres; however, a larger proportion of women work in the home, and their ability to function in the public sphere is dependent on the recognition of their rights in the private sphere.[117]

Violations by private individuals

By becoming parties to international conventions, state parties assume obligations and duties under international law to respect, to protect and to fulfil human rights. The obligation to respect means that state parties must refrain from interfering with or curtailing the enjoyment of human rights. The obligation to protect requires state parties to protect individuals and groups against human rights abuses. The obligation to fulfil means that state parties must take positive action to facilitate the enjoyment of basic human rights. However, violations of human rights by private individuals were generally outside the remit of early human rights law.[118] Human rights law was instead aimed at restraining governments from committing human rights violations against their citizens and against other countries, thus enabling the state to place low priority, in terms of their international obligations, on responding to and preventing the subordination of women in the private sphere.[119] Many violations of the rights of women occur in situations that are either outside the regulatory framework of the state or not considered important by the state and not enforced. For example, in India, abuses done to women in the name of family (honour killings), religion (*talaq*), and culture (son preference) have been largely unregulated.

However, this general principle of human rights law has been improved in two particular ways. First, *CEDAW*, in contrast to other conventions, explicitly prohibits discrimination not only by the state, but also by individuals and organisations in the political, economic, social, cultural, civil or any other field.[120] The significance of this approach lies in its recognition that, unlike for men, many violations of women's rights occur within the private sphere, and failure to address such violations undermines the exercise and enjoyment by women of their human rights in all spheres of life.[121] Examples include the failure to effectively prevent violence in the family and the failure to regulate and protect the many economic activities performed predominantly by women, such as domestic work, work in family farms or businesses, caring work and work in the unorganised sector.[122] Women workers in these fields do not receive benefits such as social security, health and safety standards, minimum pay or protection against exploitation.[123]

Second, the principle of 'due diligence' has also developed to place a greater responsibility on states for the actions of private individuals.[124] The principle of due diligence recognises that, in addition to the negative obligations imposed upon countries to refrain from violating the human rights of those within its jurisdiction, countries also have a positive obligation to exercise due diligence in securing the enjoyment of human rights of the population against violations by private individuals.[125] Women's human rights theorists have argued with some success that the principle of due diligence must be understood and extended to require not only that governments will refrain from any direct violence against their citizens, but also that they take steps to protect them against violence perpetrated by private individuals by ensuring that such violence is made punishable and prevented.[126] This requires reforming the structures and practices in social and private life that threaten the security of women, including initiatives to change social and cultural practices; reforming laws; developing policies; running campaigns against child abuse, domestic violence, sexual assault, violence against sexual minorities and gang violence and rejecting attempts to legitimise cultural and religious practices that normalise violence against women, such as forced marriage, trafficking women, widow burning, honour killings, female infanticide and domestic violence generally.[127]

First, second and third generation rights

The division of human rights into three generations was initially proposed in 1979 by the Czech jurist Karel Vasak at the International Institute of Human Rights in Strasbourg.[128]

First-generation human rights, sometimes called 'blue' rights, are primarily public sphere rights and are prioritised in the human rights system.[129] They require 'immediate realisation' without state recourse to arguments of limited resources and capacity.[130] First-generation rights include civil and political rights. Civil rights include the ensuring of peoples' physical and mental integrity, life and safety; protection from discrimination on grounds such as race, gender, national origin, colour, age, political affiliation, ethnicity, religion or disability and individual rights such as privacy and the freedoms of thought, speech, religion, press, assembly and movement. Political rights include natural justice (procedural fairness) in law, such as the rights of the accused, including the right to a fair trial; due process; the right to seek redress or a legal remedy and rights of participation in civil society and politics such as freedom of association, the right to assemble, the right to petition, the right of self-defence and the right to vote.

Second-generation human rights are (largely) private sphere rights and have less importance in the human rights framework.[131] They are characterised as aspirational rather than immutable. While they impose upon the government the duty to respect, promote and fulfill them, the obligation is to progressively (rather than immediately) realise them 'by all appropriate means', and the availability of resources determines the extent to which a state is obligated to realize them. They are economic, social and cultural and include a right to be employed in just and favourable condition and rights to food, housing and health care, as well as social security and unemployment benefits.

Third-generation rights include group and collective rights, the right to self-determination, the right to economic and social development, the right to a healthy environment, the right to natural resources and the right to participation in cultural heritage. Like second-generation rights, they are characterised as aspirational rather than immutable.[132]

Women's human rights theorists have argued that the prioritisation of civil and political rights over economic, social and cultural rights reinforces a division between the public and private spheres to the disadvantage of women. While civil and political right protection is as essential to women as to men, many of the harms and discrimination women experience are in the areas of social and economic rights. Further, the distinction between the two layers of rights makes it difficult to develop solutions because of the linkages between different inequalities. For example, the lack of political representation of Indian women can be linked to discrimination in education, violence and lack of economic independence. Women need civil and political empowerment to articulate social, economic and cultural grievances, and a hierarchy of rights in the human rights system makes this difficult to achieve.[133]

Conclusion: our views

This chapter has overviewed a range of theoretical perspectives, and in this section, we collate the core principles of women's human rights theories which we argue have most applicability to the Indian context.

We consider that liberal, radical, cultural and postmodern feminist legal perspectives all have valuable contributions to make in understanding and crafting solutions for the inequality and subordination faced by women in India. Liberal feminist legal theory, with its focus on formal equality, while insufficient, continues to have purchase in India, where many laws continue to be formally unequal. A radical feminist legal approach offers a framework for challenging the structural means by which inequality is maintained and provides an explanation of why we must strategise for and work towards substantive equality. Cultural feminist legal theory, although problematic in its assumption that differences are inherent (and therefore unchangeable), does offer insight into human characteristics that are not valued in society, such as caring for others. Rather than attributing particular behaviours or characteristics to women, we argue that human values such as caring for others should be valued, recognised and encouraged. Postmodern feminist legal approaches are limiting in their denial of a shared platform, but we argue it is important to recognise and value the differences amongst women based on factors such as caste and disability while also recognising that women have shared, but not identical experiences in relation to many issues. For example, violence against women, which, although it manifests differently in different classes and castes, at different ages and in rural and urban communities, is, however, experienced as damaging, restricting and devaluing by all women.

Women's human rights theories grew out of, and are founded on, feminist legal theories. There are three thematic areas in women's human rights theories which we argue have important applicability in the Indian context. Those thematic areas are the principles of equality and non-discrimination, the application of universalism without cultural erasure and the way in which the public and private spheres are regulated (or not).

Human rights law, the Constitution and many domestic laws in India are couched in terms of equality and non-discrimination. Strategising for happiness or well-being or focussing on the capabilities of humans is a valid alternate or complementary approach to equality. Indeed, strategies to advance women's human rights must incorporate the reality of the vulnerability of human beings at different developmental stages,[134] the differing community and family responsibilities between and amongst men and women[135] and the varied and alternate desires of different women.[136] In our view, however, the principles of equality and non-discrimination are foundational and the most relevant principles for advancing women's human rights in the Indian context for two reasons. First, they are already present in the legal and policy discourse and therefore provide a concrete base for contestation of existing legal frameworks and, second, because the principle of equality and non-discrimination, in our view, has already improved the quality of lives of women and, by extending their meaning, interpretation and application, has the potential to further improve them. For example, the right to vote, the prohibition of child marriage, the extension of birthright to daughters in joint family Hindu property and the enactment of the *Protection of Women from Domestic Violence Act* 2005 have improved the lives of women and set important, valuable standards to work towards.

We agree with Cyra Choudhury's approach to resolving the differences between women's human rights theorists in their approach to universalism and the danger of cultural erasure.[137] Central to this book is finding a balance between some strategic essentialism in cultural claims to ensure women have legal tools to guard against cultural disintegration, extinction or exploitation but finding ways of achieving this while opposing discrimination against women in all its forms. Women experience their lives differently in multiple ways; however, they also experience similar forms of discrimination. For example, women are victims of domestic violence across India in every class, caste and religious group, in slums, in rural and urban settings and in conflict zones.[138]

Her approach, which integrates aspects of the arguments of both Desai and Commaraswamy, provides a useful framework for moving forward and will be utilised in this book in the following ways. First, Choudhury argues women's human rights advocates must develop a shared platform in which they come together to engage in 'unflinching critique from positions of equality rather than civilizational superiority.'[139] In our view, theorising from the ground up and using women's lived experience are means of achieving this. They provide a more valid explanation and interpretation of culture and religion in relation to issues that particularly impact women. When states, community leaders and other powerful actors resist law reform on the basis that it is contrary to culture or religion, they are assuming the power to determine which interpretations of culture and religion are valid.[140] For example, attempts to change the Muslim personal law from both within and outside the Muslim community have been strongly resisted by religious and cultural conservatives, such as the Muslim Personal Board, based on arguments of religious adherence and orthodoxy. They argue that reforming laws governing inheritance, polygamy or women's right to divorce are contrary to Muslim religious belief and cannot be done by person-made law.[141] However, the most relevant voices are Muslim women who are discriminated against by the laws and who are articulating a very important critique of how Islam has been interpreted.[142] A study in Vadodara of 388 women from a cross-section of society found that 82.7 percent of Muslim women believed they were discriminated against by the Muslim personal laws and wanted the discriminatory aspects of the laws removed.[143] These women present a vibrant dissent from traditionalist positions and challenge their subordinations from within their communities.[144]

Second, Choudhury argues culture must be recognised and approached as fluid not bounded, unchanging and settled.[145] Indeed, in our view, local culture and universal human rights are often contraposed deploying archaic, essentialist and eternal understandings of culture. They are utilised to either justify violations of women's rights in the name of culture (cultural relativism) or to condemn (usually non-Western) cultures as being inherently primitive and violent towards women. Culture is not monolithic, and static and such constructions obfuscate alternate readings of culture as created, contested, fluid and constantly evolving over time in response to both external influences and internal movements for change. Additionally, the recognition that 'no society has "a" single culture, but each has multiple cultures – the dominant culture, the subaltern cultures and the emerging cultures of challenge,'[146] captures society much more clearly than a version of culture as static and monolithic. Resistance by government and community to human rights discourse in general and women's human rights in particular is often grounded in assertions that it is Western and contrary to Indian culture and to religion. Kamla Bhasin and Nighat Khan argue instead that the concept of feminism is not Western rather that feminist consciousness arose throughout Asia from the injustice of depriving half the population of their rights.[147] Further, human rights principles were used to struggle against British colonialism, and Western principles are readily adopted in areas such as trade and commerce, tax regimes and the regulation of contracts.[148] In our view, culture and religion can and should be seen as dynamic and fluid and capable of embracing principles such as equality and non-discrimination in all areas of people's lives.

Third, Choudhury argues women's human rights advocates should reconcile the polarised positions of cultural relativists who seek to preserve culture and universalists who seek to overcome it.[149] Indeed, we argue that while universalism sets universal standards to be achieved, it does not mean or require universality of approach. Individual rights are important, and women are individuals, more than members of a marriage, family, tribe or nation. For example, every woman has a universal right to life, a right to a life free from violence and a right to decide the course of her own life. However, how those rights are achieved, how they might operate in women's lives and how they might reflect women's experiences of relational entanglement are complexities that must be navigated as appropriate in the local context.[150] For example, giving support to women villagers so they can operate as agents of change, working with girl children and teaching them about the harms of underage marriage and the advantages of education might be a more effective response to those issues than imposing legal prohibitions on underage marriage and mandatory schooling.[151]

Fourth, Choudhury argues women's human rights advocates must resist the use of human rights, culture and civilisation as justifications for intervention and violence (in the war on terror, for example). We agree. Feminists must, in the current global context, retain their political agendas without supporting imperialist and repressive state action.[152]

We agree that human rights law has, historically, supported a divide between public and private spheres to the detriment of women's equality, first, by not making state parties accountable for the violations of women's rights by individual persons and, second, by privileging 'public sphere' rights over 'private sphere' rights. However, *CEDAW*, by requiring that state parties prevent discrimination by 'any person, organisation or enterprise' erodes the former, and there has been a definite shift towards a recognition of responsibility and accountability for private action.[153] The demarcation and privileging of civil and political rights over social, economic and cultural rights, however, continues to have profound implications for women. First-generation rights, for example, receive the strongest protection in the Indian Constitution. Although a range of social, economic and cultural rights are included in the Constitution as part of the Directive Principles, they are not enforceable by any court, although the state has a duty to apply them in making laws. The courts have been receptive to second-generation rights, illustrating the importance of utilising the courts to advance women's human rights; however, there is no guarantee of enforceability because their status is, like in human rights law, secondary to civil and political rights.[154]

However, we argue that the relationship between the public and the private is complex. The denial of second-generation rights leads to the socially constructed dependency of women on men, their underpaid labour, the non-recognition of their household contribution, the unequal economic and social distribution of resources, their lack of education and the denial of reproductive rights.[155] In turn, these limitations hinder women's access to their civil and political rights. Indeed, to secure women's civil and political rights, the state must be held to a positive duty to ensure the eradication of those social and economic conditions that maintain and perpetuate subordination.[156] Social and economic human rights cannot be detached from civil and political rights enabling citizens to enjoy their rights to life, liberty and physical security.[157]

For example, consider the following situation, which illustrates how inequality in the private sphere creates inequality in the public sphere. A person is not eligible for election to a position as a member of a panchayat in 12 states if the person has more than two children.[158] The stated policy reason for the law is population control. A number of petitioners have (unsuccessfully) challenged these laws as being in violation of article 14 (equality), article 21 (right to life) and article 25 (right to freedom of religion) of the Constitution.[159] They have argued that the number of children does not affect the capacity, competence and quality of a person to serve on any office of a panchayat and, therefore, is discriminatory since a similar provision has not been enacted for other elected positions and that it breaches a person's right to found a family. The courts have uniformly held the object of the restriction is to implement a sensible family planning programme in the public interest, and it is neither arbitrary nor unreasonable nor discriminatory.[160] The law applies equally to women and men, so it is formally equal on the grounds of sex. However, closer scrutiny reveals indirect discrimination against women and the implementation of a restriction in the public sphere that connects to performance in the private sphere, where women have much less control over their reproductive functions than men.[161] They are, through this law, given entry to the public sphere, but that entry is limited through control exerted in the private sphere in terms of their access to family planning, their ability to control decision-making around the number of children they have and the economic imperative of having children to contribute to the family income.

In considering strategies for change and reform, we argue the dualism between public and private must be dismantled so that the distinction is not cemented with women 'properly' located in the private sphere while absent from the public sphere.[162] However, we also view the public-private dualism as a useful tool to examine the private subjugation of women as an explicit part of the public agenda.[163] Recognising a dualism between public and private spheres and the differing response of the state to each does, in our view, assist in explaining how practices, doctrines and beliefs that normalise the inequalities in power, wealth and status are reflected in the inequitable order of contemporary India. For example, although women and men live across both the public and the private spheres, Indian women have a major and significant presence in and attachment to the private sphere of family and are subject to significant discrimination and abuse in that location.[164] At the same time, women have little visibility in the public political sphere.[165] While the Indian courts have been enthusiastic about enforcing gender equality using norms of international law, this has been in large part restricted to the public sphere.[166] The courts have been far less enthusiastic about gender equality in the private sphere of the family. For example, the Indian state is committed to a policy of secularism in the public sphere but has refused to regulate religious laws in the private sphere, even though those laws conflict with the constitutional guarantee of formal equality.[167] Muslim women are simultaneously included and excluded from equal citizenship as the guarantee of equality does not extend to the private sphere of the family, where Muslim women are explicitly discriminated against.[168] Consequently, the state has created a differentiated citizenship based on gender and religious identity.[169]

The theoretical framework identified in this chapter will be selectively applied to the concrete issues discussed in the chapters that follow, including equality and non-discrimination protection in the Constitution, violence against women, marriage and family relations, economic empowerment and political representation and participation.

Notes

1 Hans Kelsen (Translated by Bonnie Litchewski Paulson and Stanley L. Paulson), *Introduction to the Problems of Legal Theory* (Clarendon Press, 1992).
2 Nancy Levit, Robert R. M. Verchick and Martha Minow, *Feminist Legal Theory: A Primer* (New York University Press, 2016); Vanessa E. Munro, *Ashgate Research Companion to Feminist Legal Theory* (Routledge, 2013).
3 Niamh Reilly, *Women's Human Rights: Seeking Gender Justice in a Globalizing Age* (Polity Press, 2009) 11.
4 Rosalind O'Hanlon, *A Comparison between Women and Men: Tarabai Shinde and the Critique of Gender Relations in Colonial India* (Oxford University Press, 1994); Ratna Kapur and Brenda Cossman, *Subversive Sites: Feminist Engagements with Law in India* (Sage Publications, 1996) 43–59.
5 Katherine Bartlett, *Feminist Legal Theory: Readings in Law and Gender* (Routledge, 2018).
6 See Deborah Rhode, 'Feminist Critical Theories' (1990) 42(3) *Stanford Law Review* 617–638 for an overview of the emergence of feminist legal theories.
7 Ann Scales, 'The Emergence of Feminist Jurisprudence: An Essay' (1986) 95(7) *Yale Law Journal* 1373–1403; Katharine Bartlett, 'Feminist Legal Methods' (1990) 103(4) *Harvard Law Review* 829–888.
8 Ronald Collins and David M. Skover, 'The Future of Liberal Legal Scholarship' (1988) 87(1) *Michigan Law Review* 189–239.
9 Hilaire Barnett, *Introduction to Feminist Jurisprudence* (Cavendish Publishing, 1998) 124.
10 Kapur and Cossman, n 4, 20.
11 Ratna Kapur 'Challenging the Liberal Subject' in Maitrayee Mukhopadhyay and Navsharan Singh (eds.) *Gender Justice, Citizenship and Development* (International Development Research Centre and Zubaan, 2007) 116–170, 124. Kapur provides an overview of Indian feminist approaches within the formal equality model. See also, Scales, n 7, 1375; Margaret Thornton, 'Development of Feminist Jurisprudence' (1998) 9 *Legal Education Review* 171–194, 191.
12 Thornton, n 11, 174; Vaibhav Goel, 'Feminine Jurisprudence and Gender Justice' (2016) in Rathin Bandyopadhyay, Rajendra Dhar Dubey, Sanjay Kumar Singh and Sangeeta Manda (eds.) *Women's Rights: Human Rights* (R. Cambray and Co. Pvt. Ltd, 2010) 169–187.
13 Kapur and Cossman, n 4, 26.
14 Catharine MacKinnon, *Feminism Unmodified Discourses on Life and Law* (Harvard University Press, 1987) 38.
15 O'Hanlon, n 4, 90.
16 *Constitution of India* 1950, art 16, art 84, art 326.
17 *Hindu Minority and Guardianship Act* 1956, s 6(a). A bill, however, has been submitted to parliament to amend section 6 and make mother and father both natural guardians. http://164.100.47.4/billstexts/lsbilltexts/asintroduced/2595.pdf Accessed 17/4/19.

18 For a discussion on guardianship in Islamic law, see Asha Bajpai, 'Custody and Guardianship of Children in India' (2005) 39(2) *Family Law Quarterly* 441–457.
19 *Mines Act* 1952; *Factories Act* 1948.
20 *Beedi and Cigar Workers (Conditions of Employment) Act* 1966, s 25.
21 *Prohibition of Child Marriage Act* 2006, s 2(a).
22 Under the common law principle of *feme covert*. Lee Holcombe, *Wives and Property: Reform of the Married Women's Property Law in Nineteenth-Century England* (University of Toronto Press, 1983) 18. In *Independent Thought v. Union of India & Another* (2017) the Supreme Court held that s 375 of the *Indian Penal Code* 1860 meant that marital rape is a crime if a wife is under 18 but not if she is 18 or over.
23 Gangotri Chakraborty, 'Emerging Necessities of Gender Balance in Law' in N. Chakrabarti Sachi (ed.) *Gender Justice* (Cambray and Co, 2006) 19–39, 30.
24 Klaus Deininger, Aparajita Goyal and Hari Nagarajan, 'Women's Inheritance Rights and Intergenerational Transmission of Resources in India' (2013) 48(1) *Journal of Human Resources* 115–141.
25 Linda Alcoff, 'Cultural Feminism versus Post-Structuralism: The Identity Crisis in Feminist Theory' (1988) 13(3) *Signs: Journal of Women in Culture and Society* 405–436; Robin West, 'The Difference in Women's Hedonic Lives: A Phenomenological Critique of Feminist Legal Theory' (1987) 3 *Wisconsin Women's Law Journal* 149–216.
26 Drucilla Cornell, *Beyond Accommodation: Ethical Feminism, Deconstruction, and the Law* (Rowman and Littlefield, 1999) 50.
27 Robin West, 'Jurisprudence and Gender' (1988) 55(1) *University of Chicago Law Review* 1–72, 14, 16.
28 Ibid 66.
29 Drucilla Cornell, *Beyond Accommodation: Ethical Feminism, Deconstruction, and the Law* (Rowman and Littlefield, 1999) 50.
30 West n 27, 65.
31 Kirti Singh, *Separated and Divorced Women in India: Economic Rights and Entitlements* (Sage, 2013) 14.
32 *Family Courts Act* 1984 s 4. http://doj.gov.in/acts-and-rules/family-courts-act-1984 Accessed 18/4/19.
33 Kelly Loper, 'Constitutional Adjudication and Substantive Gender Equality in Hong Kong' in Beverley Baines, Daphne Barak-Erez and Tsvi Kahana (eds.), *Feminist Constitutionalism: Global Perspectives* (Cambridge University Press, 2012) 153.
34 Linda Alcoff, 'Cultural Feminism versus Post-Structuralism: The Identity Crisis in Feminist Theory' (1988) 13(3) *Signs* 405–436.
35 Ibid.
36 Supriya Akerkar, 'Theory and Practice of the Women's Movement in India: A Discourse Analysis' *Economic Political Weekly*, 29 April 1995, 2. www.epw.in/journal/1995/17/review-womens-studies-review-issues-specials/theory-and-practice-women-s-movement Accessed 17/4/19; Nivedita Menon, *Recovering Subversion: Feminist Politics Beyond the Law* (Permanent Black, 2004) 32, 55.
37 Catharine MacKinnon, *Women's Lives under Men's Laws* (Harvard University Press, 2005) 46.
38 Catharine MacKinnon, *Feminism Unmodified Discourses on Life and Law* (Harvard University Press, 1987) 33.
39 Catharine MacKinnon, n 38, 34.
40 Ibid.
41 Catharine MacKinnon, 'Reflections on Sex Equality under Law' (1991) 100(5) *Yale Law Journal* 1281–1328. For further discussion on radical feminist legal theory, see Suzanne Samuels, *Law, Politics and Society* (Houghton Mifflin, 2005) 48.
42 See Goel, n 12, 180–182 for an overview of Indian radical feminist approaches.
43 Goel, n 12, 169–187. See also Susan Seymour, *Women, Family, and Child Care in India: A World in Transition* (Cambridge University Press, 1999).

44 Ibid.
45 Aashish Gupta, 'Reporting and Incidence of Violence against Women in India' Working Paper (Research Institute for Compassionate Economics, 2014); Govind Kelkar, *Violence against Women* (Manohar Publishers, 1992).
46 Geetanjali Gangoli, *Indian Feminisms: Law, Patriarchies and Violence in India* (Routledge, 2016); Rituparna Bhattacharyya, 'Understanding the Spatiality's of Sexual Assault against Indian Women in India' (2015) 22(9) *Gender, Place & Culture* 1340–1356.
47 Ibid.
48 See, for example, the *Protection of Women from Domestic Violence Act* 2005.
49 Meghan Campbell, '*CEDAW* and Women's Intersecting Identities: A Pioneering New Approach to Intersectional Discrimination' (2015) 11(2) *Revista Direito GV* 479–504. https://dx.doi.org/10.1590/1808-2432201521 Accessed 17/4/19.
50 Angela Harris, 'Race and Essentialism in Feminist Legal Theory' (1990) *Stanford Law Review* 581–616; Kimberle Crenshaw, 'Demarginalizing the Intersection of Race and Sex: A Black Feminist Critique of Antidiscrimination Doctrine, Feminist Theory and Antiracist Politics' (1989) 8(1) *University of Chicago Legal Forum* 139–167; Sumi Cho, Kimberlé Crenshaw and Leslie McCall, 'Toward a Field of Intersectionality Studies: Theory, Applications and Praxis' (2013) 38(4) *Signs: Journal of Women in Culture and Society* 785–810.
51 Harris, n 50, 585.
52 Kapur and Cossman, n 4, 135.
53 Goel, n 12, 179.
54 Barnett, n 9, 199.
55 Inderpal Grewal, 'Women's Rights as Human Rights: Feminist Practices, Global Feminism and Human Rights Regimes in Transnationality' (2007) 3(3) *Citizen Studies* 337, 349.
56 Barnett, n 9, 194.
57 Aaron Xavier Fellmeth, 'Feminism and International Law: Theory, Methodology, and Substantive Reform' (2000) 22 *Human Rights Quarterly* 658–733, 688.
58 See Chapter 2 for an overview of the history of *CEDAW*.
59 Vedna Jivan and Christine Forster, 'Challenging Conventions: In Pursuit of Greater Legislative Compliance with CEDAW in the Pacific' (2009) 10 *Melbourne Journal of International Law* 655–690, 662.
60 Simone Cusack and Lisa Pusey, '*CEDAW* and the Right to Non-Discrimination and Equality' (2013) 14 *Melbourne Journal of International Law* 54–92.
61 Catherine Harnois, 'Are Perceptions of Discrimination Unidimensional, Oppositional, or Intersectional? Examining the Relationship among Perceived Racial-Ethnic-, Gender- and Age-Based Discrimination' (2014) 57(4) *Sociological Perspectives* 470–487; Martha Chamallas, 'Social Justice Feminism: A New Take on Intersectionality' (2014) 5(1) *Freedom Center Journal* 11–20.
62 Kapur and Cossman, n 4, 123.
63 Ibid.
64 73rd amendment of *Constitution of India* 1950, art 243D, 1.
65 Padmanabha Bhat, *Gender Quotas and Panchayat Raj Institutions in India: A Reflection*, 14. http://paperroom.ipsa.org/papers/paper_33276.pdf Accessed 17/4/19.
66 Ibid. However, as discussed in Chapter 7, this situation is changing as women receive training and support and build confidence and skills.
67 Elizabeth S. Anderson, 'What Is the Point of Equality?' (1999) 109(2) *Ethics* 287–337, 291.
68 Nidhi Gupta, 'Women's Human Rights and the Practice of Dowry in India' (2003) 35(48) *Journal of Legal Pluralism and Unofficial Law* 85–123, 89.
69 Sandra Fredman, 'The Potential and Limits of an Equal Rights Paradigm in Addressing Poverty' (2011) 3 *Stellenbosch Law Review* 566, 577; see also Sandra Fredman, *Discrimination Law* (Oxford University Press, 2011).
70 Ibid.

71 Ibid.
72 Ibid.
73 Ibid.
74 Manjushree Palit, Astha *Dhanda* and Garima Jain, 'Preventing Femicide in India: Valuing and Safeguarding the Girl Child and Women' (2015) *Femicide* (Academic Council of United Nations System) 106–111; Elaine Mumford, 'Growing Up Green in Rajasthan: Feminism and Grassroots Desertification Combat in Piplantri Village' (February, 2016) 61(1) *Yale Review of International Studies* 77–103. http://yris.yira.org/essays/1639.
75 Sandra Fredman, n 69, 577.
76 Ibid.
77 Ibid.
78 Ibid.
79 Kamila Klingorová and Tomáš Havlíček, 'Religion and Gender Inequality: The Status of Women in the Societies of World Religions' (2015) 23(2) *Moravian Geographical Reports* 2–11, 9.
80 Irawati Karve, 'On the Road: A Maharashtrian Pilgrimage' (1962) 22(1) *Journal of Asian Studies* 13–29. 'Over 3 Lakh Devotees of Lord Vitthal Start March on Foot to Pandharpur' *Times of India*, 7 July 2018. https://timesofindia.indiatimes.com/city/pune/over-3l-devotees-of-lord-vitthal-start-march-on-foot-to pandharpur/articleshow/64890493.cms Accessed 17/4/19.
81 Sakiko Fukuda-Parr, 'The Human Development Paradigm: Operationalizing Sen's Ideas on Capabilities' (2003) 9 *Feminist Economics* 301–317.
82 Ibid.
83 Martha Nuusbaum, *Frontiers of Justice: Disability, Nationality, Species Membership* (Harvard University Press, 2006) 71.
84 Martha Fineman, 'Equality and Difference: The Restrained State' (2015) 66(3) *Alabama Law Review* 609–626.
85 Ibid 613.
86 Ibid 614, 619.
87 Ibid 622.
88 Ibid 614.
89 Ibid.
90 Ibid 625.
91 See Johannes Morsink, *The Universal Declaration of Human Rights: Origins, Drafting, and Intent* (University of Pennsylvania Press, 1999) for a discussion on the drafting process at 1–35.
92 Cyra Choudhury, 'Beyond Culture: Human Rights Universalism versus Religious and Cultural Relativism in the Activism for Gender Justice' (2015) 30(2) *Berkeley Journal of Gender, Law and Justice* 226–267, 241.
93 Jack Donnelly, 'The Relative Universality of Human Rights' (2007) 29(2) *Human Rights Quarterly* 281–306, 288.
94 Vedna Jivan and Christine Forster, 'What Would Gandhi Say? Reconciling Universalism, Cultural Relativism and Feminism through Women's Use of *CEDAW*' (2005) 9 *SYBIL* 9 103–123, 110.
95 Ibid.
96 Bhabani Nayak, 'Challenges of Cultural Relativism and the Future of Feminist Universalism' (2013) 6 *Journal of Politics and Law* 83–90, 84.
97 Jivan and Forster, n 94, 112.
98 Jivan and Forster, n 94, 113.
99 Adel Abadeer, *Norms and Gender Discrimination in the Arab World* (Palgrave MacMillan, 2015) 53–70, 53.
100 Lauren Bock Mullins, '*CEDAW*: The Challenges of Enshrining Women's Equality in International Law' (2018) 20(3) *Public Integrity* 257–272, 262.
101 Charlotte Epstein (ed.), *Against International Relations Norms: Postcolonial Perspectives* (Routledge, 2017).

102 See Johannes Morsink, n 91, for detailed account of the implications on colonies and women's rights at 92–129.
103 Ibid 106–122.
104 Ibid.
105 Thomas Ng, 'Are Human Rights a Western Construct? From the Confucius Peace Prize to the Practice of Suttee in India' (2012) 5(21) *Journal of International Social Research* 465, 467.
106 Gupta, n 68, 98.
107 Shefali Desai, 'Hearing Afghan Women's Voices: Feminist Theory's Re-Conceptualization of Women's Human Rights' (1999) 16 *Arizona Journal of International and Comparative Law* 805–843; Yvonne Donders and Vleugel Vincent, 'Universality, Diversity and Legal Certainty: Cultural Diversity in the Dialogue between *CEDAW* and States Parties' in *The Rule of Law at the National and International Levels: Contestations and Deference* (Hart Publishing, 2015) 321–351, 324.
108 Ibid Desai 837.
109 Ibid.
110 Ibid 809.
111 Radhika Coomaraswamy, 'Identity Within: Cultural Relativism, Minority Rights and the Empowerment of Women' (2002) 34(3) *George Washington International Law Review* 483–514, 485, 499, 508.
112 Desai, n 107, 809.
113 Ursula O'Hare, 'Realizing Human Rights for Women' (1999) 21(2) *Human Rights Quarterly* 364–402, 368.
114 Christine Chinkin, 'A Critique of the Public/Private Dimension' (1999) 10 *European Journal of International Law* 387–395, 389.
115 Shazia Qureshi, 'Progressive Development of Women's Human Rights in International Human Right Law and within United Nations System' (2012) 19(2) *Journal of Political Studies* 111–124, 113.
116 Chinkin n 114, 392.
117 Martha Nussbaum, 'Women's Progress and Women's Human Rights' (2016) 38(3) *Human Rights Quarterly* 589–622, 600.
118 Charlotte Bunch, 'Women's Rights as Human Rights: Toward a Re-Vision of Human Rights' (1990) 12(4) *Human Rights Quarterly* 486–498, 488.
119 Ibid.
120 United Nations General Assembly, *Declaration on the Elimination of Discrimination against Women* (7 November 1967) (A/RES/2263(XXII)) art 2(e).
121 Bunch, n 118, 491.
122 Ibid 493.
123 Ibid 494.
124 Paulina García-Del Moral, and Megan Alexandra Dersnah, 'A Feminist Challenge to the Gendered Politics of the Public/Private Divide: On Due Diligence, Domestic Violence, and Citizenship' (2014) 18(6–7) *Citizenship Studies* 661–675.
125 Rebecca J. Cook, 'State Responsibility for Violations of Women's Human Rights' (1994) 7 *Harvard Human Rights Journal* 125–176.
126 Lee Hasselbacher, 'State Obligations Regarding Domestic Violence: The European Court of Human Rights, Due Diligence, and International Legal Minimums of Protection' (2009) 8 *Northwestern University Journal of International Human Rights* 190–215.
127 Andrew Byrnes and Eleanor Bath, 'Violence against Women, the Obligation of Due Diligence, and the Optional Protocol to the Convention on the Elimination of All Forms of Discrimination against Women – Recent Developments' (2008) 8(3) *Human Rights Law Review* 517–533.
128 Karel Vasak, 'Human Rights: A Thirty-Year Struggle: The Sustained Efforts to Give Force of Law to the Universal Declaration of Human Rights' 30(11) *UNESCO Courier* (United Nations Educational, Scientific, and Cultural Organisation, Paris, 1977).

129 Barbara Bennett Woodhouse, 'The Constitutionalisation of Children's Rights: Incorporating Emerging Human Rights into Constitutional Doctrine' (1999) 2(1) *University of Pennsylvania Journal of Constitutional Law* 1–52.
130 Stephen McCaffrey and Kate Neville, 'Small Capacity and Big Responsibilities: Financial and Legal Implications of a Human Right to Water for Developing Countries' (2009) 21(4) *Georgetown International Environmental Law Review* 679–704.
131 Vasak, n 128.
132 Jennifer Downs, 'A Healthy and Ecologically Balanced Environment: An Argument for a Third Generation Right' (1993) 3(2) *Duke Journal of Comparative and International Law* 351–386.
133 Alice Edwards, *Violence against Women under International Human Rights Law* (Cambridge University Press, 2011) 61.
134 Eva Feder Kittay, 'Searching for an Overlapping Consensus: A Secular Care Ethics Feminist Responds to Religious Feminists' (2007) 4 *University of Saint Thomas Law Journal* 468–488, 477.
135 Ibid.
136 Ratna Kapur, 'In the Aftermath of Critique We Are Not in Epistemic Free Fall: Human Rights, the Subaltern Subject, and Non-Liberal Search for Freedom and Happiness' (2014) 25(1) *Law and Critique* 25–45, 39.
137 Cyra Choudhury, 'Beyond Culture: Human Rights Universalism versus Religious and Cultural Relativism in the Activism for Gender Justice' (2015) 30(2) *Berkeley Journal of Gender, Law and Justice* 226–267, 231.
138 Maneesha Deckha, 'Is Culture Taboo? Feminism, Intersectionality, and Culture Talk in Law' (2004) 16 *Canadian Journal of Women and the Law* 14–48, 35–36.
139 Choudhury, n 137, 231.
140 Martha Nussbaum, 'Women's Bodies: Violence, Security, and Capabilities' (2005) 6(2) *Journal of Human Development* 167–183, 178.
141 Anika Rahman, 'Religious Rights versus Women's Rights in India: A Test Case for International Human Rights Law' (1990) 28 *Columbia Journal of Transnational Law* 473–498, 480.
142 Bina Srinivasan, *Negotiating Complexities: A Collection of Feminist Essays* (Promilla and Co, New Delhi, 2007) 38; Sylvia Vatuk, 'Islamic Feminism in India: Indian Muslim Women Activists and the Reform of Muslim Personal Law' (2008) 42(2–3) *Modern Asian Studies* 489–518.
143 Ibid Vatuk.
144 Sumi Madhok, 'Developmentalism, Human Rights, and Gender Politics: From a Politics of Origins to a Politics of Meaning' in Ashwani Peetush and Jay Drdyk (eds.) *Human Rights: India and the West* (Oxford University Press, 2015) 95, 100.
145 Choudhury, n 137, 231.
146 Kapur, n 136.
147 Kamla Bhasin and Nighat Khan, *Some Questions on Feminism and Its Relevance in South Asia* (Kali for Women, 1986).
148 Gupta, n 68, 93.
149 Choudhury, n 137, 259.
150 Choudhury, n 137, 252.
151 Rikki Holtmaat and Jonneke Naber, *Women's Human Rights and Culture: From Deadlock to Dialogue* (Intersentsia, 2011) 4.
152 Choudhury, n 137.
153 Dianne Otto, 'Handmaidens, Hierarchies and Crossing the Public-Private Divide in the Teaching of International Law' (2000) 1 *Melbourne Journal of International Law* 35–69, 37.
154 Pami Vyas, 'Reconceptualizing Domestic Violence in India: Economic Abuse and the Need for Broad Statutory Interpretation to Promote Women's Fundamental Rights' (2006) 13(1) *Michigan Journal of Gender and Law* 177–206, 184.

155 Ibid. Mary J. Osirim, 'Crisis in the State and the Family: Violence against Women in Zimbabwe' (2002) 7 *African Studies Quarterly* 153–169, 167.
156 Otto, n 153.
157 Vyas, n 154.
158 See, for example, *Gujarat Local Authorities Act* 2005.
159 *Bharatraj Alias Bharatram vs. Addi Civil Judge & Ors* (2012); *Javed and Others v. State of Haryana and Others* (2003).
160 Shri N. Achanta, 'Implementation of Family Planning Programmes at District Level' *Administrators in Action* (Committee on Case Studies, The Indian Institute of Public Administration, 1972) 259.
161 Marika Vicziany, 'Coercion in a Soft State: The Family-Planning Program of India: Part 2: The Sources of Coercion' (1982–1983) 55(4) *Pacific Affairs* 557–592, 574.
162 Theresa Man and Ling Lee, 'Rethinking the Personal and the Political: Feminist Activism and Civic Engagement' (2007) 22(4) *Hypatia* 163–179, 166.
163 Vrinda Narain, 'Muslim Women's Equality in India: Applying a Human Rights Framework' (2013) 35(1) *Human Rights Quarterly* 91–115, 95.
164 See United Kingdom Home Office, *Country Information and Guidance India: Women Fearing Gender-Based Harm/Violence*, April 2015 for in-depth analysis of Indian women's participation and experiences in the private, economic and political spheres. www.refworld.org/docid/553f3dfe4.html Accessed 18/4/19.
165 Sreyashi Ghosh, 'Beyond Spaces: Debunking Public/Private Divide in Understanding Violence against Women in India' (2017) 1(1) *International Journal of Gender Studies* 76–95, 90.
166 Ibid 92, fn 44; United Kingdom Home Office, n 164, 36.
167 Rajeev Bhargava, 'Political Secularism' in John S. Dryzek, Bonnie Honig and Anne Phillips (eds.) *Oxford Handbook of Political Theory* (Oxford University Press, 2008) 1–19, 13.
168 Narain n 163, 91.
169 Ibid 95.

4

RIGHT TO EQUALITY AND NON-DISCRIMINATION

Introduction

This chapter focusses on the role of the right to equality and non-discrimination guaranteed in the *Constitution of India* 1950 (Constitution) in the advancement of women's human rights. The adoption of the Constitution preceded India's accession to core human rights conventions that required guarantees of equality and non-discrimination.[1] Despite this, and although women's human rights were not a primary concern of the Indian drafters,[2] equality and non-discrimination protections were included in three separate portions of the text. The preamble states that equality of status and opportunity must be secured for all citizens. The Directive Principles direct the Parliament to make legislation to achieve the goals of equality for all persons.[3] Article 14 and article 15 of the Fundamental Rights are at the heart of equality protection in the Constitution and guarantee equality before the law and non-discrimination on the ground of sex, among other grounds.[4] In accord with most global constitutions, articles 14 and 15 occupy a prominent place at the front of the Constitution. Equality and non-discrimination provisions, particularly if embedded in a constitution, have important symbolic and practical dimensions.[5] They provide a standard of conduct to guide the state in its law and policy decision-making and to hold it accountable to that standard.[6] If an equality and non-discrimination provision places a positive obligation on the state to achieve equality and prevent discrimination, as we argue is required by *CEDAW,* this represents an active mandate for the state. The state is a powerful institution which can generate structural change because of its wide-reaching role in legitimating and regulating social roles and institutions through its laws, policies, programs and measures. In addition, women and their advocates can utilise legislative guarantees of equality and non-discrimination in advocacy, litigation, law reform and policy development to seek redress for, and to challenge, social, political or economic disadvantage.[7]

The chapter begins in 4.2 by explaining and analysing the obligations placed on India to recognise the right to equality and non-discrimination through its ratification or accession to key core conventions. In particular, 4.2 details how *CEDAW* expanded the understanding of equality in the human rights framework to include substantive equality, expanded human rights understandings of non-discrimination to include both direct and indirect discrimination, posited sex and gender as alternate sources of discrimination and inequality and, finally, identified the compounding effect of multiple discriminations. Sections 4.3, 4.4 and 4.5 consider and analyse the form and content of the equality and non-discrimination provisions contained in article 14 and article 15 of the Constitution. In these sections, we examine the context in which article 14 and article 15 were drafted and explore their interpretation in the courts and the extent to which those articles comply, both in their plain language and their interpretation, with the obligations created by the human rights framework, in particular *CEDAW*. Finally, we evaluate, with the use of case and legislative examples, the extent to which women's human rights principles and theories have been or could be utilised to broaden the scope and impact of article 14 and article 15.

Right to equality and non-discrimination: obligations of human rights law

This section examines, in general terms, the right to equality and non-discrimination as it emerged in the human rights framework and briefly plots the developing and expanding understandings of those rights. International human rights instruments are living documents and must adapt to shifting political and social norms, and therefore their interpretation is not static.[8] Equality and non-discrimination are core principles in human rights law, and all members of the UN have an obligation to incorporate equality and non-discrimination guarantees into their domestic legal systems.[9] A constitution is the most appropriate and effective place to embed the principles of equality and non-discrimination because it has supremacy over ordinary legislation, and, additionally, an extraordinary procedure is usually required to amend a constitutional provision. Such procedures, which include obtaining a two-thirds majority in the national legislature or a referendum process, thus provide the strongest means of protecting women's right to equality and non-discrimination.[10]

The principles of equality and non-discrimination are often used interchangeably by commentators, but they have subtly different meanings. We view them as follows. Equality means the absence of discrimination, and enforcing the principle of non-discrimination between groups will (theoretically) produce equality. The principles of equality and non-discrimination require individuals to pursue their rights through the courts or other judicial mechanisms and may only result in relief for an individual petitioner and not for others similarly situated. However,

CEDAW requires state parties to actively pursue the achievement of equality and non-discrimination, and it is this mandate that we argue has the potential to redress deep structural inequalities through concrete, positive, institutional and political commitments, laws, policies, programs and measures.

Right to equality and non-discrimination in human rights law

A first priority of the UN Human Rights Commission, established in 1946, was to draft a 'bill of human rights.'[11] The *UDHR* included a right to equality and non-discrimination on the grounds of sex,[12] which was subsequently enshrined in the *ICCPR* and the *ICESCR*. Article 3 of the *ICCPR* requires state parties to ensure the equal right of men and women to the enjoyment of all civil and political rights in the convention. Article 2(1) of the *ICCPR* links the prohibition of discrimination to a general obligation to implement the convention. It states that 'each state . . . undertakes to respect and to ensure to all individuals . . . the rights recognized in the present Convention, without distinction of any kind, such as race, colour, sex, language, religion, political or other opinion, national or social origin, property, birth or other statuses.' Article 2(2) of the *ICESCR* requires states to ensure all rights in the convention are exercised without discrimination of any kind as to race, colour, sex, language, religion, political or other opinion, national or social origin, property, birth or other status". Article 3 requires state parties to ensure the equal right of men and women to the enjoyment of all economic, social and cultural rights in the convention. In accord with these early conventions, most world constitutions incorporated equality and non-discrimination guarantees.

The right to equality and non-discrimination in the *ICCPR* and the *ICESCR* has resulted in direct positive outcomes for women in countries which are party to their Optional Protocols. The Optional Protocols establish a complaints process accessible to individuals who have (unsuccessfully) exhausted their domestic remedies. In *Graciela Ato del Avellanal v. Peru*,[13] for example, a Peruvian woman who owned two apartment buildings in Lima was prevented from suing the tenants to collect overdue rents because, under article 168 of the Peruvian Civil Code, when a woman is married, only her husband is entitled to pursue an action in relation to property of the marriage before the courts. After exhausting her domestic remedies as required, Avellanal sought recourse through the Human Rights Committee (HRC), claiming sex discrimination under article 14(1) of the *ICCPR*, which states that 'all persons shall be equal before the courts and tribunals'. The HRC agreed with her argument, finding that the Peruvian Civil Code meant 'the wife was not equal to her husband for purposes of suing in court' and ordered Peru to rectify the inequality and reform the law.[14]

The *ICCPR* and *ICESCR* do not, in their plain wording, define the terms 'equality' and 'non-discrimination'. Later interpretations have held the purported discriminatory or unequal treatment of one person must be measured by the relative treatment of another person similarly situated.[15] Therefore, not all differentiation of treatment constitutes unequal treatment or discrimination under the two conventions.[16] The HRC states in General Comment No. 18 that differentiation of treatment is permissible if, first, the goal is to achieve a legitimate purpose, and, second, the criteria for such differentiation are reasonable and objective. The existence of such a justification must be assessed in relation to the aims and effects of the measures under consideration.[17] Thus, only if there is an illegitimate aim and an unreasonable relationship of proportionality between the two is differential treatment unjustified, constituting discrimination.[18] In the Mauritian women case,[19] for example, 19 women complained to the HRC, arguing that the immigration law of Mauritius, which granted automatic residence rights to a foreign woman who marries a Mauritian man but did not do so in respect to a foreign man who married a Mauritian woman, was discriminatory.[20] The assumption that underscored the provision was that, upon marriage, a wife joins her husband in his country, and therefore, there is no need to grant rights to her spouse in her country of origin.[21] The HRC agreed that this assumption left women with less choice and autonomy than men after marriage and was, therefore, not reasonable or justifiable. It violated the non-discrimination provision in the *ICCPR* and supported an outdated and patriarchal notion of 'dependent nationality'.[22]

While positive decisions have been forthcoming for women under these general human rights conventions, they have been uniformly decided within a model of formal equality and direct discrimination, which is limited in its capacity to advance women's human rights.

Right to equality and non-discrimination in CEDAW

The adoption of *CEDAW* signalled the recognition that the equality and non-discrimination protection provided by the *ICCPR* and the *ICESCR* was insufficient to address the breadth and complexity of women's specific experiences of inequality and discrimination. The right to equality and non-discrimination is central to *CEDAW* and underscores each of the substantive provisions set out in articles 6 through 16, which outline state parties' obligations with respect to the most common areas of discrimination against women. Article 1 defines discrimination as:

> any distinction, exclusion or restriction made on the basis of sex which has the effect or purpose of impairing or nullifying the recognition, enjoyment or exercise by women, irrespective of their marital status, on a basis of equality of men and women, of human rights and fundamental freedoms in the political, economic, social, cultural, civil or any other field.

This is an important definition because it enables a much broader and more powerful understanding of discrimination than that provided by the earlier conventions.[23] Distinction, exclusion and restriction have been broadly interpreted by the *CEDAW* Committee. A distinction might be where a woman is not given a job despite her qualifications because the employer believes she will take time off to have children. An exclusion might be a ban on women serving in combat roles in the army. A restriction might be a maternity leave provision extended only to married women. Any distinction, exclusion or restriction that has either the effect (direct) or the purpose (indirect) of impairing or nullifying the enjoyment of rights in all spheres of women's lives is discrimination. The *CEDAW* Committee has made clear that this protection extends not only to rights enumerated in *CEDAW* but also to those rights recognised under other conventions (for example, the right to life).[24]

While article 1 provides an expansive definition of discrimination against women, article 2 creates a framework for the achievement of equality and non-discrimination in all areas of women's lives. It begins by requiring that state parties condemn discrimination against women in all its forms and agree to pursue by all appropriate means and without delay a policy of eliminating discrimination against women. This clearly requires the state to take active and positive measures to eliminate discrimination. It is not sufficient for the state to merely respond to instances of discrimination with individual remedies. To achieve this goal, article 2 then sets out the steps the state must take. Article 2(a) obligates state parties to 'embody the principle of equality of men and women in their national constitutions or other appropriate legislation' and to ensure the 'practical realisation of this principle'. This expands the meaning of equality beyond the formal understandings of the earlier conventions to that of substantive or transformative equality.[25] Article 2(b) obligates state parties to adopt appropriate legislative and other measures, including sanctions where appropriate, prohibiting all discrimination against women.[26] Article 2 subsections (d) and (e) require state parties to refrain from discrimination themselves and, uniquely, to eliminate discrimination against women 'by any person, organisation or enterprise.' This is a significant inclusion as the human rights framework focusses on the obligations of the state, rather than private individuals and organisations, to respect, protect and promote human rights.[27]

Article 3 requires state parties to 'ensure the full development and advancement of women, for the purpose of guaranteeing them the exercise and enjoyment of human rights and fundamental freedoms on a basis of equality with men'. It is insufficient to guarantee women the same treatment as men, but instead their differences (whether biological or social) must be considered. For example, it is not sufficient for the state to provide equal access to services. Instead, the state must ensure these services adequately meet the different needs of all individuals and groups of people under its jurisdiction.[28] Article 4 reinforces articles 1, 2 and 3 by providing for temporary special measures (special provisions or affirmative action) aimed at accelerating *de facto* equality between men and women. For example, the 33 percent reservation for women on panchayats is an example of a temporary special measure or 'special provision', as it is termed in the Constitution.

Right to equality in article 14 of the *Constitution of India*

Defining the right to equality

The right to equality articulated in article 14 of the Constitution states 'the state shall not deny to any person equality before the law or the equal protection of the laws within the territory of India.' We interpret the right to equality set out in article 2(a) of *CEDAW* as containing three distinct components – a right to formal equality, a right to substantive equality and a state obligation to achieve substantive equality. However, these three components are not fully articulated in article 14 of the Constitution.

A right to formal equality treats women and men as alike and deserving of equal and similar treatment. A right to formal equality is important since it guarantees important rights to women, such as the right to vote, the right to be a doctor or a lawyer and the right to own property in their own name. Article 14 of the Constitution succeeds, in its plain wording, in achieving a guarantee of formal equality. The phrases 'equality before the law' and 'the equal protection of the law' are often adopted in constitutions and have been interpreted in the global courts as equating to formal equality.[29] It is notable that, according to Jain, one of the framers of the Constitution objected to even a formal equality guarantee because a statute might need to 'make a difference . . . between men and women (as in the Factory and Labour legislation).'[30]

The Supreme Court of India, in accord with the plain language of article 14, has interpreted its meaning as a guarantee of formal equality. The Supreme Court has held, however, that formal equality does not require that all persons are treated the same, rather that persons similarly situated must be treated the same.[31] It determines which persons are similarly situated through a system of 'reasonable' classification. The court assesses whether a law or policy that differentiates between classes of persons is reasonable. To be reasonable, it must not be 'arbitrary, artificial or evasive'.[32] If the differentiation is reasonable, then there is no violation of article 14. For example, in the case of *Sanaboina Satyanarayana*, a scheme designed to reduce crime against women in prison differentiated between prisoners who had been convicted of crimes against women and those who had not. The court held this classification which differentiated between two classes of prisoners was reasonable and not, therefore, a violation of article 14.[33]

Some differences between women and men, based on either sex or gender, require legal protection in our view. Women's capacity to give birth, a difference based on sex, may require protection in employment law: for example, by the provision of maternity leave. Sexual harassment legislation is also necessary to prevent harassment in the workplace, acknowledging female vulnerability not because of biological difference, but because of gender difference. However, the Supreme Court has used the reasonable classification approach to support protectionist legislation which directly discriminates against women.[34] This, in our view, misunderstands the underlying aim of a formal equality approach, which, correctly applied, requires women's differences to be accommodated so that they can (at a formal level at least) exist equally with men. Preventing women from participating in particular occupations for their own safety does not elevate them to an equal position; it merely discriminates.[35]

A right to formal equality has been, and continues to be, significant in India because many laws do not yet deliver formal equality to women. For example, the *Prohibition of Child Marriage Act* 2006 provides an unequal marriageable age of 18 for females and 21 for males. A straightforward application of a formal equality analysis based on *CEDAW* would conclude that this legislation violates article 14.[36] Indeed, successful actions against formal inequality utilising article 14 have resulted in gains for women. For example, in 2014, a female petitioner argued that the Cine Costume Make-up Artists and Hair Dressers Association, whose rules only allowed men to be make-up artists, was, by denying her membership as a make-up artist, in breach of article 14.[37] The court agreed and held that she could not be denied membership as discrimination on grounds of gender was a clear violation of her right to equality and a denial of 'her capacity to earn her livelihood which affects her individual dignity.'[38]

> If a female artist does not get an opportunity to enter into the arena of being a member of the Association, she cannot work as a female artist. It is inconceivable. The likes of the petitioners are given membership as hair dressers, but not as make-up artist. There is no fathomable reason for the same. It is gender bias writ large. It is totally impermissible and wholly unacceptable.[39]

A right to substantive equality underscores all articles of *CEDAW*. It is important because it recognises that historical and continuing discrimination against women means that formal equality does not lead to equality in practice.[40] For example, the equal right to stand for parliament was afforded to Indian women in 1915; however, in 2019, only 12 percent of seats in the national parliament are held by women, primarily because of the range of obstacles preventing women from taking public office.[41] There is, however, no right to substantive equality in the plain wording of article 14, and the courts have not, in most instances, interpreted article 14 as extending to substantive equality.

A positive obligation on the state to advance and realise both formal and substantive equality recognises that structural change requires not just individuals seeking to enforce their rights, but also concrete and active steps by the state to enact and implement legislation, to develop and implement policies, to develop and execute national plans and to launch education initiatives and media campaigns. This vital component does not appear, in its plain wording, to be contained in article 14.

Applying women's human rights

Article 14, we suggest, despite its limited wording and interpretation by the Supreme Court, can be utilised to further women's human rights through the application of women's human rights principles and theories.[42] Although on a plain reading, article 14 does not appear to guarantee substantive equality, feminist advocates have utilised it to argue for, and briefly succeed in, the expansion of its meaning beyond formal equality to substantive equality. In the case of *T Sareetha v. T Venkata Subbaiah*,[43] a popular actor who became rich and famous was sued by her husband for restitution of conjugal rights, an action that, if successful, would order a wife or husband to resume cohabitation with her or his spouse, unless there was a 'reasonable' reason for the spouse to refuse. The Andhra Pradesh High Court noted that, although the action for restitution of conjugal rights was formally equal because both husband and wife can make use of it, the social position of women in marriage was different than that of men. The court stated that restitution of conjugal rights coerces, through the judicial process, 'the unwilling party to have sex against that person's consent and freewill'.[44] The court concluded that the enforcement of such an action would likely benefit a husband rather than a wife and, therefore, violated article 14.

This decision marked a recognition of substantive equality since it went beyond formal equality to discuss and emphasise the differential impact on women of their inferior position within marriage. Ultimately, however, in another case the following year, the Supreme Court came to a different finding and overruled the decision. 'In India . . . conjugal rights i.e. right of the husband or the wife to the society of the other spouse is not merely creature of the statute. Such a right is inherent in the very institution of marriage itself.'[45] Despite the overruling of *Sareetha*, the potential scope for article 14 to be successfully utilised by women's human rights advocates as representing a substantive equality standard remains through the original finding of the Andhra Pradesh High Court.

Article 14 does not appear to place a positive obligation on the state to achieve equality for women. This is required by *CEDAW* through the obligation placed on state parties to pursue, by all appropriate means and without delay, a policy of eliminating discrimination against women and to ensure the practical realisation of equality. The wording in the Constitution 'shall not deny' is negative, rather than imposing a positive obligation on the state to achieve equality. However, in *C. Masilamani Mudaliar and Others v. Idol Sri Swaminathaswami Thirukoil and Others*,[46] the judiciary took a different view. The petitioners argued that the *Hindu Succession Act* 1956, which has been historically interpreted along patrilineal lines, should be interpreted to provide equal succession rights to both men and women. The Supreme Court agreed and, importantly, concluded that 'the state should take all appropriate measures including legislation to modify and abolish gender-based discrimination in the existing laws, regulations, customs and practices which discriminate against women'. The judges expressly used, in support of their decision, article 2(e) of *CEDAW*, which obligates state parties 'to take all appropriate measures to eliminate discrimination against women by any person, organisation or enterprise', which they held 'enjoins the Supreme Court to breathe life into the dry bones of the Constitution'.[47]

While there has not been any further direct use of article 14 to compel the state to recognise that they have an active obligation to achieve gender equality, we argue article 14 can be characterised as a right to concrete outcomes such as resources, services and opportunity which, if not provided, can be demanded from government.[48]

Right to non-discrimination in article 15 of the *Constitution of India*

Defining non-discrimination

The right to non-discrimination set out in article 15(1) and 15(2) of the Constitution states that the 'state shall not discriminate against any citizen on grounds only of religion, race, caste, sex, place of birth or any of them' and that 'no citizen shall, on grounds only of religion, race, caste, sex, place of birth or any of them, be subject to any disability, liability, restriction or condition with regard to (a) access to shops, public restaurants, hotels and palaces of public entertainment; or (b) the use of wells, tanks, bathing ghats, roads and places of public resort maintained wholly or partly out of state funds or dedicated to the use of the general public.'

We interpret the obligations created by article 2 subsection (b) through (e) of *CEDAW* as containing four distinct components – a prohibition on both direct and indirect discrimination, a prohibition on discrimination on all the possible grounds from which discrimination arises and a recognition of the compounding effect of multiple forms of discrimination, a prohibition on discrimination by private individuals and organisations and the placement of a positive mandate on the state to achieve non-discrimination. Article 15 does not fully meet these requirements in its plain wording or in its interpretation in the courts.

The first component, the prohibition of both direct and indirect discrimination, is not expressly included in article 15(1) of the Constitution, which merely prohibits discrimination and has been interpreted by the courts as meaning direct, but not indirect, discrimination. The *CEDAW* Committee expressly states in GR 25(7) on temporary special measures that discrimination, as it is defined in article 1 of *CEDAW*, requires state parties to ensure 'that there is no direct or indirect discrimination against women in their laws'.[49] Indeed, in the 2014 concluding observations to India, the Committee expressed concern 'at the absence of a comprehensive anti-discrimination law addressing all aspects of direct and indirect discrimination against women.'[50]

Sex and gender discrimination is the different treatment of women and men leading to different and unfair outcomes.[51] Direct discrimination occurs when a difference in treatment relies directly and explicitly on distinctions based on sex or gender. For example, legislation that provides for (or does not prevent) different rates of pay for men and women undertaking the same work constitutes direct discrimination. Laws that provide unequal or no inheritance to women or prevent women from working at night or from undertaking manual labour provide further examples of direct discrimination. Indirect discrimination is much less obvious than direct discrimination. It occurs when a law, policy or programme does not appear to be discriminatory but has a discriminatory effect when implemented.[52] A policy by an employer, for example, that workers must be available for night shifts may constitute indirect discrimination against women who find it difficult to work at night due to domestic responsibilities.[53] Indirect discrimination recognises that discrimination does not always manifest in obvious or direct ways but may be disguised within laws, policies and practices which appear to apply to all persons equally but in practice do not.[54]

The second component is multiple discrimination and contains two parts. First, the prohibition of discrimination on all possible grounds of discrimination. Article 2 of *CEDAW* condemns discrimination in *all* its forms, article 2(b) refers to prohibiting *all* discrimination, and article 2(c) refers to *any* act of discrimination, anticipating the emergence of new forms of discrimination not identified at the time of its drafting. Article 15 of the Constitution does prohibit discrimination on a number of important grounds – religion, race, caste, sex and place of birth, and several further grounds have been read in by the courts, including gender[55] and sexual identity.[56] However, many other grounds of discrimination are excluded. Grounds specifically rejected by the courts include HIV status,[57] disability[58] and sexual orientation.[59]

Further grounds that give rise to discrimination experienced by women include age, marital status,[60] health status,[61] disability[62] and marginalised family forms.[63] The second part of multiple discrimination is recognition of not just the different and varied range of grounds from which discrimination can arise, but also the compounding effect of multiple forms of discrimination. When women experience discriminations on a range of grounds simultaneously, the cumulative effects can be substantial. For example, a Dalit disabled woman may be subject to discrimination because of her gender, her disability and her low caste status, and the combination of discriminations may be devastating.

The third component is the extension of the prohibition of discrimination beyond the state and its representatives to private individuals and organisations. Human rights law focusses on the obligations of the state (and not individuals) to respect, protect and promote the human rights of all persons. Article 2(e) of *CEDAW*, however, requires state parties to 'take all appropriate measures to eliminate discrimination against women by any person, organization or enterprise'. This is a significant inclusion. Many discriminatory practices are perpetrated by individuals and private organisations such as employers, banks and service providers in areas such as health, education and housing. Violence against women can be perpetrated by the state but is often perpetrated by individuals. Article 15(1) of the Constitution prohibits only the state from discriminating; however, article 15(2) prohibits discrimination in access to shops, public restaurants, hotels and palaces of public entertainment and wells, tanks, bathing ghats, roads and places of public resort maintained wholly or partly out of state funds or dedicated to the use of the general public. This represents a limited prohibition on private organisations from discriminating but falls well short of a prohibition on discrimination by all private individuals and organisations.

The fourth component, a positive obligation on the state to end discrimination against women, recognises that structural change requires not just individuals seeking to enforce their rights but also requires concrete and active steps by the state to enact and implement legislation, to develop and implement policies, to develop and execute national plans and to launch education initiatives and media campaigns. Article 15 places a positive obligation on the state not to discriminate and to ensure there is no 'disability, liability, restriction or condition' to access to certain public spaces and places. It is a very limited mandate, in our view. However, the court has interpreted the responsibilities of the state much more broadly than a plain reading of article 15(2).

Applying women's human rights

Article 15 clearly protects the right not to be directly discriminated against on the grounds of sex. In the case of *Vasantha R. v. Union of India & Ors*,[64] this guarantee was utilised successfully by the petitioner, who was a worker in a textile mill in Dharmapuri District that undertook spinning, weaving, processing and printing. She was unable to work any night shifts because of a protective provision in the *Factories Act* 1948, which banned women from working between 7:00 p.m. and 6:00 a.m. in factories.[65] The provision, although purporting to protect women from the 'dangers' of night time, is an example of direct discrimination on the grounds of sex. The Punjab-Haryana High Court agreed and held that the provision breached article 15 of the Constitution. Although the decision is positive, it provides an illustration of article 15 as a negative, rather than a positive, right. Unless a plaintiff challenges a discriminatory provision, then it remains in operation with no apparent obligation on the state to actively amend legislation that directly discriminates against women. In another example, Muthamma, a senior member of the Indian Foreign Service, brought a petition against the government, claiming she had been overlooked for promotion because she was a woman, in violation of the Constitution. She also argued that the rules that no married woman had an automatic right to be appointed to the service and that a woman employee must get written permission to marry and may be forced to resign if the government decides that her marital commitments will restrict her work were a violation of article 14. Her petition was dismissed.[66]

Also, article 15 does not expressly prohibit indirect discrimination, and the Supreme Court has not grappled with indirect sex discrimination. Indeed, given that direct discrimination is still contested, and many laws still directly discriminate against women, much work is yet to be done by women's human rights advocates to identify and showcase examples of indirect discrimination.

BOX 4.1 EXAMPLE: INDIRECT DISCRIMINATION: JALAYUKTA SHIVAR[67]

After a rush of suicides by drought-stricken farmers, the Maharashtra government introduced Jalayukta Shivar (farm full of water), a watershed development program, creating decentralised water storage. It aims to irrigate 19,059 of 40,000 villages in Maharashtra in 22 drought-affected districts. Central to the program is the participation of local beneficiary farmers in its planning, implementation and maintenance. Participation is likely to be central to its success because rural people can provide valuable social-cultural, ecological, economic and technical indigenous knowledge, ensuring consistency between objectives of development and community values and preferences. However, although women work on the land and physically contribute considerable labour in the fields, often more than even the menfolk, they do not own land. Consequently, they have been excluded from the planning, implementation and maintenance and are often excluded from decision-making. This results in indirect discrimination on the basis of gender and a consequent weakening of the programme since women's contributions are valuable and important.

Source: Authors

The *CEDAW* Committee recommended specifically to India in 2014 in its concluding observations that it should protect women from multiple or intersectional forms of discrimination and other grounds as referred to in General recommendation 28 on the core obligations of state parties under article 2 of CEDAW (GR 28).[68] We argue this requires two changes to article 15.

First, article 15 should prohibit discrimination on a much broader range of grounds than those currently articulated. Grounds identified in GR 28 of the *CEDAW* Committee which are not currently recognised include ethnicity, belief, health, status, age, class and sexual orientation and gender identity.[69] Alternately or additionally, the incorporation of an 'other status' clause, which invites the recognition of further grounds of discrimination not explicitly nominated, is an important inclusion to ensure that other grounds of discrimination can be recognised and addressed as required.

Second, article 15 requires that the multiple grounds be understood as potentially operating together to heighten the discrimination. Instead, the phrase 'on grounds only' in article 15 has directly (and perversely) not only prevented recognition of multiple discriminations, but also enabled the exclusion of any case where there are multiple discriminations. In *Mahalebs v. Dr BB Sen*,[70] for example, Justice Mukharji stated:

> The word 'only' in Article 15(1) is of great importance and significance which should not be missed. The impugned law must be shown to

> discriminate because of sex alone. If other factors in addition to sex come into play in making the discriminatory law, then such discrimination does not, in my judgment, come within the provision of Article 15(1) of the Constitution.[71]

Applying this reasoning, Justice Mukharji held a provision in the *Civil Procedure Code* 1908 which gives the court the authority in a civil suit to demand monetary security from a woman who does not possess sufficient immovable property in India but no authority to demand if from a man unless he lives outside of India does not constitute discrimination.[72] The court held that the provision did not discriminate against women only on the ground of sex since it was based not just on sex, but also on the 'important consideration of sufficient immoveable property'. The flawed reasoning, which could make any sex discrimination claim difficult to establish, explicitly used other (indirectly) discriminatory factors (women's restricted economic capacity, women's limited property ownership and women's general poverty) to exclude the claim, adopting this artificial view of sex discrimination where the category of 'sex' operates in isolation rather than in association with women's complex identities of race, religion, caste, disability and socio-political and economic contexts. The court missed the nature and complexity of discrimination against women, including the fact that multiple forms of disadvantage intersect and intensify discrimination.[73] Nothing in the drafting of the Constitution indicates an original intent for interpreting article 15(1) to exclude multi-ground discrimination. Moreover, the Constitution is a living document and must, in our view, be interpreted in light of changing social expectations.

BOX 4.2 EXAMPLE: INDIRECT AND MULTIPLE DISCRIMINATIONS: *RAJBALA V. STATE OF HARYANA*[74]

In 2015, the *Haryana Panchayati Raj Act* 1994, which regulates the election process to panchayats in Haryana, was amended to include five new disqualifications for persons seeking to stand for any post in panchayat elections. Three of those disqualifications constitute, in our view, indirect discrimination against women. They also cumulatively create multiple discriminations against women on the grounds of sex, gender, caste and class which, operating together, disproportionately impact women. Persons who have unpaid electricity bills, who do not possess the specified educational qualification and who do not have a functional toilet at their place of residence are disqualified.[75] Indeed, indications are the new qualifications have disenfranchised 68 percent of Dalit women and over 50 percent of all women from contesting panchayat elections.[76]

Three political activists who had been disqualified from standing for panchayat elections because they did not meet the educational qualifications challenged the disqualifications. The petitioners argued the disqualifications led to an arbitrary and discriminatory outcome and violated article 14. The court disagreed with the petitioners' arguments and held that the disqualifications were not arbitrary and discriminatory. The court held that 'there is nothing irrational or illegal in prescribing minimum education for contesting elections and possession of basic education would enable the candidates to effectively discharge their duties. Education gives the power to the human being to discriminate between good and bad, right and wrong.'[77] In relation to electricity bills, the court stated this was similar to insolvency that rendered people unable to contest any election. Finally, on the issue of having a toilet, the court held the primary duty of any civic body was to maintain sanitation. The elected representative should become an example for other people. 'If people still do not have a toilet it is not because of their poverty but because of their lacking the requisite will.'[78] The petitioners did not situate their argument firmly in violations of the right to equality and non-discrimination, despite claiming a violation of article 14. They did argue that 'women and scheduled castes would be worst hit by the impugned stipulation as a majority of them are the most unlikely to possess the minimum educational qualification prescribed in the impugned act'.[79] They were likely limited by the wording and interpretation of article 14 as a formal equality provision, the failure of article 15 to prohibit indirect discrimination and the interpretation of article 15(1) to specifically exclude accounts of multiple discriminations.

The impact of the educational requirement clearly does indirectly discriminate against women since statistics show that women have less access to education than men. It is also evident that there are multiple discriminations compounding the ability of women to meet these exclusions because not only are women more likely than men not to have achieved the required educational standard, but they are also more likely than men to reside in low economic housing without sanitary facilities, less likely to have the power or knowledge to take advantage of government funding for toilets and more likely than men to be unable to pay electricity bills.

Source: Authors

Finally, although article 15, on a plain reading, provides limited protection to persons from violations by individuals, the Supreme Court has interpreted it much more broadly, specifically drawing on *CEDAW* as authority for its findings.

For example, in *Vishaka*,[80] the court held that the state did have a responsibility to prevent sexual harassment perpetrated by individuals in the place of employment. Bhanwari Devi was a social worker for the Women's Development Programme in Rajasthan, working on a campaign to end child marriage. As part of her job, she worked directly with families to prevent the marriages and report cases to the police when urgent follow-up action was needed. She reported a family to the police who were arranging the marriage of a one-year-old infant. Upset with the intervention, the family rebelled against Devi. After attempting to ostracise her from her community, five men went to her home and attacked and restrained her husband while she was gang raped. Devi and her husband went to the police for help; however, no thorough investigation was launched, and police delayed taking statements regarding what had happened. Determined to receive justice for the brutal acts committed against her, Devi took her case to a trial court in Jaipur, where the court acquitted all five men. She appealed to the Supreme Court, which held it was not only a clear violation of her rights under articles 14 and 15 (and other fundamental rights) but that the state had a responsibility to take positive action to prevent further violations. They issued a comprehensive set of guidelines to protect working women from sexual harassment.[81]

Special provision in article 15(3) of the *Constitution of India*

Defining special provision

Article 15(3) states: 'Nothing in this article shall prevent the State from making any special provision for women and children.' Special provision is also known as affirmative action (or positive discrimination or, in the human rights framework, temporary special measures). The aim of special provision is to achieve substantive equality by redressing historical disadvantages faced by women or to accommodate a genuine biological difference such as pregnancy. It aims to eliminate discrimination, remedy the results of such prior discrimination and prevent such discrimination in the future.[82] A law school, for example, might make special provision by recruiting and admitting qualified female students from tribal or Dalit communities; an employer might make special provision by recruiting qualified women in an industry where only men have previously worked: for example, in a business that operates heavy equipment; the state might make special provision by legislating reserved seats for women in the national parliament.

Special provision can include targets and incentives encouraging women to apply for positions in male-dominated occupations, such as in the police force, as an engineer or as a rickshaw driver or bus driver. It can also include recruiting, training and financially assisting women candidates for election to publicly elected bodies, such as state governments and panchayats.[83] Further examples include circulating images of women in advertising material for male-dominated occupations: for example, recruitment drives for the police force depicting women on the job or political advertisements featuring women candidates. Another approach lies in using sex as a 'plus' factor, where a female applicant's sex is counted as a positive factor in her favour alongside (although not preferred over) other factors, such as experience or qualifications.[84]

Other forms of special provision which have historically been the subject of controversy and resistance due to a view that they circumvent a merit-based approach include reservations,[85] more flexible working conditions that allow women with young children to work part time and preferential treatment and targeted recruitment for appointment to public positions, such as the judiciary or other professional groups.[86]

Applying women's human rights

Special provisions are expressly supported by article 4 of *CEDAW*, which requires states to adopt temporary special measures to accelerate substantive equality between men and women. Article 4 also specifically requires that no temporary special measure should be capable of challenge on the basis that it is itself discrimination. For example, the legislation should prevent men from arguing that reserving places for women on panchayats is discrimination. Finally, article 4(2) states that temporary special measures shall be discontinued when the objectives of equality of opportunity and treatment have been achieved. For example, reserved seats might be discontinued when women are elected in equal numbers to panchayats.

We view special provisions as an important aspect of furthering women's human rights in India. In GR 5,[87] 8,[88] 23[89] and 25,[90] the *CEDAW* Committee encourages state parties to make more use of special provisions to advance women's integration into education, the economy and employment; to provide equal opportunities to represent their governments internationally; to encourage the equal participation of women in all aspects of public life and to address disadvantages faced by migrant women, women with disabilities and women in rural areas. We agree and argue that while article 15(3) of the Constitution has been utilised to authorise special provisions, which advance the rights of women, much greater use of the provisions is required. Successful examples include the following.

BOX 4.3 EXAMPLE: SPECIAL PROVISION IN GIRLS' EDUCATION

Educational access and educational opportunity are not equal for girls and boys. In 2018, 3.7 million girls eligible for school were not attending, and in rural areas, girls received an average of less than four years of formal education.[91] Improving girls' educational levels has been demonstrated to have clear impacts on the health and economic future of young women.[92] Factors which limit girls' access to education include distance to school, shortage of female teachers, lack of sanitation facilities for girls, gender bias in the curriculum, absence of family support, priority given to boys and underage marriage.[93] Special provisions adopted to address these factors include free education for girls,[94] the supply of bikes to girls to enable them to cycle to school[95] and putting money into a fixed deposit in the name of the girl for her to receive when she is 18, if she is unmarried and has completed school.[96]

Source: Authors

BOX 4.4 EXAMPLE: SPECIAL PROVISION IN WOMEN'S OWNERSHIP OF LAND

Women have suffered historic discrimination in the ownership of land, which is often held in the name of a husband, father or brother.[97] To address this, several states offer a concession in the stamp duty and registration fees payable if the property is purchased in the name of a female to 'incentivise' ownership of property by women. In Gujarat, for example, in 2004 stamp duty was reduced to 4 percent, and the registration fee was waived for property purchased by women.[98] Between 2004 and 2010, 9,77,883 women utilised the special provision, and property was purchased in their name.[99] Women who utilised the provisions reported positive outcomes across social, political and personal spheres after buying the property.[100]

Source: Authors

Article 15(3) has also been used as authority for protective legislation, which we argue is contrary to the purpose of special provision and instead constitutes direct discrimination. Protective legislation purports to protect women but denies them access to rights enjoyed by men, such as entry into the military, undertaking manual labour or working nights or in mines. In *Anuj Garg v. Hotel Association of India*,[101] for example, the petitioners challenged s 30 of the *Punjab Excise Act* 1914, which prohibited the employment of any woman in any part of premises in which liquor or intoxicating drugs are consumed by the public. The Supreme Court held the provision was unconstitutional. It violated article 15 because it constituted sex discrimination and could not be justified as a special provision under article 15(3). However, while lauded as a win for sex equality law and with a positive outcome for the petitioners, the reasoning of the Supreme Court was not in accord with *CEDAW* and problematic in part. Although finding for the petitioner, the court held that protective legislation was not inherently contrary to article 15(1) or an invalid exercise of article 15(3) but instead that protective legislation can be constitutional, provided it meets the 'legitimate aim of protecting the interests of women' and is proportionate to well-settled gender norms such as autonomy, equality of opportunity and the right to privacy.

We disagree and argue that special provision must accelerate substantive equality between men and women, a goal protective legislation cannot achieve. Preventing women, for example, from working as guards in a prison, serving in combat roles in the military, working in mines and working at night is paternalistic and reduces their opportunity for paid employment. Such laws restrict and exclude women and, as such, constitute direct discrimination. Instead of prohibiting women from night work, make safe transport provision for them, and instead of denying them the opportunity to work as prison guards, ensure the prison provides safe working conditions.

Article 15(3) has been utilised by men also. In *Dr. M.C. Sharma, Lecturer v. Punjab University*, the petitioner successfully argued that a rule that stated only women could be appointed to the position of principal of a girls' school was in breach of article 15(1) and could not constitute a special provision under article 15(3).[102] The court held that 'when any reservation is made in favour of a woman the same is to be tested on the ground of reasonableness.'[103] The court focussed on the ability of a male to hold the position of principal and saw nothing in the designated duties that could not be done by a male. In doing so, the court did not examine whether there were any historic disadvantage facing women employees in schools, whether such positions of authority were overwhelmingly held by men or whether for the pupils or parents there were symbolic and practical advantages in having a female principal.[104]

We support the greater use of special provision to advance women's human rights. The previous discussion has included examples where article 15(3) has furthered the rights of women, but it has also illustrated that article 15(3) has been misinterpreted in the courts and used inappropriately to support protective legislation that constitutes direct discrimination.

Conclusion

This chapter has explored the role of the right to equality and non-discrimination guaranteed in article 14 and article 15 of the Constitution. We conclude that they have provided some limited positive advancement of women's human rights. They have been used in the courts to change laws that discriminate against women and to authorise special provision which have advantaged women and have been utilised by women's advocates, by non-government organisations in the courts and in advocacy at the local levels of governance. Although we support legislative reform to the text of articles 14 and 15, we recognise that this is an unlikely to be realised in the foreseeable future. Alternately, women's human rights principles and theories should be utilised in the courts, in policy papers and reports and in academic literature to expand the meaning and interpretation of both articles, to accord with theories of substantive equality, to incorporate standards of indirect discrimination and to recognise the compounding effect of multiple discriminations on women.

Notes

1 For example, the *International Covenant on Civil and Political Rights* 1966 (*ICCPR*), the *International Covenant on Economic, Social and Cultural Rights* 1966 (*ICESCR*) and the *Convention on the Elimination of Discrimination against Women* 1979 (*CEDAW*).

2 Sanjay Jain and Shirish Deshpande, '"Fair Sex" and Unfair Treatment: Some Reflections on Constitutional Design and Institutional Response with Special Reference to India' in Jaya Sagade, Vedna Jivan and Christine Forster (eds.) *Feminism in the Subcontinent and Beyond: Challenging Laws, Changing Laws* (Eastern Book Company, 2014) 3–50, 13.

3 Part 4, the Directive Principles of State Policy, which guide the state to launch policies, programs and law for achieving economic social equality for all persons is not enforceable.

4 Along with articles 14 and 15, article 21, which protects 'the right to life', plays an important role in the protection of women's rights in India and has been extensively used by the Supreme Court in cases involving women's equality. See, for example, *Glory Bai v. S.K.A. Noorjakan Beevi* (2011) 2 LW 460 per D. Hariparanthaman J at [12], [19], [22].

5 Adele Cassola, Amy Raub, Danielle Foley and Jody Heymann, 'Where Do Women Stand? New Evidence on the Presence and Absence of Gender Equality in the World's Constitutions' (2014) 10(2) *Politics and Gender* 200–235, 201.

6 Ibid.

7 Ibid 203–206.

8 Daniel Moeckii, 'Equality and Non-Discrimination' in Daniel Moeckii, Sangeeta Sha and Sandesh Sivakumaran (eds.) *International Human Rights Law* (Oxford University Press, 2014) 157–173, 161.

9 Ibid 157.

10 Richard Albert, 'Amending Constitutional Amendment Rules' (2015) 13(3) *International Journal of Constitutional Law* 655–685, 656.

11 Niamh Reilly, *Women's Human Rights: Seeking Gender Justice in a Globalizing Age* (Polity Press, 2010) 48.

12 Article 1 states that all human beings are born free and equal in dignity and rights. Article 2 states that everyone is entitled to all the rights and freedoms set forth in the Universal Declaration without distinction of any kind, such as race, colour, sex, language, religion, political or other opinion, national or social origin, property, birth or other status. Article 7 states that all are equal before the law and are entitled without any discrimination to equal protection of the law.

13 Human Rights Committee, Communication No 202/1986 (UN Doc Supp. No 40 (A/44/40) at [196] 1988).

14 Ibid.

15 Lie Weiwei, 'Equality and Non-Discrimination Under International Human Rights Law' (2004) 3 *Research Notes* 1–26, 9.

16 Ibid.

17 Ibid.

18 Ibid.

19 Human Rights Committee, Communication No 35/1978 (UN Doc CCPR/C/OP/1 at [67].

20 Ibid.

21 Hugo Storey, 'The Right to Family Life and Immigration Case Law at Strasbourg' (1990) 39(2) *International and Comparative Law Quarterly* 328–344; Rebecca Cook, 'International Human Rights Law Concerning Women: Case Notes and Comments' (1990) 23 *Vanderbilt Journal of Transnational Law* 779–818.

22 Human Rights Committee, n 19.

23 Simone Cusack and Lisa Pusey, '*CEDAW* and the Right to Non-Discrimination and Equality' (2013) 14 *Melbourne Journal of International Law* 54–92, 60–62.

24 Ibid 58.

25 Rikki Holtmaat, 'The *CEDAW*: A Holistic Approach to Women's Equality and Freedom' in Anne Hellum and Henriette Aasen (eds.) *Women's Human Rights: CEDAW in International, Regional and National Law* (Cambridge University Press, 2013) 95–123, 105.
26 *CEDAW* Committee, General Recommendation No 28 *The Core Obligations of States Parties Under Article 2 of the Convention on the Elimination of All Forms of Discrimination against Women* (UN Doc CEDAW/C/GC/28) at [6].
27 Andrew Byrnes and Marsha Freeman, 'The Impact of the *CEDAW* Convention: Paths to Equality' (February 20, 2012) *UNSW Law Research Paper No 2012–7*, 1–62, 7. https://ssrn.com/abstract=2011655 Accessed 17/4/19.
28 Cusack and Pusey, n 23.
29 Wouter Vandenhole, *Non-Discrimination and Equality in the View of the UN Human Rights Treaty Bodies* (Intersentia, 2005) 18; James Kelly, *Governing with the Charter: Legislative and Judicial Activism and Framers' Intent* (University of British Columbia Press, 2005).
30 Jain and Deshpande, n 2, 15.
31 Ratna Kapur and Brenda Cossman, *Subversive Sites: Feminist Engagements with Law in India* (Sage Publications, 1996) 177–178.
32 *Paradise Printers v. Union Territory of Chandigarh*, AIR 1988 SC 354: (1988) 1 SCC 440. See Jatrindra K. Das, 'Examining the Concept of Equal Opportunity and the Application of 'Protective Discrimination to 'Vulnerable Groups'' (2017) 9(2) *Contemporary Voice of Dalit* 136–147, 140 for a broader discussion of reasonableness.
33 *Sanaboina Satyanarayana v. Government of Andhra Pradesh* 2003 Supp (1) SCR 874.
34 Kapur and Cossman, n 31, 181.
35 Ibid 176.
36 *Charu Khurana v. Union of India* (2014) SCC Online SC 900.
37 Ibid.
38 Ibid.
39 Ibid 41.
40 Anu Saksena, '*CEDAW*: Mandate for Substantive Equality' (2007) 14(3) *Indian Journal of Gender Studies* 481–498, 484.
41 Carole Spary, 'Women Candidates and Party Nomination Trends in India: Evidence from the 2009 General Election' (2014) 52(1) *Commonwealth and Comparative Politics* 109–138.
42 Kapur and Cossman, n 31, 178.
43 *T Sareetha v. T Venkata Subbaiah* (1983) AIR AP 356.
44 Ibid.
45 *Saroj Rani v. Sudarshan Kumar Chadha* (1984) 4 SCC 90.
46 *C. Masilamani Mudaliar and Others v. Idol Sri Swaminathaswami Thirukoil and Others* (1996) 8 Supreme Court Cases 525.
47 Ibid.
48 Helen Irving, *Gender and the Constitution: Equity and Agency in Comparative Constitutional Law* (Cambridge University Press, 2008) 3.
49 *CEDAW* Committee, General Recommendation No 25: *Temporary Special Measures*, 27 May 2008 (UN Doc HRI/Gen/1/Rev.9).
50 Hugh Collins and Tarunabh Khaitan (eds.) 'Indirect Discrimination Law: Controversies and Critical Questions' in *Foundations of Indirect Discrimination* (Hart Publishers, 2018) 1–31, 2, 3.
51 General Recommendation 25, n 49, at [365].
52 Collins and Khaitan, n 50, 2, 3.
53 Joni Hersch, 'Employment Discrimination, Economists, and the Law' in Karine Moe (ed.) *Women, Family and Work: Writings on the Economics of Gender* (Blackwell Publishing Ltd, 2003) 217, 228.
54 Vanderhule, n 29, 35.
55 *Madhu Kishwar and Ors. Etc v. State of Bihar and Ors* (1996) AIR 5.
56 *National Legal Services Authority v. Union of India* Writ Petition (Civil) No 400 of 2012.
57 *MX v. ZY* AIR (1997) Bom 406.

58 *Ranjit Kuman Rajak v. State Bank of India* (2009) (5) Bom CR 227.
59 *Naz Foundation v. Delhi Administration* (2009) 160 *Delhi* Law Times 277.
60 Although *CEDAW* refers only to sex-based discrimination, the Committee stated in GR 28 (n 26, at [5]) that the Convention extends to gender-based discrimination against women.
61 *CEDAW* Committee, General Recommendation 15 *Avoidance of Discrimination against Women in National Strategies for the Prevention and Control of Acquired Immunodeficiency Syndrome (AIDS)* 1990 (UN Doc A/45/38).
62 The *CEDAW* Committee states in General Recommendation 18, *Disabled Women* 1991 (UN Doc A/46/38), that women with disabilities suffer from a 'double discrimination linked to their special living conditions'.
63 *CEDAW* Committee, General Recommendation 21, *Equality in Marriage and Family Relations* 1994 (UN Doc A/49/38) at [13], where the Committee recommends the recognition of *de facto* relationships.
64 *Vasantha R. v. Union of India and Ors* (2001) II ILJ 843.
65 *Factories Act* 1948, s 66(1)(b).
66 *C. B. Muthamma v. Union of India and others* (1979) AIR 1868.
67 Gopal Bagdi and Ravi S. Kurothe, 'People's Participation in Watershed Management Programmes: Evaluation Study of Vidarbha Region of Maharashtra in India' (2014) 2(3) *International Soil and Water Conservation Research* 57–66; Shreya Atrey, 'Through the Looking Glass of Intersectionality: Making Sense of Indian Discrimination Jurisprudence under Article 15' (2016) 16 *Equal Rights Review* 160–185.
68 Concluding Observations of the *CEDAW* Committee: India (28 July 2014) 58th Session (UN Doc CEDAW/C/IND/CO/45) at [4].
69 See GR 28, n 26, at [18].
70 *Mahadeb v. Dr BB Sen* (1951) AIR Cal 563.
71 Ibid.
72 *Civil Procedure Code*, order 25, rule 1, sub-rule 3.
73 Atrey n 67, 168.
74 *Rajbala v. State of Haryana* (2016) 1 SCC 463.
75 The educational qualification is specified as passing the 'matriculation examination or its equivalent examination from any recognised institution/board: Provided that in case of a woman candidate or a candidate belonging to Scheduled Caste, the minimum qualification shall be middle pass: Provided further that in case of a woman candidate belonging to Scheduled Caste contesting election for the post of Panch, the minimum qualification shall be 5th pass.' *Haryana Panchayati Raj Act* 1994, s 175.
76 Analysis of the Case of *Rajbala v. State of Haryana* (2016). https://amangowda.wordpress.com/2016/06/26/analysis-of-the-case-of-rajbala-v-state-of-haryana/ Accessed 17/4/19.
77 *Rajbala v. State of Haryana*, n 74.
78 Ibid.
79 Ibid.
80 *Vishaka and Others v. State of Rajasthan and Others* (1997) 6 SCC 241.
81 Ibid at [16].
82 Zoya Hasan, *Politics of Inclusion: Castes, Minorities, and Affirmative Action* (Oxford University Press, 2011) 3–6.
83 Catherine Casey, Renate Skibnes and Judith Pringle, 'Gender Equality and Corporate Governance: Policy Strategies in Norway and New Zealand' (2011) 18(6) *Gender, Work and Organization* 613–630, 627.
84 Ritika Kansal, 'The Meaning and Scope of Temporary Special Measures in the Convention on the Elimination of All Forms of Discrimination against Women' (2013). http://ssrn.com/abstract=2257316 Accessed 17/4/19.
85 Mona Krook, 'Empowerment versus Backlash: Gender Quotas and Critical Mass Theory' (2015) 3(1) *Politics, Groups, and Identities* 184–188, 185; Mona Krook and Diana Z. O'Brien, 'The Politics of Group Representation: Quotas for Women and Minorities Worldwide' (2010) 42(3) *Comparative Politics* 253–272.

86 Christopher McCrudden, Raya Muttarak, Heather Hamill and Anthony Heath, 'Affirmative Action without Quotas in Northern Ireland' (2010) 4 *Equal Rights Review* 7–14, 9.

87 *CEDAW* Committee, General Recommendation 5, *Temporary Special Measures* 2008 (UN Doc HRI/Gen/1/Rev.9).

88 *CEDAW* Committee, General Recommendation 8, *Implementation of Article 8 of the Convention* 2008 (UN Doc HRI/Gen/1/Rev.9).

89 *CEDAW* Committee, General Recommendation 23, *Women in Public Life* 1997 (UN Doc A/52/38/REV.1 at [15]).

90 General Recommendation 25, n 4.

91 Ministry of Resource Development, Educational Statistics at a Glance. https://mhrd.gov.in/educational-statistics-glance-2018 Accessed 17/4/19.

92 Esther Duflo, 'Women Empowerment and Economic Development' (2012) 50(4) *Journal of Economic Literature* 1051–1079; Jad Chaaban and Wendy Cunningham, *Measuring the Economic Gain of Investing in Girls: The Girl Effect Dividend* (World Bank, 2011).

93 Peggy Froerer, 'Education, Inequality and Social Mobility in Central India' (2011) 23(5) *European Journal of Development Research* 695–711; Annemie Maertens, 'Social Norms and Aspirations: Age of Marriage and Education in Rural India' (2013) 47 *World Development* 1–15, 14–15.

94 John C. Caldwell, Prasuna H. Reddy and Pat Caldwell, 'Educational Transition in Rural South India' (1985) 11(1) *Population and Development Review* 29–51, 33; Duncan Wilson, 'Human Rights: Promoting Gender Equality in and through Education' (2004) 34(1) *Prospects: Quarterly Review of Comparative Education* 11–27.

95 Karthik Muralitharan and Nishith Prakash, 'Cycling to School: Increasing Secondary Enrolment for Girls in India' (2017) 9(3) *American Economic Journal: Applied Economics* 321–350. The authors found that a cycle program in Bihar increased girls' age-appropriate enrolment in secondary school by 32 percent and reduced the corresponding gender gap by 40 percent.

96 Garima Jain, Manjushree Palit and Astha Dhanda, 'Preventing Femicide in India: Valuing and Safeguarding the Girl Child and Women' (2015) *JUG Research Publications* 106–110, 108.

97 Rob Langham, *Good Women Do Not Inherit Land: Politics of Land and Gender in India* (Routledge, 2017).

98 Prem Singh, Varsha Ganguly and Saroj Arora, *Concession in Registration Charges Including Stamp Duty to Women Property Buyers: A Tool for Empowerment: A Case of Gujarat* (Centre for Rural Studies, NIAR, 2013) 109. http://centre.lbsnaa.gov.in/crs/admin/upload/Publication_Int/Gujarat_book.pdf Accessed 17/4/19; Meera Velayudhan, 'Contextualising Women's Rights and Entitlements to Land: Insights from Gujarat' (2012) 42(4) *Social Change* 505–526.

99 Ibid.

100 Ibid. See Prem Singh and Saroj Arora, *Concession in Stamp Duty Including Registration Charges to Women Property Buyers: A Tool for Empowerment a Case Study of Uttar Pradesh* (Centre for Rural Studies, 2013) for a discussion of similar measures in Uttar Pradesh.

101 *Anuj Garg v. Hotel Association of India* (2008) 3 SCC 1. Gautam Bhatia, 'Sex Discrimination and the Anti-Stereotyping Principle: *Anuj Garg v. Hotel Association of India*' (September 3, 2017). https://ssrn.com/abstract=3031374 or http://dx.doi.org/10.2139/ssrn.3031374 Accessed 17/4/19.

102 *Dr. M.C. Sharma, Lecturer v. Punjab University* (1997) AIR P H 87.

103 Ibid.

104 Karuna Chanana, 'Visibility, Gender, and the Careers of Women Faculty in an Indian University' (2003) 38(3) *McGill Journal of Education* 381–389, 385.

5

RIGHT TO A LIFE FREE FROM VIOLENCE

Introduction

This chapter focusses on violence against women. We define violence against women as any act, omission or threat that results in, or is likely to result in, physical, sexual, psychological or economic harm or suffering to women, either in public or in private life.[1] It includes violence perpetrated by individuals, organisations, the state and state representatives.[2] Violence against women is widespread in India.[3] Although its impact differs across disparities in location (rural and urban) and across caste, religion and class, all women are vulnerable to violence.[4] The 2016 figures from the National Crime Bureau (India) indicate that a crime is recorded against a woman every three minutes, every hour at least two women are sexually assaulted and every six hours, a married woman is beaten to death, burnt or driven to suicide.[5] The chapter assesses the extent to which women's human rights principles, particularly those detailed in GR 19 on violence against women[6] and GR 35 on gender-based violence against women[7] and women's human rights theories have been or could be utilised to advance women's right to a life free from violence. We understand violence against women as integrally linked to other gender inequalities, as a manifestation of women's exclusion from power structures in both public and private spheres,[8] as a reflection of models of masculinity and femininity[9] and, finally, as the result of an institutional power dynamic in which women are subordinate to men.[10] The chapter examines violence against women through selected (representative) forms of violence – domestic violence including dowry violence, sexual violence and honour crimes. In each of these areas, using examples of feminist-driven law reform, policy and judicial reasoning we illustrate how principles and theories of women's human rights can be used to understand and strengthen the state response to violence against women and to develop strategies for reducing and ultimately ending violence against women.

The chapter begins in 5.2 by outlining, in general terms, India's international obligations to respond to and eradicate violence against women. We argue a right to a life free from violence is a universal right, and we reject any argument that it can be tempered by contextual and cultural considerations.[11] Indian women are entitled to enjoy equally with all other women a right to life, human dignity and physical and emotional integrity.[12] Section 5.3 maps out three central structural and institutional theories of violence against women, which we argue assist understanding why it continues and how to strategise to reduce and ultimately end violence against women. Section 5.4 maps out changing legislative responses to domestic violence evidenced by the shift from a criminal law response to a civil law response, fuelled and animated by women's human rights principles and feminist intervention. We utilise the *Protection of Women from Domestic Violence Act* 2005 (*DV Act*) to illustrate how principles and theories of women's human rights can lead to positive law reform. We also focus on dowry-related violence, a form of domestic violence, tracking the evolution of the laws criminalising dowry violence and concluding that further reform based on women's human rights perspectives could strengthen women's rights in this area. Section 5.5 focusses on sexual violence and examines how a horrific gang rape in Delhi led to legislative and policy changes in the criminal justice system, marking a shift from an outdated and moralistic sexual offences framework to new sexual assault provisions much more reflective of contemporary women's human rights standards. Section 5.6 focusses on so-called honour crimes and, utilising women's human rights perspectives, illustrates how the threat of dishonour underscoring these crimes is not unique to India and can be located in institutional structures which regard women as the property of men. Section 5.7, the conclusion, sums up our understanding of the utility of women's human rights principles and theories in crafting solutions for reducing and ending violence against women.

Violence against women: obligations of human rights law

This section examines the obligations, in general terms, to end violence against women created by key international instruments in the human rights framework, ratified and acceded to by India. According to GR 19 and GR 35 of the *CEDAW* Committee, the *CRC*[13] and the *CRPD*,[14] India must take effective measures to reduce and end violence against women in all its forms. Although these instruments do not themselves set out in detail the specific measures to be taken, including appropriate legislative standards, it is possible through analysing GR 19 and GR 35, the concluding observations of the *CEDAW* Committee and research by gender scholars to identify good practice standards.

No specific article on violence against women was included in *CEDAW*. Indeed, it was not until the 1990s that violence against women emerged as a major focus for women's rights.[15] Accordingly, its gravity was recognised by the *CEDAW* Committee in GR 19, which was specifically adopted to provide guidance on state obligations in relation to violence against women. Importantly, GR 19 defines violence against women as a form of discrimination and makes clear that states are responsible for eliminating violence, regardless of whether it is perpetrated by an individual or by the state.[16] GR 19 requires state parties to enact a strong system of laws to protect women from family violence and abuse, rape, sexual assault and other gender-based violence.[17] Such laws should include specific and targeted domestic violence legislation in both criminal and civil law frameworks[18] and the criminalisation of all forms of sexual abuse,[19] including child sexual abuse.[20] As well as a strong system of laws, states should also, according to GR 19, establish services to ensure the safety and security of victims of gender-based violence, including refuges and counselling and rehabilitation programmes, and implement preventive measures, including public information and education programmes, to change attitudes concerning the roles and status of men and women.[21]

In 1993 the *Declaration on the Elimination of Violence against Women* (Declaration) was adopted by the United Nations General Assembly as a means of further highlighting the importance of ending violence against women. The Declaration defines violence against women as any act of gender-based violence that results in, or is likely to result in, physical, sexual or mental harm or suffering to women, including threats of such acts, coercion or arbitrary deprivation of liberty.[22] Like *CEDAW*, the Declaration makes clear that, in relation to violence against women, the principle of due diligence (what a duty bearer, generally the state, must do to fulfil their international obligations) applies.[23] The due diligence framework in relation to violence against women has been summarised as requiring prevention, protection, punishment, reparations and compensation.[24] States are required to exercise due diligence 'to prevent, investigate and in accordance with national legislation, punish acts of violence against women, whether these acts are perpetrated by the state or by private persons'.[25] This is important because the structural and widespread nature of violence against women means it is unlikely to be ended through the actions of individuals. State action, in contrast to individual action, has the capacity to be systematised, countrywide and properly resourced.[26]

In 2017 the *CEDAW* Committee issued another General Recommendation focussed on violence against women. GR 35 complements and updates GR 19. It makes clear that violence is a critical obstacle to the achievement of substantive equality between men and women.[27] In particular, it outlines the responsibilities of the state at the executive, legislative and judicial levels to end violence against women.[28]

India has reported thrice to *CEDAW* – in 2000, in 2007 and in 2014 – and there is evidence that civil societal pressure in the form of shadow reports, combined with the *CEDAW* Committee's concluding observations, have influenced some limited law and policy reforms in relation to violence against women. Of note are the following recommendations and responses from the Indian state.

In 2007 the *CEDAW* Committee in its concluding observations, while commending the enactment of the *DV Act*, a civil domestic violence law, expressed concern that the various states and union territories had not put into place mechanisms to effectively enforce it.[29] The Committee called upon India to develop, in consultation with women's groups, a coordinated and comprehensive plan to combat all forms of violence against women, taking a life-cycle approach.[30] It urged implementation and enforcement of the *DV Act* and requested that the state ensure that all victims of domestic violence, including scheduled caste, scheduled tribes, backward classes and minority women, benefit from the legislative framework.[31] It requested India to provide in its next periodic report information, disaggregated by caste, minority status and ethnicity, on the number of cases of domestic violence reported to the police and other relevant authorities, the number of protection and other orders granted under the *DV Act* and the number of convictions of offenders of domestic violence under the *Penal Code* 1860 (Penal Code).[32] The Committee also urged India to widen the definition of rape in the Penal Code to reflect the realities of sexual abuse experienced by women and to remove the exception for marital rape from the definition of rape.[33] It also requested the criminalisation of all other forms of sexual abuse, including child sexual abuse.[34] It recommended that India consult widely with women's groups in its process of reform of laws and procedures relating to rape and sexual abuse.[35]

In 2014 the *CEDAW* Committee in its concluding observations commended India for its overhaul of sexual assault offences and specifically for enacting a legislative framework targeted at sexual offences against children as recommended in 2007.[36] It again recommended that India define marital rape as a criminal offence and recommended that gang rape be included as an aggravating factor for sexual offences.[37] It noted the high number of dowry deaths since 2008, the persistence of so-called 'honour' crimes perpetrated by family members against women and girls and the stark increase in violent crimes against women, especially rape.[38] It recommended India enact specific legislation to introduce heavier sentences for acid attack offenders, regulate the sale and distribution of acid substances and conduct large-scale campaigns to raise public awareness of the criminal nature of such attacks.[39] It recommended strengthening the efficiency of the police, ensuring that police officers fulfil their duty to protect women and girls against violence and are held accountable, adopt standard procedures for the police in each state on gender-sensitive investigations and treatment of victims and of witnesses; ensuring that 'First Information Reports' are filed;[40] establishing one-stop crisis centres providing victims of violence and rape with free and immediate access to medical attention, psychological counselling, legal aid, shelters and other support services;[41] providing systematic training on women's rights to all law enforcement personnel, medical staff and judicial officials and allocating sufficient resources for the immediate enforcement of legislation on violence against women.[42] Finally, the Committee recommended that India establish special courts and complaints procedures as envisaged under the legislation in a time-bound manner.[43] Some of the recommended changes have been incorporated, as discussed throughout the chapter.

Two further conventions to which India is a party are relevant to violence against women. The *CRC*, acceded to in 1996, obligates India to:

> take all appropriate legislative, administrative, social and educational measures to protect the child from all forms of physical or mental violence, injury or abuse, neglect or negligent treatment, maltreatment or exploitation, including sexual abuse, while in the care of parent(s), legal guardian(s) or any other person who has the care of the child.[44]

Finally, the *CRPD* provides a comprehensive framework of India's obligation to prevent violence against persons with disabilities and takes particular cognisance of the vulnerability of women who have disabilities.[45] In particular, the *CRPD* requires India to 'put in place effective legislation and policies, including women and child-focussed legislation and policies, to ensure that instances of exploitation, violence and abuse against persons with disabilities are identified, investigated and, where appropriate, prosecuted',[46] 'take all appropriate legislative, administrative, social, educational and other measures to protect persons with disabilities, both within and outside the home, from all forms of exploitation, violence and abuse, including their gender-based aspects'[47] and 'take all appropriate measures to prevent all forms of exploitation, violence and abuse by ensuring, inter alia, appropriate forms of gender- and age-sensitive assistance and support for persons with disabilities and their families and caregiver, including through the provision of information and education on how to avoid, recognize and report instances of exploitation, violence and abuse.'[48]

In 1994 the Human Rights Council established the position of Special Rapporteur on Violence against Women.[49] The special rapporteur is mandated to seek and receive information on violence against women; recommend ways to eliminate violence against women at national, regional and intersectionality levels and work collaboratively with the other United Nations human rights mechanisms. There have been four special rapporteurs, and they have published a series of influential reports.[50]

International and domestic pressure to address violence against women has increased in India. Women's advocates, politicians and lawyers and civil society have called for measures – legal and non-legal – in response to highly publicised examples of violence against women.[51] We argue that, although the right to a life free from violence is a universal right, this does not mean uniformity of approach to achieving enjoyment of the right. Therefore, the solutions, remedies and strategies for change, to be effective, must account for and incorporate India's diverse social and cultural context.[52] The right to a life free from violence is linked to women's subordinate status across society in all areas of their lives, and, therefore, women's rights to equal political representation and participation, economic independence and equality in marriage and family relations are also critical to the enjoyment of a life free from violence. Other chapters, however, focus on the recognition of these rights.

Understanding violence against women

Violence against women in India occurs throughout their life-cycle, in a range of forms in every aspect of their lives, in both public and private spheres.[53] It begins before conception with the practice of preconception selection, where prospective parents preselect chromosomes to ensure a boy child.[54] It continues after conception with sex-selection practices that determine the sex of the foetus for the purpose of aborting female foetuses.[55] During pregnancy and birthing, many women are not provided with adequate maternity facilities and services and suffer death or serious morbidity issues and other harms in childbirth, and infants are born with preventable conditions.[56] After birth, foeticide (where female children are killed in favour of sons) is still widespread.[57] The girl child, if not a victim of abortion or foeticide, experiences violence in the form of discrimination in the provision of healthcare[58] and access to education[59] and basic nutrition.[60] As the female child grows, she may be married underage or forced into marriage.[61] Within marriage (and live-in relationships), domestic and family violence (including dowry violence) is widespread.[62] She may be a victim of sexual violence by persons known to her and, less frequently, by strangers.[63] Before marriage, she is vulnerable to acid attacks when she rebuts sexual advances,[64] and after marriage, she is vulnerable to honour crimes when she chooses to marry into a different religion or caste.[65] At educational facilities and at places of employment, she is a victim of sexual harassment.[66] Single women are particularly vulnerable to violence,[67] and for a married woman who survives her husband, violence against widows is endemic.[68] As a female senior citizen, she experiences neglect and abuse.[69]

There are a range of feminist theories which seek to understand and explain violence against women. We briefly overview a selection of theories we view as relevant in the Indian context. We exclude those theories that focus on the individual characteristics of offenders and victims as we view them as lacking explanatory value.[70] These theories suggest that violence against women is caused by factors such as excess alcohol, individual deviant male aggression, poverty and loss of self-esteem. While we agree these factors may heighten violence in some contexts, we do not regard such factors as causative as they do not explain why men, rather than women, are the main offenders. Instead, we focus on theories that locate the primary causes of violence against women in structural and institutional systems, bodies and practices. For example, men's power and dominance in the family and within marriage, men's disproportionate economic wealth and control over resources, men's dominance in political representation and participation are structural inequalities. They are structural inequalities because men's dominance is systemically grounded and reproduced in the normal operations of dominant social institutions, such as the family, the education system, the healthcare system, the criminal justice system and the political system.

The representative theories we have chosen are not mutually exclusive but overlap thematically. They have, however, differing approaches moored in a range of concepts, including exclusion and subordination, difference, masculinity, femininity, power to and power over.

First, some feminist scholars argue that violence against women results from women's systematic exclusion from economic and political power structures, which leaves them subordinate to men and vulnerable to violence in both public and private spheres.[71] This approach is closely aligned with theories of the public and private which connect women's location in the home and exclusion from economic and political positions of power in the public realm to her subordination and vulnerability to violence in the private sphere. Men dominate in the marketplace and places of employment, parliament and government, local and national, both in number and in power. Consequently, the policies and practices of these institutions are likely to embody, reproduce and legitimate male domination over women, including violent practices.[72] That 'natural' public sphere power then extends to social spheres, such as the family, where it is 'natural' that men also dominate.[73]

Women are certainly excluded from many political and economic power structures in India. They have limited mobility and lack access to the public sphere. They are under-represented in the national and local parliaments and have little economic independence.[74] They are separated, therefore, from networks and social capital that might enhance their standing in the home and community.[75] Women have, however, an increasing presence in the village panchayats due to the gender reservations introduced in 1994, and, according to this theory, this increased political power should translate to reduced violence against women in those communities. However, no systematic research has been undertaken to date.

A second approach, rather than focussing on the exclusion of women from economic and political power structures, examines the differing social roles, behaviours and attributes considered appropriate for men and women.[76] 'Masculinity' is the theoretical term used to describe those attributes, behaviours and roles associated with maleness while 'femininity' is the term used to describe those attributes, behaviours and roles associated with femaleness.[77] For example, masculinity is associated with assertiveness and competitiveness, while femininity is associated with gentleness and compliance.[78] Although many different ways of being a man (multiple masculinities) exist within a society, dominance and control over women are frequently part of the set of male attributes and behaviours (masculinity) that are recognised and accepted as a shared social ideal.[79] Importantly, masculinity is often not overtly imposed but is absorbed during childhood from multiple sources and aspired to by most men, even those who, for various reasons, cannot fulfil all the associated expected roles (for example, poverty preventing a man from being a provider).[80] Although differences between men and women are much less notable in more equitable societies, all societies confer a higher social value on the attributes of masculinity than those of femininity. In the Indian context, masculinity and femininity, particularly as they pertain to marriage, order social life in the family.[81] Women are expected to demonstrate early fertility and are tasked with child rearing, food preparation and other domestic duties. Ideologies surrounding sexual access support the unfettered conjugal rights men have to their wives' bodies, and women are generally unable to make decisions regarding contraceptive use, family planning or pregnancy without explicit permission from husbands. Subservience, compliance, subordination and passivity are expected and enforced by fathers, brothers, husbands and, if applicable, in-laws who may be residing within the family household.[82] These gender norms have created a power dynamic in which a wife or daughter is left with few resources and little agency in the family context.[83] The lack of value placed on the attributes of femininity, coupled with the value placed on the activities of men in the public sphere, creates different expectations of women compared to men. According to this theoretical approach, violence is used to control those women who do not or cannot meet the expectations of femininity.

Some Indian feminist scholars argue that the intersection of caste, religion, social position and geographic location (whether rural or urban) complicate and challenge any analysis that is based simply on masculinity and femininity.[84] A Dalit man, for example, is subordinate to a Brahmin woman. We agree, but an analysis of masculinity and femininity is still useful in identifying the differing socialisation of males and females in all contexts. While an upper-caste woman may be more powerful than a lower-caste man in certain ways, she is still more vulnerable to violence in her home than the lower-caste man in his home. She is also vulnerable to violence in public spaces in different forms than the lower-caste man in the same public space. For example, a Brahmin woman is much more likely than a Dalit man to experience sexual harassment in the place of employment or in a public space, such as on public transport, in the market or on the street.

A third related approach focusses on women's lack of 'power to' and men's 'power over'.[85] 'Power to' is defined as the ability to resist violence or escape an abusive situation, based on factors such as age, income, education level and occupational status.[86] Women often do not have 'power to' because of lack of resources, resulting in economic or social dependency.[87] Men typically have 'power over', meaning the ability to control or change women's behaviour, to override their decisions or to prevent them from recognising there is a conflict of interest through coercion, threat or violence.[88] Although these are more individually focussed than the previous two theoretical frameworks, we view the concepts of 'power to' and 'power over' as systematic and institutionalised through such factors as spousal differences in resource contribution, differences in control over household decision-making, differences in household responsibilities and duties and control by one spouse over the other in relation to behaviour and mobility.[89] Some feminist scholars have referred to contrary yet compelling research which has shown that women who earn more money or contribute more to household expenditures, are better employed or have higher levels of education than their spouses, report greater levels of physical violence than women who do not have spousal differences in these indicators of power.[90] Some have argued that men may see women's successes as illegitimate due to internalised beliefs about male superiority and feel entitled to use violence to (re) assert 'power over' the household and over women.[91] In India, marriage is a site of both women's lack of 'power to' and male 'power over' women. Women lack 'power to' after marriage as they typically move to their husbands' homes and are separated from their natal families, leaving them isolated from their support systems.[92] Women have little 'power to' leave a violent situation as it is shameful for a woman to return to her natal family and, without access to financial support, she may have no other choice.[93] Additionally, the fear of ridicule and stigma attached to rebutting social traditions and the family honour discourage women from reporting abuse and violence.[94] Indeed, a victim of violence may prioritise her family – her husband's family first and then her natal family.[95] Men and other family members have 'power over' married and unmarried women who have subordinate status as wives, daughters-in-law, sisters-in-law and mothers. Women's subordinate place and role in the family is supported by religious and cultural norms and beliefs which focus on self-sacrifice, duty and responsibility to the family and community.[96] Gupta explains that, as women's agency increases and women become less passive, new forms of violence emerge, such as acid attacks when girls reject romantic advances.[97]

We view these three interconnected and overlapping theories as providing useful explanatory frameworks for analysing violence against women. While none of these theories provides a complete explanation for violence against women, each can provide a partial explanation or, in a given situation, a viable explanation. For example, violence against women manifests differently in urban and rural areas; in slums; amongst pavement dwellers; between castes, religions, classes and genders and in border areas and conflict zones, such as Kashmir, Chhattisgarh, Odisha and Andhra Pradesh.[98] A lack of 'power to' and 'power over' might provide a convincing framework for understanding violence in a particular rural community while a theory of exclusion from political and economic structures might provide a convincing framework for understanding violence against women in urban households.[99]

Domestic and family violence

Defining domestic and family violence

Domestic and family violence is the intentional use of violence, threats, force or intimidation to control or manipulate a family member, spouse, former spouse or household member.[100] We use the dual term 'domestic and family' to include all violence against women in all domestic situations. This includes within and across family relationships, both natal and marital, and also includes violence against caregivers and domestic servants in the home. The *CEDAW* Committee states in GR 19: 'Family violence is one of the most insidious forms of violence against women. It is prevalent in all societies. Within family relationships, women of all ages are subjected to violence of all kinds, including battering, rape, other forms of sexual assault, mental and other forms of violence, which are perpetuated by traditional attitudes. Lack of economic independence forces many women to stay in violent relationships . . . The effect of such violence on the physical and mental integrity of women is to deprive them [of] the equal enjoyment, exercise and knowledge of human rights and fundamental freedoms.'[101]

Although statistics are difficult to obtain, domestic and family violence is clearly prevalent across India.[102] There are no statistics, however, on violence against domestic servants and caregivers in the home, and in the Indian context, the term 'domestic violence' is used to mean violence in family relationships, natal and marital. When discussing the Indian context, therefore, we use the term 'domestic violence', but when referring to the global context, we use the term 'domestic and family violence'. The National Family Health Survey conducted by the Ministry of Health and Family Welfare in 2015–2016,[103] which surveyed data from all 29 states, found very high rates of domestic violence.[104] Overall the survey found that the percentage of ever-married women who have experienced spousal violence is 28.8 percent.[105] Although high, this is lower than 2005–2006, when the national rate was 37.2 percent.[106] In particular states, the rate was very high. In Manipur for example the rate of domestic and family violence experienced by ever-married women between the ages of 15 and 49 was 54.7 percent; in Bihar, it was 45.2 percent and in Andhra Pradesh 45.2 percent.[107] Overall, the survey revealed that scheduled caste women, slum women and Muslim women suffered the highest rates of all forms of violence, that rural women experienced higher rates than urban women and that the lower the educational levels, the higher the likelihood of violence although, conversely, engaging in paid employment is a risk factor in all settings, including slums.[108]

The legal response to domestic and family violence has been, in most jurisdictions globally, historically dealt with (if at all) in the criminal justice system.[109] India's initial legal response to domestic violence is, therefore, unsurprising. A criminal offence of a husband or relative of a husband subjecting a woman to cruelty was introduced in the Penal Code in 1983.[110] Cruelty is expressly defined as 'any wilful conduct which is of such a nature as is likely to drive the woman to commit suicide or to cause grave injury or danger to life, limb or health (whether mental or physical) of the woman'. It also includes 'harassment of the woman where such harassment is with a view to coercing her or any person related to her to meet any unlawful demand for any property or valuable security or is on account of failure by her or any person related to her to meet such demand',[111] which we will discuss more fully in 5.4.3 and 5.4.4 next. The provision makes 'cruelty' a cognisable, non-bailable offence punishable with imprisonment up to three years and a fine.

Section 498A is not the result of women's advocacy or crafted from a feminist perspective and is very limited in several ways. It is restricted to violence against a married woman by her husband or a relative of her husband. It does not, therefore, extend to violence that occurs in natal relationships or to live-in relationships. It does not include violence against daughters, mothers and other female relatives or domestic helpers and carers. The definition of 'cruelty' is also specific and has been interpreted in the courts narrowly as serious injury to life or limb and, therefore, excludes many of the behaviours commonly associated with domestic violence, such as economic and psychological violence.[112] The requirement that the injury is serious excludes the patterned minor violence that often characterises domestic violence, which can be harmful and often escalates to serious violence. In 2016, the National Crime Records Bureau recorded a total of 12,218 cases of the offence of cruelty by a husband or his relatives, indicating that the offence has some utility.[113]

Applying women's human rights

The state's response to domestic violence was initially in the criminal justice system. However, after sustained pressure from women's organisations, a civil law response followed. The criminal justice system is limited in its capacity to prevent violence against women because it is grounded in an understanding of violence against women as perpetrated by deviant individuals rather than as a result of structural and institutional inequalities.[114] The individual victim must lodge a complaint with police against an individual offender, the police must investigate the complaint and then decide to prosecute. The court must hear the case and convict. In India, as it is worldwide, women are reluctant to report to the police. Women often do not report to the police because they believe it would have an irreversible negative effect on marital relations.[115] When they report, the police often do not prosecute as they have power to counsel and reconcile the parties.[116] When cases do reach the courts, conviction rates are extremely low.[117] This is because of a combination of factors, including lack of evidence because domestic violence often occurs in the home without witnesses and because women, even if they have complained, may not appear in court as witnesses; police corruption and/or apathy, lack of community support, delays in judgments, lack of resources available for women, particularly rural, semi-literate women, to approach the formal legal system and customary norms which favour settlement of family matters within the community without recourse to the formal system.[118] If, despite the barriers, a conviction ensues, then punishment is of the individual offender, and there is no broader response which challenges the structural inequalities we argue are central to understanding violence against women in the Indian context.

The criminal justice system has a limited capacity to reduce and eradicate violence against women. However, despite its individual focus, victims may be individually aggrieved and deserve individual redress.[119] There are also symbolic reasons for recognising domestic and family violence as a crime which may have some positive impact on violence against women. The application of criminal law to domestic and family violence (arrest, prosecution and conviction) carries the clear condemnation of society for the conduct of the abuse. It is a clear public statement that domestic and family violence is a crime, is wrong and should be punished. This undermines the ability of offenders and others to argue that what happens in the home is private and counteracts the social message that violence in a domestic setting is not as 'serious' as violence between strangers.[120] We do not propose, therefore, the removal of domestic and family violence as a serious crime which can be prosecuted in the criminal justice system. Instead, we recommend that section 498A be reformed in accord with women's human rights principles. First, it should extend to all women, including natal relationships, live-in relationships, daughters, mothers and other female relatives or domestic helpers and carers. This recognises the scope of domestic and family violence. Second, the definition of 'cruelty' should include economic and psychological harm and be broadened to include patterns of violence regardless of 'seriousness'. A number of acts that form part of a pattern of behaviour may amount to abuse, even though some of those acts, when viewed in isolation, may appear to be minor or trivial. Additionally, supporting women to report, encouraging police to pursue prosecutions and training judges to respond appropriately to offences may increase the rate of convictions and have an important deterrent effect.[121]

Research suggests that the civil law, which provides protective and compensatory remedies rather than focussing on the punishment of the offender, is a more effective response than the criminal law.[122] As the Supreme Court stated in reference to domestic violence in 2016: '[t]he idea therefore is to provide various innovative remedies in favour of women who suffer from domestic violence, against the perpetrators of such violence.'[123] The civil law has, in our view, much more capacity than the criminal law to challenge critical institutions which support violence against women, such as the police, the courts and the family.

Therefore, we view the introduction of the *DV Act* as a positive state response which (unlike section 498A of the Penal Code) is an active and positive result of women's advocacy and feminist intervention.[124] The *DV Act* was enacted 'to protect women from violence within the family, to ensure their safety and dignity and to safeguard their right to live a life free from violence as guaranteed by the Constitution under Articles 14, 15 and 21.'[125] It was enacted after a lengthy period of activism from feminist organisations throughout India.[126] The first bill was prepared by the government; however, it was poorly drafted, and the Lawyers Collective, a Mumbai NGO, prepared an alternate bill.[127] After a lengthy period of regional consultations around the country with many stakeholders, the Lawyers Collective Bill was submitted to government. The government reworked and modified it and then enacted it. The *DV Act* was the first piece of legislation to be passed after a process of democratic participation of community and civil society rather than by the Law Commission.[128] Further pieces of legislation followed, adopting the same consultative process.[129]

The *DV Act*, despite its shortcomings, showcases both women's human rights principles and women's human rights theories as frameworks that can be utilised to achieve positive law reform outcomes. It challenges constructions of femininity and masculinity in powerful institutions, such as the family and marriage, which Indian feminists argue maintain gender inequalities and support violence against women.[130] Domestic violence, as recommended by the *CEDAW* Committee, is defined comprehensively in the *DV Act* to include 'physical abuse, sexual abuse, verbal and emotional abuse and economic abuse'.[131] Each of these forms of abuse is further defined to include a broad and exhaustive range of circumstances.[132] Importantly, marital rape, although still not recognised in the Penal Code as a sexual offence despite the express recommendations of the *CEDAW* Committee in 2007 and 2014, is recognised in the *DV Act* as a form of domestic violence.[133] This marks a departure from the view of women as male property within marriage, acknowledging their right to refuse sexual relations. In sum, by recognising the variety of ways in which domestic violence can occur, the legislation openly lays out the forms by which male members of Indian households may hold 'power over' women.

To claim protection under the *DV Act*, a person must establish they are an aggrieved person which is defined as 'any woman who is, or has been, in a domestic relationship with the respondent and who alleges to have been subjected to any act of domestic violence by the respondent'.[134] A respondent was initially defined as an adult male who is in a domestic relationship with the aggrieved person or a relative of the husband or male partner.[135] The legislation was criticised for restricting potential respondents to men, and a subsequent recent case replaced the term 'adult male' with 'adult person'.[136] This is an important acknowledgement of the complex and layered nature of domestic violence in India that while most victims are female, some offenders are female. A domestic relationship is defined as 'a relationship between two persons who live or have, at any point of time, lived together in a shared household, when they are related by consanguinity, marriage, or through a relationship in the nature of marriage, adoption or family members living together as a joint family.'[137] This means that a woman can seek relief under the *DV Act* in relation to all family members, natal and marital, but servants and caregivers who work in many Indian households cannot.[138] Although the scope of the *DV Act* extends to live-in relationships, this has been interpreted narrowly in the courts, requiring both parties to be 'free' to marry, excluding, therefore, persons still technically married to another.[139]

The legislation creates a new role in protection officers, appointed by each state government,[140] who have wide-ranging responsibilities including creating awareness of domestic violence, protecting women who approach them, assisting the judicial officer when the case reaches the court and, finally, once the case is decided, making sure the remedy is implemented.[141] Protection officers shall as far as possible be women[142] and officers of the state government not below the rank of Deputy Tehsildar, block development officers, representatives of non-governmental organisations or representatives of service providers registered under the *DV Act*, provided they have been serving in the organisation for at least two years and have been working in the area of empowerment of women.[143] However, by 2016 only a few states had appointed full-time protection officers, despite the requirement for every state to do so.[144] Initially, the legislative provision was interpreted as meaning a magistrate must consider the domestic incident report from the protection officer before making any order. This delayed many applications where there was no report. However, a subsequent court case held the provision meant that only if there is a report must it be considered.[145]

The *DV Act* provides for a protection order[146] and a residence order.[147] A protection order can be issued by a magistrate after a hearing and if the magistrate is satisfied that domestic violence has taken place or is likely to take place. The order prohibits the respondent from committing domestic violence, entering the aggrieved person's place of employment or any other place she frequents, communicating in any form or alienating assets including from bank accounts jointly owned or owned singly by the respondent, including *stridham* or other property.[148] A magistrate has 60 days to finalise a matter.[149] Ghosh found in her research in West Bengal, however, that procedures under the *DV Act* were slow, that the 60-day limit for resolution was not adhered to and that many cases remained unresolved.[150]

Interim protection orders are also available under the *DV Act* on an ex parte basis (without a requirement that the respondent be present at the hearing). This measure is central to domestic violence legislation globally, recognising that many victims of domestic violence need immediate protection.[151]

A residence order can also be issued by the magistrate, restraining the respondent from dispossessing or 'disturbing the possession' of the aggrieved person from the shared household, directing the respondent to remove himself from the shared household, restraining the respondent and any of his relatives from entering an identified portion of the shared household, restraining the respondent from alienating or disposing of the shared household or directing the respondent to secure alternate accommodation for the aggrieved person of the same standard as that currently enjoyed by her if no separate space is available.[152] Residence orders are very important in the Indian context where shared homes remain common and where women typically move from their natal family home to their husband's family home on marriage. Women who are victims of domestic violence in the husband's family home are in a difficult position as they may be unable to move back to their natal home, and they may have no means of supporting themselves in the community.[153] While the residence order can exclude the husband and provide a portion of the home from which his family members are excluded, women are nevertheless left vulnerable.[154] In a very small home, there may not be any possible space from which the family can be excluded.[155]

Other orders can also be made by the court under the *DV Act*, including compensation orders and maintenance orders recognising the financial barriers facing women who report domestic violence and seek a remedy from the formal legal system and custody orders enabling women to retain custody of their children.

The *DV Act* provides an excellent example of positive law reform. It can be strengthened and already has been in a number of court actions, through advocacy that draws on women's human rights principles and arguments.

It could be argued that the strength of customary law in parts of India diminishes the usefulness of a formal law response (criminal and civil) to domestic violence and that, if victims are unlikely to use the formal law system, then there is little value in strengthening it. However, we argue that the strength of customary law itself makes formal law reform initiatives critical. Even if disputes continue to be primarily settled in customary ways, the symbolic impact of the formal law system should not be discounted or underestimated. Although the prevailing legal culture (ideas, attitudes, values and expectations regarding law) is important to the success of law reform initiatives, a targeted civil domestic violence law and well-crafted targeted domestic violence criminal offences make a strong and visible public statement of the seriousness with which the state views domestic violence.[156] Importantly, they highlight and acknowledge the structural dimensions of domestic violence, rather than viewing it as an 'addition' to other societal crimes.[157] Across India, prevailing social beliefs about family relations include the view that men have a right or obligation to punish and discipline female family members in order to maintain order at home and in society at large,[158] that domestic relationships are legitimately hierarchical[159] and that God made men and women 'essentially' different, and these differences contribute to different familial roles, rights and duties, which are crucial to the cohesion and stability of the family.[160] Challenging those norms through law can, we argue, lead to changes in socio-cultural norms, including accepted traditional practices and customary law, thereby building a general ethos against domestic violence.

Defining dowry violence

Dowry violence is a form of domestic violence. We include it separately because of its distinctive features and the independent body of literature that has emerged to explain its incidence and to posit strategies for change. The system of dowry compels a bride's family to give to the bridegroom, his parents or his relatives, as a condition of the marriage, goods, cash, jewelry and real or movable property.[161] In India, dowry can be traced historically to traditional (high-caste) Hindu practices, including the *kanyadan* (gift of the virgin bride to the groom) *varadakshina* (gifts given to the groom) and *stridhan* (gifts given to the bride but typically controlled by the groom's family).[162] In independent India, however, dowry is an integral part of all marriages, regardless of caste, class or religion, consisting of what is given to the bride before the marriage; what is given to the bridegroom before, at and after the marriage and what is given to the bridegroom's family before, at and after the marriage.[163] The association of the system of dowry with violence against women is a modern phenomenon, wielded as a punishment for insufficient dowry or as a mechanism for extortion at the time of the marriage or for failing to meet demands for dowry after the marriage.[164] It can take the form of daily humiliation, harassment and verbal and physical abuse, including burning and sometimes ending in murder or abetment to suicide.[165]

An increase in dowry-related injuries and deaths led to the regulation of the giving and taking of dowry and the creation of targeted offences for cruelty and deaths associated with demands for dowry.[166] The *Dowry Prohibition Act* 1961 (*Dowry Act*) made the giving and taking of dowry a criminal offence.[167] However, the *Dowry Act* exempts 'voluntary and customary gifts of love and affection' given by the bride's family to her or her husband from the definition of 'dowry' if the gifts are not excessive in financial value.[168] A record of the gifts must be maintained and held in trust for the bride. It has become very difficult in practice to distinguish a gift that is lawful from dowry which is demanded unlawfully.[169] Between its enactment in 1961 and 1981, no reported cases against the *Dowry Act* were documented.

In 1983, after sustained pressure from the Indian women's movement, s 498A a new offence of a 'husband or his relative subjecting a woman to cruelty' was introduced in the Penal Code (as discussed previously in 5.4.1 and 5.4.2).[170] Cruelty includes 'harassment of the woman where such harassment is with a view to coercing her or any person related to her to meet any unlawful demand for any property or valuable security or is on account of failure by her or any person related to her to meet such demand' and was clearly intended as an offence to curb dowry violence.[171]

In 1986, the *Dowry Act* was amended, increasing the penalties for giving or taking dowry to up to five years imprisonment or a fine of up to 15,000 IR.[172] The penalty for demanding dowry was increased from up to six months imprisonment to up to two years imprisonment and a fine of up to 10,000 IR.[173] The same amendment also made a postmortem mandatory and empowered magistrates to hold an inquiry if a woman dies in suspicious circumstances within seven years of her marriage.[174] The amendment also created a new official position – the dowry prohibition officer – who was given the role of ensuring the provisions of the *Dowry Act* are complied with, preventing, as far as possible, the taking or abetting the taking of, or the demanding of, dowry and collecting evidence necessary for the prosecution of persons committing offence under the *Dowry Act*.[175] However, full-time dowry officers are rarely appointed anywhere in the country.[176]

A specific dowry death offence s 304B was also created in the Penal Code through the same 1986 amendment, complementing the requirement of a mandatory postmortem.[177] If the death of a woman is caused by any burns or bodily injury or occurs otherwise than under normal circumstances within seven years of her marriage, and it is shown that soon before her death, she was subjected to cruelty or harassment by her husband or any relative of her husband for, or in connection with, any demand for dowry, it is a 'dowry death', and the husband or relative of the husband shall be deemed to have caused her death.[178] The penalty is a minimum of seven years imprisonment to life imprisonment. Prosecutions have been increasing under this provision, and the judiciary has interpreted the provision to mean that if there is evidence of harassment related to dowry before the death, if the death is suspicious (including a possible suicide), then it is up to the accused to prove that the death was not suspicious or to prove there was no harassment connected with dowry.[179] The reversal of the onus is crucial and has resulted in convictions that would have been unlikely to have otherwise succeeded.[180] However, it is difficult in some cases to link the harassment to demands for dowry because of the inability to produce proof.

BOX 5.1 DOWRY EXAMPLE: *JITENDER SRIVASTAV & ORS V. STATE OF DELHI*[181]

The female victim died of poisoning after two years of marriage. Evidence was presented establishing that the husband and father-in-law made repeated requests for money from the victim's father. Some amounts were paid, but other requests were not fulfilled. There was considerable evidence of harassment of the victim.[182] The Delhi High Court upheld s 304B dowry death convictions that had been found in the lower court against the husband and the father-in-law but dismissed convictions of other members of the family, including the victim's mother-in-law, on the basis that, although there was clearly harassment, it could not be connected to dowry.[183] It was not possible to prove in this case whether the victim drank the poison voluntarily or whether she was forced to drink it, but the offence can be made out in either situation if proof of harassment related to dowry is established.[184]

Source: Authors

Applying women's human rights

Dowry is integrally connected to a social norm that daughters should 'marry up', either into a higher caste or into a wealthier family, in order to maintain or promote the social status of her natal family. The transfer of wealth to facilitate that aim marks her, the bride-to-be, as a 'transacted object'.[185]

Legislative reform to counter the practice of dowry and to challenge its underlying assumptions of women as property with the ultimate goal of ending dowry-related violence against women has had some limited success. The offence of dowry death (s 304B) has led to an increasing number of convictions. In 2016, the National Crime Bureau recorded 1,354 cases of murder related to dowry.[186] However, there are also some obvious flaws in the Penal Code and in the *Dowry Act*.

First, in a number of cases, the failure to prove a link between the harassment and dowry has resulted in no convictions for dowry deaths under s 304B of the Penal Code. It can be difficult to establish a suspicious death if the family state, as they often do, that it was caused by a kitchen kerosene accident.[187] Fire-related injuries are the leading cause of death amongst married women ages 15 through 34 years who are living in poor conditions and work in small kitchen spaces.[188]

Second, the *Dowry Act* treats the giver and the taker of dowry equally as potential offenders.[189] However, they are not equally positioned as giving dowry is necessary for parents to enable the marriage of their daughter.[190] Marriage is a cultural necessity, and an unmarried daughter is not only a financial and social burden but also a source of religious shame for her family.[191] For many families, marriage is a means to achieve greater prestige through marrying a daughter into a higher caste or into a wealthier family.[192] The giver, therefore, has little scope for bargaining and is unlikely to report any prohibited demand for dowry. The law, therefore, is impervious to the power imbalance between the families and unable to effectively challenge the cultural norms which are reinforcing the practice.

Third, permitting gifts while prohibiting dowry makes it difficult to distinguish gifts from dowry. Indeed, research in rural Bengal reveals that community members understand the *Dowry Act* and avoid its reach in several ways: for example, by demanding and receiving gifts before the marriage.[193]

In addition to the legislative flaws, the practice of dowry is deeply rooted in societal norms. Dowry-related deaths are notoriously underreported as a result.[194] The police, neighbours and family members are often reluctant to get involved in a dowry dispute as it is viewed as a private matter.[195] Women are regarded as property and of lower status than men.[196] The concept of dowry is not unique to India, however.[197] Indeed, in Great Britain, until the early twentieth century, a marriage settlement, which was a comparable practice, was common.[198] Gender equality, increases in women's rights and the ability of women to own property in their own right led to the practice being gradually discarded.[199] We argue that, similarly, increasing women's rights, particularly their economic empowerment, will likely be the most effective means of reducing the practice of dowry and dowry-related violence.

Sexual violence

Defining sexual violence

Sexual violence is defined as a sexual act committed against a person without that person's freely given consent. The main legal response to sexual violence globally is criminalisation.[200] In India, as in many countries, the sexual assault criminal law framework historically reflected the perceived gravity of the breach of morality or honour (to the girl or woman, her husband and her family), rather than the degree of invasion of personal integrity and the harm suffered by the victim. That breach of morality was conveyed through offences such as defilement, assault with intent to outrage the modesty and indecent assault. For example, the term 'defilement' implies that the victim is 'spoilt' by the sexual assault and no longer 'pure', rather than approaching it as harmful and an unacceptable invasion of the personal integrity of the victim.[201]

In 2012, the *Protection of Children from Sexual Offences Act* (*POCSO Act*) was enacted, defining different forms of sexual abuse of children, including penetrative and non-penetrative assault, shifting the focus to the victim and away from a morality or honour-based approach. Shortly after the enactment of the *POCSO Act*, a controversial gang rape and murder of a young woman on a bus in New Delhi (popularly known as the 'Nirbhaya case') was widely reported in local and international media.[202] Due to international and local outrage, a three-member committee (Verma Committee) was constituted by the central government to 'explore amendments to the criminal law to provide for quicker trial and enhanced punishment for criminals accused of committing sexual assault of extreme nature against women.'[203] Despite the relatively narrow instructions the Verma Committee was given, in the ensuing report, they made a wide range of recommendations, including reform to the sexual offences framework.[204]

In response, the Indian parliament enacted a series of reforms to the offences of rape and assault with intent to outrage the modesty of a woman. The reforms are in accord with recommendations made to India by the *CEDAW* Committee and shifted the focus firmly (although not entirely) to one that more effectively represents the invasion of the physical integrity of the victim rather than the perceived breach of morality.

The National Crime Records Bureau in 2016 recorded very high rates of cases in relation to rape (now termed 'sexual assault' in the *Criminal Law (Amendment) Act* 2013 and assault on a woman with intent to outrage her modesty. A total of 123,693 sexual offences were reported to police authorities in 2016.[205] There were 38,947 rapes reported, of which 94.6 percent were perpetrated by someone known to the victim, indicating that the private sphere is the most dangerous space for women.[206] There were 84,746 reports of assaults on a woman with intent to outrage her modesty.[207] Madhya Pradesh reported the highest number of rape cases in 2016 (4,882 cases), and Maharashtra reported the highest number of assaults on a woman with intent to outrage her modesty (11,396 cases).[208] These figures, despite being high, are unlikely to represent the full extent of sexual violence against women due to the reluctance and inability of many women to report sexual crimes to authorities.[209] For example, while five Dalit women report rape every day, research shows that 67.1 percent of rapes are not reported by Dalit women because of fear or because dominant castes intervene to prevent registration of cases.[210] In relation to children, 36,022 cases of sexual assault were reported under the *POCSO Act* 2012.

Applying women's human rights

According to Brownmiller, 'rape entered the law . . . as a property crime of a man against man'. Women were viewed as the property.[211] Sexual violence against women has been a strongly visible and articulated issue in the Indian women's movement for decades.[212] Despite this, reform has come slowly. Basu argues that, historically, rape was viewed as sex rather than violence in India, and because the right to sex was vested in men – husbands and fathers – rape was a violation of their right.[213] The *Criminal Law Amendment Act* 2013 introduced standards more reflective of women's human rights principles that uphold the autonomy, dignity and physical integrity of women. For example, before reform, rape was defined as the forceful penile penetration of a woman by a man. The focus on penile penetration is grounded in a view of rape as a violation of the property rights of men, which may lead to pregnancy and threaten that power structure.[214]

The new definition of rape (now termed 'sexual assault') in the Penal Code expands it to include the penetration of a woman's vagina, urethra, mouth or anus by a man to any extent with his penis;[215] the insertion by a man of any object into a woman's vagina, urethra, mouth or anus[216] and the application by a man of his mouth to the vagina, urethra, mouth or anus of a woman.[217] It is also sexual assault if a man makes a woman do any of the above acts with any other person. This model moves away from rape as the violation of a man's right to property in his wife or daughter to focussing on the victim, the invasion of the victim's personal and physical integrity and the harm suffered by the victim.[218]

Additionally, sexual assault can occur in any of seven 'non-consensual' circumstances, including against her will or without her consent.[219] The rules of consent in sexual offences are highly contested by feminist scholars, and the new rape provision adopts the following definition of consent as 'the unequivocal voluntary agreement when the woman by words, gesture or non-verbal communication communicates willingness to participate in the specific sexual act.'[220] Consent under this definition constitutes a positive 'communicative' standard, which places emphasis on a woman freely choosing whether or not to engage in sexual activity. The basic principle underlying this model of consent requires a man to establish that he has obtained agreement before the sexual relations occur, in effect creating a presumption of lack of consent.[221] Thus, no indication from the woman of either consent or lack of consent would result in a finding that consent had not been obtained, which is a stark departure from the previous approach which required 'force, fear or fraud' by the offender and evidence that the victim physically resisted sexual relations. This model, in contrast to the former, recognises the inherent power imbalance between men and women and the non-violent ways in which women are coerced into sexual relations.

The penalty for sexual assault is seven years to life imprisonment.[222] However, once sexual assault is established, aggravating factors make the offence more serious and raise the penalty. If the sexual assault was perpetrated by a public servant, a police officer, a member of the armed forces, a staff of a jail or remand home, a relative, a guardian, a teacher or a person in a position of authority; during communal or sectarian violence; on a female under 18[223] or incapable of giving consent or by a person in a position of dominance or control over a woman or if a woman is repeatedly sexually assaulted, the penalty is raised to ten years to life imprisonment.[224] If, during a sexual assault, the offender inflicts an injury which causes the death of the person or causes the person to be in a persistent vegetative state, the penalty is raised to twenty years to life imprisonment.[225] If it is a 'gang rape', the penalty is raised to twenty years to life imprisonment, and the offenders may be ordered to pay 'reasonable' compensation to the victim to meet her medical expenses and rehabilitative costs.[226] This accords with the specific recommendations by the *CEDAW* Committee to India in 2014 and with research which suggests that particular contextual (or aggravating) factors are very relevant to both the level of harm suffered by the victim and the culpability of the offender.[227] For example, research has indicated that sexual violations that are perpetrated by persons in a position of trust and authority (such as fathers or other senior relatives, priests, doctors, teachers, counsellors and police officers) are likely to result in a greater impact upon the victim than assaults by persons unknown or unconnected to the victim because of the devastating effects of the breach of trust implicit in the assault.[228] Research also suggests that multiple sexual assaults by multiple offenders (such as gang rape) and multiple rapes perpetrated over a period of time by the same offender often result in more extensive and cumulative harm.[229] Importantly, the differential penalties reflect the greater harm to the victim and the greater breach of her right to physical and personal integrity, reflecting a shift away from a perception of rape as a violation of a husband's or father's right over a women's sexuality.

The *POCSO Act* defines a child as anyone below the age of 18, and there are no consent provisions, which means any sexual activity with a child below the age of 18 constitutes an offence.[230] The age below which child sexual assault offences should apply without consideration of consent and whether any exception should be made to accommodate sexual exploration between young people (and, if so, in what circumstances) remain controversial.[231] Many argue that the increase of sexual activity amongst teenagers and the important and growing recognition of the sexual rights of young people necessitate an exception for sexual relations between consenting young persons.[232]

Indeed, the *CRC* provides that children should be involved in the decision-making process in matters affecting their lives, which lends support to providing them with some autonomy and choice in relation to their sexual selves, provided they have the requisite physical and emotional maturity. However, the *CRC* also states that children need protection from sexual abuse and defines 'child' as 'every human being below the age of eighteen years unless under the law applicable to the child, majority is attained earlier.'[233] Clearly, therefore, the most difficult legal issue is to strike an appropriate balance between protecting children from sexual abuse and exploitation on the one hand and permitting the sexual expression of young persons as they proceed through adolescence into young adulthood on the other. We recommend revision of the legislation, perhaps in the form of an age difference exception, to recognise changing norms around sexual exploration by young persons.

There are two categories of sexual offences in the *POCSO Act*. The first category, termed 'penetrative sexual assault', includes the penetration of a child's vagina, urethra, mouth or anus by a man to any extent with his penis;[234] the insertion by a man of any object into a child's vagina, urethra, mouth or anus[235] and the application by a man of his mouth to the vagina, urethra, mouth or anus of a child.[236] The penalty is seven years to life imprisonment.[237] As in the new sexual assault framework, aggravating factors make the offence more serious and raise the penalty to ten years to life imprisonment:[238] for example, if the rape was perpetrated by a police officer, a member of the armed forces, a staff of a jail or remand home or hospital, school or religious institution; uses deadly weapons, fire, heated substance or corrosive substance; causes bodily harm and injury or injury to the sexual organs; infects the child with HIV or if the child is pregnant.[239] Since the vast majority of child sexual assaults are perpetrated over a period of time by persons known and trusted by the child, often with the use of 'grooming techniques' (which are used to gain the trust of the child to facilitate the abuse and prevent its discovery), the list of relationships that might give rise to a breach of trust and authority in the legislation and serious penalties recognising the devastating impact of the breach of trust in such circumstances is a strong feature of the legislation.[240]

A second offence, termed sexual assault, includes touching of the vagina, penis, anus or breast of a child, with a penalty of three to five years imprisonment.[241] If the touching is associated with any of the aggravated factors listed above, the penalty increases to five to seven years imprisonment.[242] The *POCSO Act* requires each state government to establish a special court to try offences under the act.[243] That court must create a child-friendly atmosphere, allowing the child to have support, prohibiting aggressive questioning, providing frequent breaks for the child and enabling the child's evidence to be presented through video conferencing.[244] The *POCSO Act* also introduces procedural changes, including mandatory reporting by anyone who has knowledge of an offence under the act and a duty on the police to report the matter to the Child Welfare Committee and the special court and to provide appropriate care and protection to the child.[245] A failure to report may attract a penalty of up to six months imprisonment or a fine or both.[246] Recording the statement of the child is done at the residence of the child by an officer not in uniform, and the child must not, during the examination, meet the offender.[247] The legislation provides for trials in camera that do not reveal the identity of the child, in a manner that is as child-friendly as possible.

These reforms and new offences focus on the child as a victim, highlighting the intrusive and harmful impact of such assaults in accord with the human rights principle of the paramountcy of the best interests of the child.

Honour crimes

Defining honour crimes

An honour crime is defined in the Indian context as the injury or murder of a family member (most often a female member) by other members of the family, community or caste, due to a belief that the victim has brought shame or dishonour upon the family or has violated the principles of a community or a religion.[248] The reasons for honour crimes include a refusal to enter an arranged marriage; entering a relationship that is disapproved by family or community, often outside the person's caste or religion; having sex outside marriage; becoming the victim of rape; dressing in ways which are deemed inappropriate; engaging in non-heterosexual relations and renouncing a faith.[249] There is no targeted 'honour crime' offence in India.[250] Victims have legal protection through article 21 (the right to life) in the Constitution and the criminal offences of murder, assault, false imprisonment and kidnapping. Although statistics in relation to honour crimes are hard to obtain, in 2014 the National Crime Records Bureau created a category in which they distinguished honour killings from other murders but recorded only 28 nationwide.[251] In 2015 that number rose to 189.[252] However, three other murder categories may also include honour killings. The bureau in 2016 recorded murders related to 'love affairs', murders related to 'illicit relations' and murders after kidnapping and abduction.[253] Cases of abetment of suicide of women (often related to either honour or dowry) were recorded by the bureau as 4,485 in 2016, and cases of kidnapping and abduction of women for 'marriage purposes' were recorded as 33,769.[254]

Applying women's human rights

Feminist scholars who examine honour crimes in the Indian context link them with a desire to preserve the ownership of property in familial male control by ensuring women marry appropriate partners.[255] Frequent killings by spouses and ex-spouses of women, children and other family members in Western countries, although not called honour crimes, rest on similar assumptions.[256] Often these killings in Western countries begin by stalking and possessive behaviour and escalate to killing after rejection by the ex-spouse, after the ex-spouse forms a new relationship or if the ex-spouse denies access to children.[257] Although the different cultural context of India at family, community and state levels requires targeted solutions, the underlying cultural assumptions of these killings rest on the ownership of women,[258] men's honour and the sexual regulation of women, especially sexual relationships outside social norms.[259] To maintain family honour, men must constantly supervise their female relatives and take all necessary measures to restrict their mobility. Every movement outside the house might risk a meeting with men, leading to improper behaviour of the female relative and the potential threat of dishonour. Any suspicion that their daughters, wives or sisters have defied the accepted social norms will provide strong grounds for punishing or even killing them. As men have assumed the responsibility of protecting the honour of female relatives, men are in a difficult and fragile position that requires them always to be vigilant. The killings enforce women's inferiority, preserve male supremacy and maintain codes of acceptable behaviour, particularly in relation to women's sexuality.[260]

Shifting these norms and assumptions is unlikely to be achieved through the criminal justice system, although it has a valuable role to play. Strengthening the formal law so it does not reflect such assumptions and compelling police to enforce the formal law are important challenges to the informal organisations operating in this space, such as the caste panchayats. Clearly, there is a contradiction between legal sanctions as they currently exist and social sanctions. For example, the law provides for interfaith or inter-caste marriage, but social norms do not. Customary and personal law practices regulate relations in the private sphere and wield significant 'power over' women.[261] Unfortunately, like 'protective' laws, honour crimes are justified as protecting women from perceived threats to their security and livelihood.[262]

Conclusion

This chapter has examined violence against women through selected (representative) forms of violence – domestic violence, including dowry violence, sexual violence and honour crimes. In each of these areas, using examples of feminist-driven law reform, policy and judicial reasoning, we have illustrated how principles and theories of women's human rights can be used to understand and strengthen the state response to violence against women and to develop strategies for reducing and ultimately ending violence against women. The right to a life free from violence is a universal right that should be afforded equally to all women across India. No claim to culture or tradition can be maintained to support any practice that violates the personal integrity of another person. Indian women, however, are subject to gender-based violence throughout their life-cycle across caste and religious divides. The most dangerous place is in the home, but women are also subject to violence outside the home and in many public spaces. International human rights law provides a framework that sets out the steps the state must take in order to reduce and ultimately end violence against women. While law reform provides only one step toward ending violence against women, it is, in our view, an essential first step. It provides a mandate for the state to act, it sets the standard for acceptable community behaviour and it provides a mechanism through which individuals and organisations can seek justice. Pursuing further law reform measures in accord with international women's human rights standards is, therefore, an important aspect of recognising a women's right to a life free from violence. However, there is a significant gap between the law and lived lives of women. In particular, in many parts of India, both rural and urban, customary practices that are unrepresentative of women's human rights standards are enforced by informal institutions. In addition to law reform, therefore, structural change to public institutions, such as the police, the courts, medical centres, schools and other service providers is required. In the private sphere, social and cultural norms that support violence against women and girls at individual, family, community and political levels must be shifted alongside change to social institutions such as marriage and the expectations of women in marriage and religious institutions and norms.

Notes

1 Declaration on the Elimination of All Forms of Discrimination against Women 1993 (UN Doc A/RES/48/104) art 1.
2 Ibid art 4(c).
3 Barbara Burton, Nata Duvvury, Anuradha Rajan and Nisha Varia, 'Violence against Women in India: Evidence from Rural Gujarat' in *Domestic Violence in India: A Summary Report of Three Studies* (International Center for Research on Women, 1999). See also Thomas Reuters Foundation, 'The World's Most Dangerous Countries for Women 2018' (Survey, 2018), where India was rated the most dangerous country for women based on statistics of sexual violence, human trafficking, domestic work, forced marriage and forced labour. http://poll2018.trust.org/ Accessed 17/4/19.
4 Bina Srinivasan, *Negotiating Complexities: A Collection of Feminist Essays* (Promilla and Co, 2007) 188.
5 National Crime Records Bureau, Ministry of Home Affairs, 'Crime in India–2016'. http://ncrb.gov.in/StatPublications/CII/CII2016/pdfs/NEWPDFs/Crime%20in%20India%20-%202016%20Complete%20PDF%20291117.pdf Accessed 18/4/19.
6 *CEDAW* Committee, General Recommendation 19, *Violence against Women* 1992 (UN Doc A/47/38).
7 *CEDAW* Committee, General Recommendation 35: *On Gender-Based Violence* 2017 (UN Doc CEDAW/C/GC/35).
8 Myra Marx Ferree, 'Beyond Separate Spheres: Feminism and Family Research' (1990) 52(4) *Journal of Marriage and the Family* 866–884.
9 James Messerschmidt and Stephen Tomsen, 'Masculinities and Crime' in Walter S. DeKeseredy and Molly Dragiewicx (eds.) *Handbook of Critical Criminology* (Routledge, 2018) 83–95.
10 Amanda Burgess-Proctor, 'Intersections of Race, Class, Gender, and Crime: Future Directions for Feminist Criminology' (2006) 27(1) *Feminist Criminology* 27–46, 36.
11 Radhika Coomoraswamy and Brian Earp, 'Female Genital Mutilation and Male Circumcision: Toward an Autonomy-Based Ethical Framework' (2015) 5(1) *Medicolegal and Bioethics* 89–104, 91.
12 Nidhi Gupta, 'Women's Human Rights and the Practice of Dowry in India' (2003) 35(48) *Journal of Legal Pluralism and Unofficial Law* 85–123, 95, 101.
13 *Convention* on *the Rights of the Child* 1990 (UN Doc A/44/49).
14 *Convention on the Rights of Persons with Disabilities* 2007 (UN Doc A/RES/61/106).
15 Majorie Agosín, *Women, Gender and Human Rights: A Global Perspective* (Rutgers University Press, 2001) 87.
16 General Recommendation 19, n 6, at [6], [8] and [9].
17 Ibid at [24(r)].
18 Ibid at [24(b)], [24(r)] and [24(t)].
19 Ibid at [24(r)].
20 Ibid at [12].
21 Ibid at [24(r)].
22 Declaration on the Elimination of All Forms of Discrimination against Women, n 1.

23 Yakin Erturk, 'Special Rapporteur on Violence against Women' (2006) *The Due Diligence Standard as a Tool for the Elimination of Violence against Women* 35 (UN Doc E/CN4/2006/61).
24 Ibid.
25 General Recommendation 19, n 6, at [4(c)].
26 Ibid at [4(e)]; Charlotte Bunch, 'Women's Rights as Human Rights: Toward a Re-Vision of Human Rights' (1990) 12(4) *Human Rights Quarterly* 486–498.
27 General Recommendation 35, n 7, at [10].
28 Ibid at [24].
29 Concluding Observations of the *CEDAW* Committee: India 2007 37th Session (UN Doc A/62/38) at [202].
30 Ibid at [157–158].
31 Ibid at [267].
32 Ibid at [151], [156], [170], [205].
33 Ibid at [160].
34 Ibid at [159].
35 Ibid at [160].
36 Concluding Observations of the *CEDAW* Committee: India (28 July 2014) 58th Session (UN Doc CEDAW/C/IND/CO/4-5) at [4].
37 Ibid at [11(c)].
38 Ibid at [10(e)].
39 Ibid at [11(d)].
40 Ibid at [11(e)].
41 Ibid at [11(f)].
42 Ibid at [11(g), (h)].
43 Ibid at [11(k)].
44 *Convention on the Rights of the Child*, n 13, art 19.
45 *Convention on the Rights of Persons with Disabilities*, n 14, annex 1 (d), (q).
46 Ibid art 16(5).
47 Ibid art 16(1).
48 Ibid art 16(2).
49 *Question of Integrating the Human Rights of Women into the Human Rights Mechanisms of the United Nations* 1995 (UN Doc E/CN4/RES/1995/86).
50 See, for example, Rashida Manjoo, *Reparations to Women Who Have Been Subjected to Violence* 2010 (A/HRC/26/38); Yakin Ertürk, *Intersections between Culture and Violence against Women* 2007 (A/HRC/4/34). See also Sally Engle Merry, *Human Rights: Gender Violence: Translating International Law into Local Justice* (Oxford University Press, 2006) 61–65 for discussion on the work of the Special Rapporteurs.
51 Ibid.
52 Suvarna Menon and Nicole E. Allen, 'The Formal Systems Response to Violence against Women in India: A Cultural Lens' (2018) 41(3–4) *American Journal of Community Psychology* 304–313.
53 Sanjukta Chaudhuri, 'A Life Course Model of Human Rights Realisation, Female Empowerment and Gender Inequality in India' (2013) 52 *World Development* 55–70.
54 Sharada Srinivasan, *Daughter Deficit: Sex Selection in Tamil Nadu* (Women Unlimited, 2012) 1–6.
55 Ibid Mohit Sahni, Neeraj Verma, Dherian Narula, Raji Mathew Varghese, Vishnubhatla Sreenivas and Jacob M. Puliyel, 'Missing Girls in India: Infanticide, Feticide and Made-to Order Pregnancies? Insights from Hospital-Based Sex Ratio-at-Birth over the Last Century' (2008) 3(5) *PLoS One*. https://doi.org/10.1371/journal.pone.0002224 Accessed 17/4/19.
56 Ana Flávia Pires, Lucas d'Oliveira, Simone Grilo Diniz and Lilia Blima Schraiber, 'Violence against Women in Health-Care Institutions: An Emerging Problem' (2002) 359 *The Lancet* 1681–1685.
57 Sahni et al., n 55.

58 Priya Banerjee, 'Dowry in 21st-Century India: The Sociocultural Face of Exploitation' (2014) 15(1) *Trauma, Violence and Abuse* 34–40; Luojia Hu and Analía Schlosser, 'Prenatal Sex Selection and Girls' Well-Being: Evidence from India' (2015) 125(587) *Economic Journal* 1227–1261.
59 Monica Das Gupta, 'Selective Discrimination against Female Children in Rural Punjab, India' (1987) 13(1) *Population and Development Review* 77–100, 80.
60 Hu and Schlosser, n 58.
61 Anita Raj, Niranjan Saggurti, Michael Winter, Alan Labonte, Michele R. Decker, Donta Balaiah and Jay G. Silverman, 'The Effect of Maternal Child Marriage on Morbidity and Mortality of Children under 5 in India: Cross Sectional Study of a Nationally Representative Sample' (2010) 340 *British Medical Journal* 1–9. https://doi.org/10.1136/bmj.b4258 Accessed 17/4/19.
62 Sundari Anitha, Harshita Yalamarty and Anupama Roy, 'Changing Nature and Emerging Patterns of Domestic Violence in Global Contexts: Dowry Abuse and the Transnational Abandonment of Wives in India' (2018) 69 *Women's Studies International Forum* 67–75.
63 Michael Koenig, Rob Stephenson, Saifuddin Ahmed, Shireen Jejeebhoy and Jacquelyn Campbell, 'Individual and Contextual Determinants of Domestic Violence in North India' (2006) 96(1) *American Journal of Public Health* 132–138.
64 Lisa M. Taylor, 'Saving Face: Acid Attack Laws after the U.N. Convention on the Elimination of All Forms of Discrimination against Women' (2001) 29(2) *Georgia Journal of International and Comparative Law* 395–426, 402.
65 Inderpal Grewal, 'Outsourcing Patriarchy' (2013) 15(1) *International Feminist Journal of Politics* 1–19.
66 Varun Kap and Kanika Dhingra, 'Sexual Harassment against Women in India' (2013) 6(10) *OIDA International Journal of Sustainable Development* 85–92.
67 Deepthi Varma, Prabha S. Chandra and Tinku Thomas, 'Intimate Partner Violence and Sexual Coercion among Pregnant Women in India: Relationship with Depression and Post-Traumatic Stress Disorder' (2007) 102(1–3) *Journal of Affective Disorders* 227–235.
68 Ibid.
69 See, generally, Mike Brogden and Preeti Nijhar, *Crime, Abuse and the Elderly* (Willan, 2000).
70 Tony Ward, 'Sexual Offenders' Cognitive Distortions as Implicit Theories' (2000) 5(5) *Aggression and Violent Behaviour* 491–507.
71 Martha Albertson Fineman and Raxanne Mykitiuk, *The Public Nature of Private Violence* (Routledge, 1994).
72 Jan Pahl, *Private Violence and Public Policy: The Needs of Battered Women and the Response of the Public Services* (Routledge, 1985).
73 Nancy Fraser, 'Rethinking the Public Sphere: A Contribution to the Critique of Actually Existing Democracy' (1999) 25(26) *Social Text* 56–80.
74 Suzanne Gleason, 'Female Political Participation and Health in India' (2001) 573 *Culture and Development: International Perspectives* 105–126.
75 Michael A. Koenig, Saifuddin Ahmed, Mian Bazle Hossain and Khorshed Alam Mozumder, 'Women's Status and Domestic Violence in Rural Bangladesh: Individual- and Community-Level Effects' (2003) 40(2) *Demography* 269–288; Rituparna Bhattacharyya, 'Understanding the Spatialities of Sexual Assault against Indian Women in India' (2015) 22(9) *Gender, Place and Culture* 1340–1356.
76 Agustin Echebarria Echabe, 'Role Identities versus Social Identities: Masculinity, Femininity, Instrumentality and Communality' (2010) 13(1) *Asian Journal of Social Psychology* 30–43.
77 Ibid; Kirsten Anderson, 'Violence against Women: State Responsibilities in International Human Rights Law to Address Harmful "Masculinities"' (2008) 26(2) *Netherlands Quarterly of Human Rights* 173–197.
78 Anjali Dave, 'Listening to Women's Voices: Domestic Violence and Women's Negotiations with Law and Public Institutions' in Flavia Agnes, Shoba Venkatesh Ghosh

and Majlis (eds.) *Negotiating Spaces, Legal Domains, Gender Concerns and Community Constructs* (Oxford University Press, 2012) 223–245, 226. Dave explains how the cultural construction of women in Indian society presents them as calm, accepting and subordinate, which constrains them from making any abuse public.

79 Rachel Jewkes Robert Morrell, Jeff Hearn, Emma Lundqvist, David Blackbeard, Graham Lindegger, Michael Quayle, Yandisa Sikweyiya and Lucas Gottzén, 'Hegemonic Masculinity: Combining Theory and Practice in Gender Interventions' (2015) 17(2) *Culture, Health and Sexuality* 112–127, 112–127, 114.

80 Clarinda Still, *Dalit Women: Honour and Patriarchy in South India* (Routledge, 2014) 163.

81 Sitawa R. Kimuna, Yanyi K. Djamba and Gabriele Ciciurkaite, 'Domestic Violence in India: Insights from the 2005–2006 National Family Health Survey' (2012) 28 *Journal of Interpersonal Violence* 773–807; Amitav Mukherjee, 'Transmission of Intergenerational Violence against Women in India' in Yanyi Djamba and Stawa Kimuno (eds.) *Gender-Based Violence: Perspectives from Africa, the Middle East and India* (Springer, 2015) 215–238, 216.

82 Akiko Kamimura, Maziar M. Nourian, Nushean Assasnik and Kathy Franchek-Roa, 'Intimate Partner Violence, Childhood Abuse, and In-Law Abuse among Women Utilising Community Health Services in Gujarat, India' (2015) 32(24) *Journal of Interpersonal Violence* 3778–3796.

83 Brittany E. Hayes and Cortney Franklin, 'Community Effects on Women's Help-Seeking Behaviour for Intimate Partner Violence in India: Gender Disparity, Feminist Theory, and Empowerment' (2017) 41(1–2) *International Journal of Comparative and Applied Criminal Justice* 79–94, 81.

84 Manisha Gupte, 'Why Feminism Should Inform Our Routine Interventions in Domestic Violence' in Padma Bhate-Deosthali, Sangeeta Rege and Padma Prakash (eds.) *Feminist Counselling and Domestic Violence in India* (Routledge, 2013) 48–85, 60.

85 Rawyn Connell, 'Gender, Health and Theory: Conceptualizing the Issue, in Local and World Perspective' (2012) 74 *Social Science & Medicine* 1675–1683.

86 Ibid 1680.

87 Ibid 1677.

88 See, generally, Michael Koenig et al., n 75.

89 Shireen J. Jejeebhoy, 'Wife-Beating in Rural India: A Husband's Right?' (1998) 33 *Economic and Political Weekly* 855–862.

90 Sofia Amaral, 'Do Improved Property Rights Decrease Violence against Women in India?' (July 1, 2017). https://ssrn.com/abstract=2504579 Accessed 17/4/19.

91 Lakshmanan Jeyaseelan, Shuba Kumar, Nithya Neelakantan, Abraham Peedicayil Rajmohan Pillai and Nata Duvvury, 'Physical Spousal Violence against Women in India: Some Risk Factors' (2007) 39 *Journal of Biosocial Sciences* 657–670.

92 Ibid 660.

93 Ibid 666.

94 Ibid 658.

95 Nidhi Gupta, 'Women's Human Rights and the Practice of Dowry' (2003) 35(48) *Journal of Legal Pluralism and Unofficial Law* 85, 87, 89.

96 Gupta, n 95, 98.

97 Gupte, n 84, 58.

98 Shahina Begum, Balaiah Donta, Saritha Nair and C. P. Prakasam, 'Socio-Demographic Factors Associated with Domestic Violence in Urban Slums, Mumbai, Maharashtra, India' (2015) 141(6) *The Indian Journal of Medical Research* 783–788.

99 Sreyashi Ghosh, 'Beyond Spaces: Debunking Public/Private Divide in Understanding Violence against Women in India' (2017) 1(5) *International Journal of Gender Studies* 76–95; see also Lakshmanan Jeyaseelan et al., n 91, for discussion on cross-sectional household research and the differentiating results on rates of violence between rural, urban and urban-slum areas.

100 Malavika Karlekar, 'Domestic Violence' (1998) 33(27) *Economic and Political Weekly* 1741–1751; see also Ameeta S. Kalokhe, Ratnaprabha R. Potdar, Rob Stephenson,

Kristin L. Dunkle, Anuradha Paranjape, Carlos del Rio and Seema Sahay, 'How Well Does the World Health Organization Definition of Domestic Violence Work for India?' (2015) 10(3) *PLoS One* for a comprehensive discussion on defining domestic and family violence in India. http://journals.plos.org/plosone/article?id=10.1371/journal.pone.0120909 Accessed 17/4/19.

101 Anju Khosla, Deepta Dua, Lajya Devi and Shyam Sudd, 'Domestic Violence in Pregnancy in North Indian Women' (2005) 59 *Indian Journal of Medical Science* 195–199.

102 Amy Piedalue, 'Understanding Violence in Place: Travelling Knowledge Paradigms and Measuring Domestic Violence in India' (2015) 22(1) *Indian Journal of Gender Studies* 63–91, 71. Currently, there are only two sources of data on violence against women: the National Crime Records Bureau, which reports annually on the number of reported cases against each offence and the number of convicted, and the National Family Health Survey, which is conducted every five years. Both sources provide useful information and data but are below the standard expected by international norms. The National Family Health Survey, for example, while yielding statistics, is premised on a model of violence as individual acts. For example, the survey asks about specific individual physical acts but does not ask whether there is a pattern of violent behavior or about the context of the violence.

103 Ministry of Health and Family Welfare, 'National Family Health Survey 4, 2015/2016' (International Institute for Population Sciences, Mumbai). http://rchiips.org/nfhs/pdf/NFHS4/India.pdf/ Accessed 26/03/19.

104 Ministry of Health and Family Welfare, 'Key Findings from NFHS-4'. http://rchiips.org/nfhs/factsheet_NFHS-4.shtml Accessed 26/03/19.

105 Ministry of Health and Family Welfare, n 103, 6. Although high, this is lower than 2005–2006, when the national rate was 37.2 percent.

106 Ministry of Health and Family Welfare, n 103.

107 Ibid; Bushra Sabri and Jacquelyn Campbell, 'Intimate Partner Violence against Women in Slums in India' (2015) 141(6) *Indian Journal of Medical Research* 757–759.

108 Ministry of Health and Family Welfare, n 103. See also Koustuv Dalal and Kent Lindqvist, 'A National Study of the Prevalence and Correlates of Domestic Violence in India' (2012) 24(2) *Asia Pacific Journal of Public Health* 265–277, 269, 271, in which the authors analysis the results of the survey; Sabri and Campbell, n 107.

109 John Barner and Michelle Mohr Carney, 'Interventions for Intimate Partner Violence: A Historical Review' (2011) 26(3) *Journal of Family Violence* 235–244.

110 *Criminal Law (Second Amendment) Act* 1983, s 498A.

111 Ibid.

112 *State v. Mr Sona Ram Son of Mr Nimba Ram* 27 (August 2010) Sessions Case Number: 96 of 2009; *State v. Vishesh Chaushary* (16 May 2008) SC No: 29/06.

113 National Crime Records Bureau, 'Crime in India-2016' (Government of India, Mahipalpur, New Delhi), xix, Table E. http://ncrb.gov.in/StatPublications/CII/CII2016/pdfs/NEWPDFs/Crime%20in%20India%20-%202016%20Complete%20PDF%20291117.pdf Accessed 26/03/19.

114 See Claire M. Renzetti, Jeffrey L. Edleson and Raquel Kennedy Bergen, *Sourcebook on Violence against Women* (Sage Publications, 2011) 16 for a discussion on the tension between structural and personal factors affecting violence against women. http://dx.doi.org/10.4135/9781452224916 Accessed 26/03/19.

115 Achyuta Suneetha and Vasuda Nagaraj, 'Dealing with Domestic Violence towards Complicating the Rights Discourse' (2010) 17(3) *Indian Journal of Gender Studies* 451–478, 457.

116 Sudhir Singh and Meerambika Mahapatro, 'Institutions and Abused Women: An Interactional Model to Access Justice in India' (2018) 28(4) *Development in Practice* 574–583, 581.

117 Suneetha and Nagaraj, n 115, 469.

118 Ibid 466.

119 Alice Edwards, *Violence against Women Under International Human Rights Law* (Cambridge University Press, 2010) 59.

120 Ronagh McQuigg, *International Human Rights Law and Domestic Violence: The Effectiveness of International Human Rights Law* (Routledge, 2011).
121 Deborah Epstein, 'Effective Intervention in Domestic Violence Cases: Rethinking the Roles of Prosecutors, Judges, and the Court System' (1999) 11(1) *Yale Journal of Law and Feminism* 3–50.
122 David Garland, 'The Limits of the Sovereign State: Strategies of Crime Control in Contemporary Society' (1996) 36 *British Journal of Criminology* 445–471.
123 *Hiral P. Harsora and Ors vs Kusum Narottam Das Harsora and Ors* (2016) 10 SCC 165 at [14].
124 *The Protection of Women from Domestic Violence Act* 2005 (Maharashtra State Handbook on Protocols, Best Practices and Reporting Format 2014).
125 Ibid 4.
126 Amy Horbeck, Bethany Johnson, Michelle LaGrotta and Kellie Sellman, 'The Protection of Women from Domestic Violence Act: Solution or Mere Paper Tiger?' (2007) 4(2) *Loyola University Chicago International Law Review* 273–307.
127 Ibid.
128 Ibid 276.
129 See Prianka Rao, 'Parliament as a Law-Making Body Background Note for the Conference on Effective Legislatures' (PRS Legislative Research, Institute for Policy Research Studies, 2014), which demonstrates the role of public scrutiny and debate in pre-legislative consultation. The *Prevention of Communal Violence Bill* 2013 was challenged on grounds of legislative competence, and the minister decided not to introduce the bill. The *Civil Liability for Nuclear Damage Bill* 2010 was opposed on grounds that it violated the Constitution. See her report for an analysis of public engagement with the legislative process in India. www.prsindia.org/administrator/uploads/general/1417684398~~Parliament%20as%20a%20Law%20Making%20Body.pdf Accessed 26/03/19.
130 Gupte, n 84.
131 *Protection of Women from Domestic Violence Act* 2005, s 3(a).
132 Ibid s 3 under headings 'definition of domestic violence' and 'explanation II'.
133 Ibid. Note that there are no legislative exclusions within definitions of domestic violence with regard to marital relations; see also Deborah Kim, 'Marital Rape Immunity in India: Historical Anomaly or Cultural Defence?' (2018) 69(1) *Crime, Law and Social Change* 91–107.
134 *Protection of Women from Domestic Violence Act* 2005, s 2(a).
135 Ibid s 2(q).
136 *Hiral P. Harsora & Ors v. Kusum Narottam Das Harsora & Ors* (2016) 10 SCC 165.
137 *Protection of Women from Domestic Violence Act* 2005, s 2(f).
138 Ibid s 2(a). The definition of an 'aggrieved person' is restricted to a female in a domestic relationship.
139 In *Narayan Jangluji Thool and 2 v. Sou Mala W/O Chandan Wani* (27 January 2015) Criminal Writ Petition No 773 of 2014. The court held that to attract the protection of the act, as well as living together in a relationship as husband and wife, the potential 'aggrieved person' must also show that both parties are legally qualified to marry. As the victim was still legally married to another, she could not and therefore she was not an 'aggrieved person' under the act.
140 *Protection of Women from Domestic Violence Act* 2005, s 8.
141 Ibid s 9.
142 Ibid s 8(2).
143 Ibid Rule No 3.
144 Indira Jaising, 'Violence against Women: The Indian Perspective' in J.S. Peters and Andrea Wolper (eds.) *Women's Rights, Human Rights* (Routledge, 2018) 51–56.
145 *Protection of Women from Domestic Violence Act* 2005, s 12(1).
146 Ibid s 18.
147 Ibid s 19.

148 Ibid s 18(a),(c),(e).
149 Ibid s 12(5).
150 Biswajit Ghosh and Tanima Choudhuri, 'Legal Protection against Domestic Violence in India: Scope and Limitations' (2011) 26 *Journal of Family Violence* 319–330.
151 Ibid 322. Kit Kinports and Karla Fischer, 'Orders of Protection in Domestic Violence Cases: An Empirical Assessment of the Impact of the Reform Statutes' (1993) 2(2) *Texas Journal of Women and the Law* 163–276.
152 *Protection of Women from Domestic Violence Act* 2005, s 19.
153 Jeyaseelan et al., n 99, 660.
154 Biswajit Gosh, 'How Does the Legal Framework Protect Victims of Dowry and Domestic Violence in India? A Critical Review' (2013) 18 *Aggression and Violent Behaviour* 409, 414.
155 Ibid 413.
156 Suneetha and Nagaraj, n 115, 475.
157 Renzetti, Edleson and Bergen, n 114.
158 Tim Dyson and Mick Moore, 'On Kinship Structure, Female Autonomy, and Demographic Behaviour in India' (1983) 9 *Population and Development Review* 35–60.
159 Ibid.
160 Lisa Hajjar, 'Religion, State Power, and Domestic Violence in Muslim Societies: A Framework for Comparative Analysis' (2004) 29(1) *Law & Social Inquiry* 1–38.
161 Ghosh, n 154, 410.
162 Ibid. Priya Banerjee, n 58, 34, 35; In *Krishna Bhatacharjee v. Sarathi Choudery* Criminal Appeal No 1545 of 2015, the Supreme Court held that if a gift is categorised as *stridham*, then a wife retains full rights of alienation during the marriage, and then it passes to her heirs. The husband could only make use of it during financial distress and must pay it back as soon as possible.
163 Ghosh, n 154, 411.
164 Banerjeee, n 58, 36.
165 Ghosh, n 154, 410.
166 Robyn Wyatt and Nazia Massood, *Broken Mirrors: The 'Dowry Problem' in India* (Sage Publications, 2010) 18.
167 *Dowry Prohibition Act* 1961, s 3.
168 Chand R. Jilova, *Law of Cruelty in India* (Universal Law Publishing, 2016) 27.
169 Ghosh, n 154, 411.
170 *Criminal Law (Second Amendment) Act* 1983.
171 *Penal Code* 1860, s 498A(b).
172 *Dowry Prohibition Act* 1961, s 3.
173 Ibid 4.
174 *Penal Code*, s 304B inserted by the *Dowry Prohibition (Amendment) Act 1986*; *Evidence Act*, s 113A.
175 *Dowry Prohibition (Amendment) Act* 1986, s 8; *Dowry Prohibition Act* 1961, s (8)(2)(c).
176 Ghosh, n 155, 411.
177 *Penal Code* 1860, s 304B.
178 Ibid; *Dowry Prohibition Act* 1961, s 8A.
179 *Penal Code* 1860, s 304B(2).
180 *Dowry Prohibition Act* 1961, s 8A.
181 *Jitender Srivastav and Ors v. State of Delhi* (30 August 2017).
182 Ibid.
183 Ibid at [67].
184 Ibid.
185 Srimati Basu, 'Legacies of the Dowry Prohibition Act in India in Dowry' in Tamsin Bradley, Emma Tomalin and Mangala Subramaniam (eds.) *Bridging the Gap between Theory and Practice* (Women Unlimited, 2009).
186 National Crime Bureau, Ministry of Home Affairs, 'Crime in India-2016' (Government of India) 4. http://ncrb.gov.in/StatPublications/CII/CII2016/pdfs/NEWPDFs/

Crime%20in%20India%20-%202016%20Complete%20PDF%20291117.pdf Accessed 17/4/19.

187 Linda Stone and Caroline James, 'Dowry, Bride-Burning, and Female Power in India' (1995) 18(2) *Women's Studies International Forum* 125–134.

188 Ibid.

189 *Dowry Prohibition Act* 1961, s 3.

190 Ghosh, n 154, 410.

191 Stone and James, n 187, 130.

192 Banjeree, n 58, 35.

193 Ghosh, n 154, 411.

194 Virendra Kumar and Sarita Kanth, 'Bride Burning' (2004) 362 *The Lancet* 18.

195 Katerina Standish, 'Understanding Cultural Violence and Gender: Honour Killings, Dowry Murder, the Zina Ordinance and Blood-Feuds' (2014) 23(2) *Journal of Gender Studies* 111–124, 112.

196 Ghosh, n 154, 411.

197 Stephanie Coontz, 'The World Historical Transformation of Marriage' (2004) 66(4) *Journal of Marriage and Family* 974–979; Stevan Harrell and Sara A. Dickey, 'Dowry Systems in Complex Societies' (1985) 24(2) *Ethnology* 105–120.

198 See Barbara J. Harris, 'A New Look at the Reformation: Aristocratic Women and Nunneries' (1992) 32(2) *Journal of British Studies* 89–113, which describes how the English dowry system was used to marry off daughters from noble families. Daughters became commodities to fathers of the English aristocracy, enabling them to gain kin and strengthen patronage ties.

199 Siwan Anderson, 'The Economics of Dowry and Brideprice' (2007) 21(4) *Journal of Economic Perspectives* 151–174, 169–171.

200 Kimberly A. Lonsway and Joanne Archambault, 'The "Justice Gap" for Sexual Assault Cases: Future Directions for Research and Reform' (2012) 18(2) *Violence against Women* 145–168.

201 Christine Forster, 'Sexual Offences Law Reform in Pacific Island Countries: Replacing Colonial Norms with International Good Practice Standards' (2010) 33(3) *Melbourne University Law Review* 833–864.

202 Ashutosh Misra and Simon Bronitt, 'Reforming Sexual Offences in India: Lessons in Human Rights and Comparative Law' (2014) 2(1) *Griffith Asia Quarterly* 37–56, 40; Thomas Poell and Sudha Rajagopalan, 'Connecting Activists and Journalists: Twitter Communication in the Aftermath of the 2012 Delhi Rape' (2015) 16(5) *Journalism Studies* 719–733; Soma Chaudhuri and Sarah Fitzgerald, 'Rape Protests in India and the Birth of a New Repertoire' (2015) 14(5) *Social Movement Studies* 622–628.

203 Justice Verma, Justice Seth, and Gopal Subramaniam, *Report of the Committee on Amendments to the Criminal Law*, January 23 2013.

204 Ibid.

205 National Crime Records Bureau, 'Crime in India-2016', Table 3A2(i). http://ncrb.gov.in/ Accessed 17/4/19.

206 Ibid.

207 Ibid.

208 Ibid.

209 Prakash Behere, T. S. Sathyanarayana Rao and Akshata N. Mulmule, 'Sexual Abuse in Women with Special Reference to Children: Barriers, Boundaries and Beyond' (2013) 55(4) *Indian Journal of Psychiatry* 316–319; Shana Maier, '"I Have Heard Horrible Stories . . . " Rape Victim Advocates' Perceptions of the Revictimization of Rape Victims by the Police and Medical System' (2008) 14(7) *Violence against Women* 786–808.

210 Jayshree Mangubhai and Chiara Capraro, 'Leave None Behind and the Challenge of Intersectionality: Christian Aid's Experience of Working with Single and Dalit Women in India' (2015) 23(2) *Gender and Development* 261–277, 265.

211 Susan Brownmiller, *Against Our Will* (Simon & Schuster, New York, 1975) 8.

212 Vivedita Menon, *Recovering Subversion: Feminist Politics beyond the Law* (Permanent Black, New Delhi, 2004) 108.
213 Srimati Basu, 'Sexual Property: Staging Rape and Marriage in Law and Feminisms' in Srimati Basu and Lucinda Ramberg (eds.) *Conjugality Unbound: Sexual Economies, State Regulation and the Marital Form in India* (Women Unlimited, 2015) 76–99, 77.
214 Flavia Agnes and Vivedita Menon, *Recovering Subversion: Feminist Politics Beyond the Law* (Permanent Black, 2004) 109.
215 *Penal Code* 1860 s 375.
216 Ibid.
217 Ibid.
218 Misra and Bronitt, n 198, 39, 51; Rituparna Bhattacharyya, 'Understanding the Spatialities of Sexual Assault against Indian Women in India' (2015) 22(9) *Gender, Place and Culture* 1340–1356.
219 *Penal Code* 1860, s 375.
220 Ibid s 375, explanation 3.
221 Sharon Cowan, 'Freedom and Capacity to Make a Choice: A Feminist Analysis of Consent in the Criminal Law of Rape' in Vanessa Munro and Carl Stychin (eds.) *Sexuality and the Law* (Routledge and Cavendish, 2007) 69–90. model.
222 *Penal Code* 1860, s 376.
223 Ibid s 376; *Independent Thought v. Union of India* (2017) SCC OnLine SC 1222.
224 Ibid s 376A.
225 Ibid.
226 Ibid s 376, s 376AB.
227 Patricia Coburn, Kristin Chong and Deborah A. Connolly, 'The Effect of Case Severity on Sentence Length in Cases of Child Sexual Assault in Canada' (2017) 26(3) *Journal of Child Sexual Abuse* 319–333.
228 Kim Stevenson, Judith Rowbotham and Jason Lowther, 'Reparation for Betrayal of Trust in Child Sexual Abuse Cases: The Christian Duty of Care, Vicarious Liability and the Church of England' (2015) 41(2) *Australian Feminist Law Journal* 253–270.
229 Louise Morgan, Bernadette Brittain and Jan Welch, 'Medical Care Following Multiple Perpetrator Sexual Assault: A Retrospective Review' (2015) 26(2) *International Journal of STD and AIDS* 86–92; Louise Morgan, Bernadette Brittain and Jan Welch, 'Multiple Perpetrator Sexual Assault: How Does It Differ from Assault by a Single Perpetrator?' (2012) 27(12) *Journal of Interpersonal Violence* 2415–2436.
230 *POCSO Act* 2012, s 2(d).
231 Gautum Ghosh, 'Addressing the Sex Related Problems among Adolescents in India' (2013) 1–10, 3. https://ssrn.com/abstract=2226777 Accessed 17/4/19.
232 Jyoti Belur and Brijesh Bahadur Singh, 'Child Sexual Abuse and the Law in India: A Commentary' (2015) 4(26) *Crime Science* 1–6, 3.
233 *CRC*, n 13, art 1.
234 *POCSO Act* 2012, s 3(a).
235 Ibid s 3(b).
236 Ibid s 3(d).
237 Ibid s 4.
238 Ibid s 6.
239 Ibid s 5.
240 Anne-Marie McAlinden, '"Setting' Em Up": Personal, Familial and Institutional Grooming in the Sexual Abuse of Children' (2006) 15(3) *Social and Legal Studies* 339–362; Satinder Bhullar, P. Mittal and Aditya Singla, 'Child Sexual Abuse in India: A Review' (2015) 1(2) *International Journal of Ethics, Trauma and Victimology* 38–44.
241 *POCSO Act* 2012, s 7.
242 Ibid s 9, s 10.
243 Ibid s 28.
244 Ibid chapter VIII.

245 Ibid chapter V, chapter VII.
246 Ibid s 21.
247 Ibid s 24.
248 Geeta Ramaseshan, 'Changing the Law? Current Developments in India Relating to Honour Crimes' in Manisha Gupte, Ramesh Awasthi and Shraddha Chickerur (eds.) *Honour and Women's Rights: South Asian Perspectives* (MASUM Publications, 2012) 219–254, 250, 219.
249 Anuja Agrawal, 'Ideologies of "Honour" and Prostitution of Women: The Bedia Case' in Gupte, Awasthi and Chickerur, n 248, 83–114, 84.
250 Geeta Ramaseshan, above n 248, 238.
251 National Crime Records Bureau, 2014, Table 3.2. http://ncrb.gov.in/ Accessed 17/4/19.
252 National Crime Records Bureau, 2015, Table 3.2. http://ncrb.gov.in/ Accessed 17/4/19.
253 National Crime Records Bureau, 2016, Table 3.2. http://ncrb.gov.in/ Accessed 17/4/19.
254 Ibid.
255 Inderpal Grewal, 'Outsourcing Patriarchy: Feminist Encounters, Transnational Mediations and the Crime of Honour Killings' (2013) 15(1) *International Feminist Journal of Politics* 1–19, 6; Manisha Gupte, 'Codes of Daily Conduct: Patriarchal and Caste Honour in Rural Maharashtra' in Gupte, Awasthi and Chickerur n 285,35–69, 35, 36.
256 Desmond Ellis, Noreen Stuckless and Carrie Smith, *Marital Separation and Lethal Domestic Violence* (Routledge, 2015); Allie Shier and Eran Shor, 'Shades of Foreign Evil, Honor Killings and Family Murders in the Canadian Press' (2016) 22(10) *Violence against Women* 1163–1188.
257 Laurence Miller, 'Stalking: Patterns, Motives, and Intervention Strategies' (2012) 17(6) *Aggression and Violent Behavior* 495–506.
258 Inderpal Grewal, n 255, 6.
259 Jyothi Vishwanath and Srinivas C. Palakonda, 'Patriarchal Ideology of Honour and Honour Crimes in India' (2011) 6(1) *International Journal of Criminal Justice Sciences* 386–395, 387.
260 Ibid 389–391.
261 Navsharan Singh, 'Of Crimes of "Honour" and Impunity' 143–151, 146 in Gupte, Awasthi and Chickerur, n 245.
262 Ibid 151.

6

RIGHT TO EQUALITY IN MARRIAGE AND FAMILY RELATIONSHIPS

Introduction

This chapter focusses on women's right to equality in marriage and family relationships. Marriage and family are powerful social institutions in Indian society where women experience subordination and discrimination. The perception of the family as a private space and the construction of women within the family as dependent and in need of protection has resulted in a legal framework reinforcing that perspective. India has no universal family law. Rather, there are different personal laws for each religious community – Muslim, Hindu, Buddhist, Jain and Sikh, Lingayat, followers of Arya and Prarthana and Brahmo Samaj and a secular personal law. Each offers differing levels of human rights protections for women.[1] These personal laws, except for Muslim law, reflect a combination of local norms and British law as it was during the colonial period.[2] Although article 44 of the *Constitution of India* 1950 (Constitution) requires the state to 'endeavour to secure for the citizens a uniform civil code throughout the territory of India', no uniform civil code has eventuated in the context of fierce debate both inside and outside the different religious communities.[3] The chapter assesses the extent to which women's human rights principles – particularly those detailed in article 16 of *CEDAW* on marriage and family relations, GR 21 on equality in marriage and family relations[4] and GR 29 on economic consequences of marriage, family relations and their dissolution[5] – and women's human rights theories have been or could be utilised to advance the rights of women in key illustrative areas. We argue that equality in marriage and family relations is a universal value and, therefore, support the introduction of a secular uniform family law code that meets international norms, particularly those set by article 16 of *CEDAW*. We also argue, however, that cultural and religious practices that do not erode or infringe upon women's human rights should be retained in each community's family law framework.

The chapter begins in 6.2 by outlining in general terms the obligations placed on India by article 16 of *CEDAW* and other international instruments to advance women's rights in marriage and family relations. In sections 6.3 through 6.9, we consider and assess those obligations through a series of illustrative examples. Those examples include the formation of marriage, live-in relationships, matrimonial remedies including the action for restitution of conjugal rights, divorce, spousal and child maintenance, the marital property division regime after divorce and, finally, inheritance. In each of these areas, using examples of feminist-driven law reform, policy and judicial reasoning, we illustrate how principles and theories of women's human rights, particularly theories of public and private and equality and non-discrimination, can be used to advance women rights in marriage and family relations. In particular, we illustrate how the economic regulation of women and the application of laws that support a version of women as dependent and in need of care and protection together retain women's subordination and marginalisation in the family.

Marriage and family relations: obligations of human rights law

This section examines, in general terms, the obligations to advance women's human rights in marriage and family relations created by key international conventions in the human rights framework, ratified or acceded to by India. The *ICCPR* and the *ICESCR* provide general standards on the right to protection and assistance in the family and the requirement for the free consent of both parties to marriage. The preamble of the *ICCPR* states that the purpose of the *ICCPR* is to recognise 'the inherent dignity and . . . the equal and inalienable rights of all members of the human family', and article 23(1) of the *ICCPR* states that the family is the natural and fundamental group unit of society and is entitled to protection by society and the state. Article 23(2) provides for the recognition of the right of men and women of marriageable age to marry and to found a family. It does not specify, however, what the marriageable age should be or that the age should be the same for women and men. India is not a signatory to the UN *Convention on Consent to Marriage, Minimum Age for Marriage and Registration of Marriages* 1962, which requires a minimum age for marriage to be clearly specified and the elimination of child marriage. Article 23(3) states that marriage must be entered into with the free consent of both spouses.

The *ICESCR* states in article 10(1) that 'the widest possible protection and assistance should be accorded to the family, which is the natural and fundamental group unit of society, particularly for its establishment and while it is responsible for the care and education of dependent children.' Both the *ICCPR* and the *ICESCR* support, in general terms, therefore, women's equality in marriage and family relations but do not contain targeted nuanced guarantees of equality in the family for women.

The *CRC* is also relevant to women's human rights in marriage and family relations. The preamble notes that a child, 'for the full and harmonious development of his or her personality, should grow up in a family environment'. Article 2 prohibits discrimination on the grounds of sex, and article 3 states that: '[i]n all actions concerning children, whether undertaken by public or private social welfare institutions, courts of law, administrative authorities or legislative bodies, the best interests of the child shall be a primary consideration'. Additionally, a child is protected from 'arbitrary or unlawful interference with his or her privacy, family, home or correspondence'.[6] The *CRC* Committee noted in 1994 that the concept of 'family' includes diverse family structures 'arising from various cultural patterns and emerging familial relationships', stating that the *CRC* is relevant to 'the extended family and the community and applies in situations of nuclear family, separated parents, single-parent family, common-law family and adoptive family'.[7]

Article 16 of *CEDAW*, which focusses exclusively on discrimination against women in all matters relating to marriage and family relations; GR 21; GR 29 and the concluding observations of the *CEDAW* Committee represent, however, the most developed statements on the rights of women in marriage and family relations. We adopt in the chapter the specific norms and standards endorsed by *CEDAW* to assess the level of recognition of women's human rights in the Indian context and to illustrate how women's human rights principles can be utilised to effect change.

Human rights law, therefore, requires universal minimum standards to be integrated into domestic legislation in relation to marriage and family relations. The *Constitution of India* 1950 (Constitution) recognises the requirement for a universal standard in article 44, which requires the state to 'endeavour to enact a uniform civil code that ensures that all personal laws are the same for all communities.' There has, however, been fierce and oppositional debate surrounding the introduction of a uniform civil code. Feminists who support a uniform civil code base their arguments on the universality of women's human rights norms;[8] feminists who oppose a uniform civil code argue that the rights of women in minority religions (such as Muslim women) will be subsumed into a universal law which will inevitably reflect the norms and beliefs of the Hindu majority and not recognise the diversity of women across India.[9] Hindu nationalists have also demanded a uniform civil code that eliminates religious-based family law and forces assimilation into a 'neutral' (but not necessarily secular) family code.[10] The debate that surrounds the possible introduction of a uniform civil code can be examined in the context of the universalism versus cultural relativism debate laid out in Chapter 2. A uniform civil code will contain one law for all and will, as cultural relativists argue, overrule some cultural and traditional practices. We argue for a uniform civil code, but not from the cultural relativist position, instead arguing that a uniform civil code should set minimum standards for all in accord with the standards set by *CEDAW*. Beyond those minimum standards, communities should be free to practice their own cultural and religious practices. For example, in the formation of marriage, the minimum standards that we argue for are: an equal marriageable age of 18, the voiding of underage marriage, a requirement for full and free consent by both parties, compulsory registration of marriage and the prohibition of polygyny. Other aspects of the formation of marriage – for example, the form of the ceremony, the clothes worn by the bride and groom and the choice of who performs the ceremony – can continue according to local custom, religious norms or personal choice. Arranged marriages, provided they are accompanied by genuine consent from the respective parties, can also continue according to local custom.

In the following sections, which focus on key aspects of women's human rights in marriage and family relations, we will primarily focus on article 16 of *CEDAW* and its interpretation in light of the *CEDAW* Committee's concluding observations, GR 21 and GR 29 and argue for the introduction of a secular uniform civil code that sets 'minimum' standards for all.

Formation of marriage

This section considers the formal requirements of marriage. Marriage in India, despite wide social changes, remains caste endogamous, universal, early and involves active participation of kin and family in spouse selection.[11] Marriage law is not universal across India, with different marriage laws for members of different religions. The *Hindu Marriage Act* 1955 (*Hindu Marriage Act*) regulates marriage for persons who are Hindu, Buddhist, Jain and Sikh, Lingayat and followers of Arya, Prarthana and Brahmo Samaj. Muslims are governed by the customary law of sharia.[12] The Parsi *Marriage and Divorce Act* 1936 (*Parsi Marriage and Divorce Act*) regulates the marriage of Parsis. The *Indian Christian Marriage Act* 1872 (*Christian Marriage Act*) regulates marriage for Christians, and the *Special Marriage Act* 1954 (*Special Marriage Act*) is a secular law of marriage which allows persons to marry irrespective of their religion.

Marriage law does not consistently meet the standards set by *CEDAW* and other international norms, as illustrated in the sections that follow, including equal marriageable age of 18, the voiding of underage marriage, a requirement for full and free consent by both parties, the compulsory registration of marriage and the prohibition of polygyny.

Marriageable age

Defining marriageable age

Marriage is between a man and a woman in all the personal laws. The *Prohibition of Child Marriages Act* 2006 (*Prohibition of Child Marriage Act*), designating an (unequal) marriageable age of 21 for males and 18 for females, applies to all citizens regardless of religion.[13] The legislation additionally provides that underage marriage is voidable at the request of the underage spouse up until two years past the age of majority.[14] However, despite the law, the courts have made decisions which appear to contradict the plain meaning of the law. In May 2012, the Delhi High Court held that a 15-year-old girl has the right to marry under Muslim personal law if she has attained puberty.[15]

Applying women's human rights

The law on marriageable age is contrary to international norms, which require an equal marriageable age of 18. In GR 21(36), the *CEDAW* Committee states that international standards require that the minimum age of marriage for both men and women be set at 18 years since marriage carries with it important responsibilities which require maturity and capacity to act.[16] An early marriage can have negative effects on girls' 'enjoyment of their human rights, especially their rights to health and education',[17] in part because of the increased likelihood of early motherhood and the associated health risks, including an increased risk of HIV/AIDS.[18] Although many countries worldwide continue to have different marriageable ages for males and females (typically younger for females), the *CEDAW* Committee explicitly rejects any justification for this on the basis that women have a different rate of intellectual or physical development from men.[19]

The unequal marriageable age of 21 for males and 18 for females is an illustration of a failure to achieve formal equality. It reflects a stereotypical view that men require more time to equip themselves for the financial support of the marriage and a complementary view that women will be economically dependent on their husbands during marriage and do not need the extra time to prepare financially.[20] As well as being out of step with international norms, the unequal marriageable age is contrary to the guarantees of equality and non-discrimination in article 14 and article 15(1) of the Constitution, but it has not to date been challenged in the courts on this basis.[21]

Article 16(2) of *CEDAW* states that the betrothal and marriage of a child shall have no legal effect. The *CEDAW* Committee has expressed concern with legal systems that do not render child marriages void, rejecting the justification that their aim is to avoid illegitimacy of any offspring of such unions.[22] Reform to the *Prohibition of Child Marriages Act*, influenced by feminist arguments relying on the international standard set by *CEDAW*, has rendered child marriages voidable 'at the option of the contracting party, provided that such marriage, whether consummated or not, was repudiated within two years of either of them attaining the marriage age.'[23] Those who conduct child marriages commit offences, which is positive; however, the underlying reasons for child marriage – poverty, poor educational options, a family's fear of harassment and safety concerns for their daughter(s), fear of losing control over sexuality, social norms and patriarchal values – are not addressed.[24]

We argue that child marriages should be void, rather than voidable. The practice of underage marriage is unlikely to cease unless firm legislative action is taken. This position is supported by the report conducted by the Core Committee on the Prevention of Child Marriages constituted by the government of Karnataka, which concluded that child marriages should be void.[25] They based their recommendation on the reality that few women exercise the option of filing a decree of nullity in the court to annul their marriages once they are consummated.[26] They also noted that courts are reluctant to declare child marriage void unless the facts of the case fall conclusively within the circumstances provided under s 12 of the act.[27] On 26 April 2017, the *Prohibition of Child Marriage (Karnataka Amendment) Act* 2016 was passed in accord with the Committee's recommendations, declaring child marriages void.

Another impact of reform on the civil law relating to underage marriages can be seen in the criminal law in relation to marital rape. In *Independent Thought v. Union of India*,[28] the Supreme Court of India modified s 375 of the *Penal Code* 1860 (Penal Code), which provides that sexual intercourse with a wife under 15 years of age (but not over 15 years of age) is rape to 'sexual intercourse by a man with his wife, the wife not being less than 18 years of age, is not rape'. This means that marital rape is an offence if the wife is under 18 years of age but not if she is 18 years of age or over. While still problematic, since women 18 years of age or over cannot refuse sexual relations with their husbands, it does represent a positive shift, in particular because the Supreme Court considered the standards set by the *CRC* and *CEDAW*. Since the marital rape exemption legitimised the practice of child marriage, it was found to be in contravention of the obligations imposed by these instruments.[29] The exemption was also found to be in breach of article 14 (right to equality) and article 21 (right to life) and, therefore, unconstitutional.[30]

Full and free consent

Defining full and free consent

A requirement for full and free consent to marriage by both parties ensures that a marriage is voluntary and is particularly important in the Indian context of arranged marriages. Arranged marriages are not problematic in our view, provided they are fully consensual.[31] The full and free consent to marriage is not, however, a specific requirement under the Parsi *Marriage and Divorce Act* and the *Christian Marriage Act*. Although capacity to consent is required for a Hindu marriage under the *Hindu Marriage Act* and a secular marriage under the *Special Marriage Act*, actual full and free consent is not a requirement.[32] It is, however, a requirement for Muslim marriages under sharia law. Indeed, marriage/'*Nikah*', according to sharia law, is a contract underscoring a permanent relationship based on mutual consent. A Muslim marriage requires a proposal (*Ijab*) from one party and acceptance (*Qubul*) from the other as is required for any contract.[33]

A marriage without free and full consent (and such consent cannot be obtained by means of coercion, fraud or undue influence) is void.[34]

Applying women's human rights

Article 16(1)(b) of *CEDAW* requires state parties to ensure, on a basis of equality with men, that women have the same right to freely choose a spouse and to enter marriage only with their free and full consent. GR 21(16) states that a woman's right to choose a spouse and enter freely into marriage is 'central to her life and to her dignity and equality as a human being', and a woman's right to choose 'when, if and whom she shall marry must be protected and enforced at law'. In accord with *CEDAW*, the BPA recommends that governments 'enact and strictly enforce laws to ensure that marriage is only entered into with the free and full consent of the intending spouses.'[35]

The failure to require the full and free consent of both parties to a marriage in any of the personal laws, except for Muslim law, is problematic, particularly in the context of arranged marriages. Although formally equal, because it applies equally to males and females, it is women and girls who are disproportionately impacted, given the widespread practice of young girls being married to much older men.[36] We argue that a uniform civil code should require full and free consent to marriage from both parties for all marriages, and, additionally, there should be no requirement for consent from parents or any other third party for either party.

Polygyny

Defining polygyny

Polygamy is the practice of having more than one spouse. Polygyny, the practice of having more than one wife, leads to discrimination and harms against women including economic disadvantage[37] and negative effects on mental, sexual and reproductive health[38] and, in some instances, is harmful to children.[39] A legal framework that permits polygyny may also be used to control and limit women's ability to assert their rights during marriage since 'the threat of the husband taking another wife may be used to ensure women stay obedient.'[40]

The Penal Code prohibits bigamy.[41] All the marriage laws void any marriage if a person is married to another.[42] However, for Muslim men, polygyny is lawful. Men are permitted to have four wives, but women can only have one husband.[43] If a Muslim woman marries a second husband, like any non-Muslim, she can be prosecuted for bigamy under the Penal Code, the marriage is void and children of such a marriage are 'illegitimate'.[44] On 10 February 2015, the Indian Supreme Court ruled that polygyny was not an integral part of Islam and justified the firing of an Uttar Pradesh government employee for violating Government Servant Rules following his marriage to a second woman. Justices

TK Thakur and AK Goel stated, 'What was protected under article 25 (right to practice and propagate any religion) was the religious faith and not a practice which may run counter to public order, health or morality. Polygamy was not an integral part of religion and monogamy was a reform within the power of the State under Article 25.'[45] Despite the ruling weakening the legitimacy of polygyny, it does not make it unlawful in Muslim communities.

Applying women's human rights

CEDAW does not expressly mandate the prohibition of polygyny. However, in GR 21(14), the *CEDAW* Committee states that a polygamous marriage 'contravenes a woman's right to equality with men and can have such serious emotional and financial consequences for her and her dependents that such marriages ought to be discouraged and prohibited'.[46] The HRC has also stated that 'polygamy violates the dignity of women. It is an inadmissible discrimination against women. Consequently, it should definitely be abolished wherever it continues to exist'.[47] In our view, polygyny should be prohibited in all communities. Many Muslim women's organisations have also called for reform.[48]

Registration of marriage

Defining registration of marriage

The registration of a marriage enables the state to keep check on the validity of marriages,[49] to enforce the minimum age of marriage,[50] to protect the rights of spouses in regard to property issues upon dissolution by death or divorce[51] and to prevent polygyny.[52] The *Hindu Marriage Act* and the *Special Marriage Act* require the registration of marriage. None of the other marriage frameworks require registration of marriage, although Muslims, Christians and Parsi priests do keep marriage registers.[53] Some states have enacted compulsory marriage registration legislation; however, a failure to register a marriage attracts only a fine and does not invalidate a marriage.[54]

Applying women's human rights

Article 16(2) of *CEDAW* obligates state parties to take all necessary action, including the enactment of legislation, to make the registration of marriages in an official registry compulsory. The *CEDAW* Committee continually urges state parties to take 'proactive measures to speedily enact legislation to require compulsory registration of all marriages',[55] including customary marriages.[56] In India, it is primarily customary marriages for which registration is considered difficult because of the informal and diverse systems of marriage in rural and tribal areas.[57] The Law Reform Commission in July 2017 recommended central legislation making registration of marriages compulsory through an online portal.[58] It further recommended that unregistered marriages should not be voided but rather subject to a small fine.[59] We support a much firmer approach to registration, given its significance in preventing underage marriage, polygyny and other practices that are harmful to women. If a marriage is not registered, in our view, it should be void.[60]

Live-in relationships

Defining live-in relationships

Live-in relationships, once uncommon and unacceptable, are becoming increasingly common,[61] although still considered 'immoral' in many communities.[62] In many Western countries live-in relationships have increasingly been recognised in law for the purposes of financial benefits, power of attorney, adoption and maintenance and property division after relationship breakdown.[63] In India, although live-in relationships have had recent legal recognition, it is only in specific circumstances. There is no comprehensive protection of rights and obligations for persons in live-in relationships.

Three contexts in which live-in relationships have been recognised include, first, the *Protection of Women from Domestic Violence Act* 2005 (*DV Act*), which enables women in a live-in relationship to apply for a protection order.[64] Second, there has been a gradual but limited recognition of the rights of persons in live-in relationships by the Supreme Court. In a recent case, grandchildren argued that their grandfather was not legally married to a woman he had lived with for 20 years and that she was his 'mistress', despite living in the joint family with them.[65] Drawing on a lengthy precedent of earlier cases, the Supreme Court concluded that 'it is well settled that the law presumes in favour of marriage and against concubinage, when a man and woman have cohabited continuously for a long time.'[66] The court recognised the live-in relationship and afforded her the same rights as a married person. Although this case and the precedent which came before are positive for women in live-in relationships, they are limited in their scope. The live-in wife had resided with her partner for over 20 years and had been accepted in the joint family home during that period. The community had accepted them as a married couple. A relationship of lesser duration or a relationship in which the parties are not co-habiting would not be protected by this precedent. Finally, other cases have determined that children born from live-in relationships have the same rights as children born within marriage, although no claim can be made on Hindu joint property.[67]

Applying women's human rights

CEDAW does not expressly mandate the protection of women in live-in relationships. In GR 21(13), however, the *CEDAW* Committee supports the recognition of live-in relationships, stating that the form and concept of the family can vary, and in whatever form it takes, the treatment of women at law and in private must accord with the principles of equality and justice for all. In GR 21(18), the Committee states that women in live-in relationships should 'have their equality of status with men both in family life and in the sharing of income and assets protected by law.'[68] Additionally, the *CEDAW* Committee has recently expressed concerns about the implications of the lack of legal framework for live-in relationships.[69]

Women's human rights standards, therefore, support affording women in live-in relationships the same rights and protections as married women. The combination of the case of *Dhannulal* described earlier, the obligation to comply with *CEDAW* and article 14 of the Constitution which requires equal protection before the law provides a solid base for legislative reform. We support legal recognition of live-in relationships as an important first step. However, we acknowledge that, without support in the community, it may be difficult to achieve in practice.

Additionally, although the recognition of same-sex relationships has not yet been explicitly addressed by the *CEDAW* Committee, many consider there is sufficient support in *CEDAW* and other human rights instruments (such as *ICESCR*, *ICCPR* and the *CRC*) through a broader interpretation of terms such as 'family' and 'discrimination on the grounds of sex or marital status' to obligate state parties to introduce protection for those in same-sex relationships.[70] In increasing recognition of such obligations, there has been rapid and widespread recognition of same-sex relationships in many Western countries, particularly in Europe, but also the United Kingdom, Canada and some parts of the United States, Australia and New Zealand.[71] At the United Nations (UN) level, increasing promotion and acceptance for the protection of LGBTI rights is occurring. In 2010, UN Secretary-General Ban Ki-moon presented a landmark speech on the need for LGBTI rights to be regarded as human rights; in 2011, the Human Rights Council adopted a resolution on human rights, sexual orientation and gender identity[72] and, in 2016, the Human Rights Council adopted a further resolution entitled 'Protection against Violence and Discrimination Based on Sexual Orientation and Gender Identity.'[73]

Matrimonial remedies

Restitution of conjugal rights

Defining restitution of conjugal rights

Restitution of conjugal rights refers to an action for an order to compel a married person who has left a marital home to return to the marriage and resume a sexual relationship with her or his spouse. Typically, such an order is made when the court deems there is no valid reason (such as desertion, cruelty or adultery) for the spouse to have left. Restitution of conjugal rights was transplanted into Indian law by Great Britain.[74] In British law, it was historically an action in the ecclesiastical courts which was later transferred into the secular law.[75] It could be brought against a husband or wife who was living away from their spouse without a 'good' reason.[76] If the suit was successful, the errant spouse would be required to live with her or his spouse again. In 1969, in the United Kingdom, a law commission report recommended the abolition of the action on the basis that there were more appropriate means of restoring and rehabilitating relations than forcing couples to resume cohabitation, and it was subsequently abolished in 1970.[77]

It has, however, remained in Indian law despite being called by Khardekar (MP), at the time of the drafting of the *Hindu Marriage Act* (which contains it) 'uncouth, barbarous and vulgar'.[78] In 1983, in *T. Sareetha v. T. Venkata Subbaiah*, P Choudary held the action violated article 21 (the right to life) of the Constitution.[79] Sareetha, aged 16, was married to Venkata Subbaiah. Almost immediately after the marriage, they separated from each other and continuously lived apart for five years. Venkata filed an action for restitution of conjugal rights. Sareetha argued the action violated her right to life protected by article 21 of the Constitution and her right to equality in article 14. The court agreed.

However, in 1984, the Supreme Court of India overrode *T. Sareetha* and upheld the constitutionality of the action in *Saroj Rani v. Sudarshan Kumar Chadha*.[80] The court found that the action of restitution of conjugal rights does not violate article 14 or article 21 of the Constitution and is therefore constitutional.[81]

Applying women's human rights

Restitution of conjugal rights is an action that literally operates to confine women to the marital family. The findings of P Choudhary in the Andhra High Court, although ultimately overruled, are important. They illustrate how feminist arguments can sway a court, if the arguments are persuasive and the judge receptive. P Choudhary stated 'sexual expression is so integral to one's personality that it is impossible to conceive of sexuality on any basis except on the basis of consensual participation of the opposite sexes. No relationship between man and woman is more rested on mutual consent and freewill and is more intimately and personally forged than sexual relationship.'[82] The court also acknowledged that the action is not grounded in any Indian cultural practice, rather that its origin 'is the medieval ecclesiastical law of England.' Indeed, the 'ancient Hindu system of matrimonial law never recognised the institution of conjugal rights although it fully upheld the duty of the wife to surrender to her husband. In other words, the ancient Hindu law treated the duty of the Hindu wife to abide by her husband only as an imperfect obligation incapable of being enforced against her will. It left the choice entirely to the free will of the wife.'[83] This is an important recognition, in our view, because many aspects of the personal laws reflect British law rather than the cultural norms of India and cannot be defended on the basis of a cultural relativist perspective.

The Supreme Court ultimately held that the action of restitution of conjugal rights was not contrary to article 14 because the action is available to women and men and therefore formally equal. However, we argue that while it is formally equal, it leads to substantive inequality because it disproportionately impacts women in a number of ways. First, women cannot obtain spousal maintenance if they refuse to comply with an order, and given their relative lack of economic security compared to men, this places them in a more vulnerable and unequal position. Husbands often use the action when women seek maintenance.[84] Second, the action is conceptually grounded in the primacy of the unity of the family and historical notions of the proprietary rights of men over women by treating a married person (but typically the wife) and their fidelity as the property of the other.[85] Finally, forcing a woman to resume sexual relations with her husband deprives her of sexual choice and control over her reproductive functioning. Since Indian law does not recognise marital rape of a woman 18 years of age or over, she is left with no protection from unwanted sexual relations.

Divorce

Defining divorce

Divorce is the final termination of a marriage. It cancels the legal duties and responsibilities created by marriage and dissolves the bonds of matrimony between married persons. The 2011 census indicated that 1.36 million people in India are divorced, which is equivalent to 0.24 percent of the married population and 0.11 percent of the total population.[86] Divorce rates in north-east states are relatively higher than elsewhere in India. Mizoram has the highest divorce rate (4.08 percent), more than four times that of Nagaland, the state with the second highest rate (0.88 percent). Hindus account for 76 percent of divorced persons, Muslims 12.7 percent and Christians 4.1 percent.[87] In global terms, the divorce rate is very low.[88] There are likely a range of reasons for the low rate of divorce, including the strict regulation of women's sexuality and the high cost of divorce for women socially, the lack of economic support for women who leave marriages, Hindu notions of duty and keeping the family together and the complicated divorce processes contained in the different divorce laws.[89]

Divorce, like marriage, is principally regulated by religious personal laws. None are fully compliant with *CEDAW* and other international norms. The *Hindu Marriage Act*, the Parsi *Marriage and Divorce Act*, the *Divorce Act* and the *Special Marriage Act* have similar grounds for granting divorce if there is no mutual consent, including matrimonial fault (adultery, cruelty, desertion) unsound mind, communicable venereal disease, incurable leprosy, renunciation of the world by entering religious orders, not having been seen alive for seven or more years, special circumstances (if the husband has been found guilty of rape, sodomy or conversion to another religion) and mutual consent.[90] Divorce is also permissible (without fault) under the *Hindu Marriage Act* if there is no resumption of cohabitation or order granted for restitution of conjugal rights for one year after a decree of judicial separation is granted.[91]

Divorces can, in most instances, only be obtained in the courts, complicating the process.[92] Courts are obligated by law to promote reconciliation and resolution of marital disputes by developing consensus between spouses.[93] Despite the law requiring fault or satisfaction of one of the other factors listed in the legislation, the courts do sometimes grant divorces when 'convinced of the impossibility of reconciliation'.[94] The *Hindu Marriage Act* and the *Special Marriage Act* also recognise customary divorces granted by village councils, caste organisations and quasi-legal and non-formal institutions.[95] This recognition of customary divorces means that divorces can be obtained in panchayats or village councils without approaching the courts.[96] This provides a cheaper and informal means of negotiating marital disputes and ending of marital relationships within individuals' own 'sociocultural spheres'.[97] Although the legality of divorces obtained from non-state forums is not fully clear, such divorces are accepted within their communities.[98]

For Muslims in India, sharia provides three forms of unilateral divorce for husbands. The first, *Talaq-e-Ahsan*, requires the husband to pronounce *talaq*, followed by a three-month *iddat* period, the equivalent of three menstrual cycles.[99] *Iddat* is for reconciliation and arbitration and, if the marriage resumes, the *talaq* is considered revoked.[100] The second *Talaq-e-Hasan* – requires *talaq* to be pronounced once in each of three menstrual cycles. The first and second pronouncements of *talaq* may be revoked by the husband. Indeed, if he does so, either expressly or by resuming conjugal relations, the words of *talaq* become ineffective. If no revocation is made after the first or second declaration and the husband makes the third pronouncement, the *talaq* becomes irrevocable.[101] The final form is *Talaq-e-Biddat*, in which a husband pronounces *talaq* thrice in one sitting, sometimes in a written note or even by phone or text message.[102] The divorce is immediate and irrevocable. All forms of *talaq* can be given for any or no cause, in the presence or absence of his wife.[103] Recently the Supreme Court held that *Talaq-e-Biddat* (triple *talaq*) is unconstitutional.[104]

A wife can unilaterally divorce her husband if she has negotiated to have such powers in the marriage contract.[105] She can initiate divorce and request the husband to free her from the marriage, and if he agrees, then divorce takes place (known as *Khula*).[106] She can also seek a divorce under the *Dissolution of Muslim Marriages Act* 1939 under specified conditions, including apostasy, failure to provide maintenance, unknown whereabouts, cruelty, failure to perform marital obligation without reasonable cause, impotence, insanity, severe disease or any grounds recognised by Muslim law.[107] This requires going through the judicial process which is expensive and often involves mental harassment and humiliation, adding another layer of discrimination.[108]

Wives and husbands can together initiate divorce through mutual consent (known as *mubarat*).[109] Divorces mostly happen without going to court through non-state dispute resolution forums such as the *dar ul qaza*, run by the All India Muslim Personal Law Board, and *Imaarat Shariah*.[110]

Applying women's human rights

We suggest that those divorce laws that are fault based or enable unilateral divorce by men but not by women do not meet international norms. The *CEDAW* Committee has called upon state parties to abolish fault-based divorce.[111] There is no provision under any of the personal laws for granting divorce because of irreconcilable breakdown of the marriage (despite the court recognising this option) or without mutual consent in the absence of fault or special circumstances. Fault-based divorce was introduced into many world legal systems based on a religious belief that divorce is a sin and that, accordingly, the rules of divorce should punish the matrimonial crime[112] freeing an 'innocent spouse from the contractual obligation of a lifelong marriage to a guilty spouse.'[113]

Fault-based divorce discriminates against women because it can be difficult for women to leave violent relationships if they have to provide evidence of situations that are humiliating, embarrassing, or frightening or that may interfere with their dignity[114] and because it interferes with women's autonomy and right to choose when to enter and leave relationships.[115] The practice of judicial encouragement of reconciliation during divorce proceedings aims at protecting family unity, which could be detrimental to women who are victims of domestic violence or other forms of abuse.[116] Indeed, the state, by placing a duty on the court to promote reconciliation between divorcing parties, may be perpetuating violence and discrimination against women and placing them in vulnerable and fearful situations.[117]

Divorces are increasing, and we suggest that the combination of greater participation of women in the workforce, increasing gender equality, individualism and the gradual dismantling of both arranged marriages and the joint family will lead to ongoing increases in the rate of divorce. We argue that divorce law should uniformly reflect the autonomy of both consenting adults who entered the marriage by enabling the spouses to withdraw from marriage on similar terms. Many countries have replaced fault-based divorces with a system that merely requires proof that a marriage has broken down in such a way that it is 'irretrievable', without reference to spousal conduct and typically upon the request of either spouse. Given that the courts have already moved towards granting divorce if a marriage is irretrievable, we recommend it be embedded uniformly in legislation.

A recent Supreme Court case on triple *talaq* highlights the shifting norms in Indian society around divorce. India's international and constitutional obligations to achieve formal and substantive equality for women must include the enactment of laws that provide women with equality with men and the means to leave marriages they do not want to continue with. However, we recognise that changing the law to facilitate an easier divorce process must be accompanied by reform that enables women to access spousal and child support and to divide property equally and fairly with recognition of non-financial contributions.

BOX 6.1 CASE EXAMPLE: TRIPLE *TALAQ*: *SHAYARA BANO V. UNION OF INDIA*

Facts

Shayara Bano, after a 15-year marriage, was divorced by her husband, Rizwan Ahmed, through triple *talaq* in October 2015. Shayara filed a petition in the Supreme Court in 2016, arguing that triple *talaq* violates the rights guaranteed by the Constitution under article 14 (the right to equality), article 15 (non-discrimination) and article 21 (the right to life). Rizwan Ahmed contested her petition, relying on article 25 (the right to religious freedom) and argued that Muslims are lawfully governed by Muslim personal law, which authorises triple *talaq*. The Constitution Bench of the Supreme Court heard the case in 2017.

Shayara Bano Arguments	*Rizwan Ahmed Arguments*
Shayara Bano argued, using a formal equality argument, that under the Constitution, religious freedom in article 25 is subject to all other Fundamental Rights including article 14 and article 15. These override article 25. Triple *talaq* denies a Muslim woman's equality before the law, and because articles 14 and 15 are superior rights to the right to religion, triple *talaq* violates the Constitution. Similarly, article 25 is subject to article 15(1), which says that the State 'shall not discriminate against any citizen on grounds only of religion, race, caste, sex . . .' Triple *talaq* discriminates on the ground of sex and, therefore, is contrary to article 15(1).	Rizwan Ahmed did not deny that triple *taliq* is contrary to the formal equality right in article 14; rather, he argued that the issues raised in the petition were matters of legislative policy and could not be addressed by the court. He referred to *CEDAW* and noted that India had made an express reservation with regard to its policy of non-interference in the personal affairs of any community without its initiative and consent.

Applying Women's Human Rights

Rizwan Ahmed cleverly utilised *CEDAW* to support his arguments. However, in August 2017, the Supreme Court, by a majority of 3–2, set aside the practice of triple *talaq*. The majority held that triple *talaq* violated article 14 of the Constitution. Of the justices who voted against the practice, two held it to be unconstitutional, while the third relied on case precedents to reiterate that such practice was impermissible under Islamic law. The case was driven by feminist activism and led by Muslim women affected by the practice. It is an example of Choudhury's position that theorising from the ground up and using women's lived experience are more valid explanations and interpretations of culture and religion in relation to issues that particularly impact women. Male leaders in the Muslim community who are resisting law reform in family and personal relations are assuming the power to determine what Islam means. Instead, the relevant voices are Muslim women who are discriminated against by the laws and who are challenging their subordination from within.[118]

Source: Authors

Spousal and child maintenance

Defining spousal and child maintenance

Spousal maintenance is the provision of financial support by one party to a marriage to the other party after nullity, separation and/or divorce while child maintenance is support paid to the person who has the day-to-day care of a child. There is a confusing array of laws that provide for spousal and child maintenance, all with different criteria and procedures. Some laws are formally equal, providing for both the husband and the wife to claim for maintenance. Others provide only for the wife to claim.

The *Muslim Women (Protection of Rights on Divorce) Act* 1986 provides that a divorced Muslim woman is entitled to reasonable and fair provision and maintenance to be made and paid by her former husband during the period of *iddat* (approximately three months).[119] No maintenance is payable after *iddat*.[120] The *Hindu Marriage Act* provides for maintenance payable after the decree is passed by the competent court, either for restitution of conjugal rights or judicial separation or divorce to both the wife and the husband. The amount is determined on the basis of what the court thinks 'just' having regard to the respondent's own income and other property of the applicant, the conduct of the parties and other circumstances of the case.[121] The *Hindu Adoption and Maintenance Act* 1956 also provides for maintenance for a Hindu wife and children, calculated on the basis of a number of factors, although maintenance is not payable if she is unchaste or ceases to be a Hindu by conversion to another religion.[122] She can receive maintenance under this legislation whether she is still living with him or not, and no judicial separation, divorce or nullity is required before eligibility ensues.[123] The Parsi *Marriage and Divorce Act*, the *Divorce Act*[124] and the *Special Marriage Act* (covering marriages not covered by the other religious laws) provide maintenance for a wife only payable after judicial separation or divorce on the basis of what is 'just'.[125]

The *Code of Criminal Procedure* 1973 enables the court to order a monthly allowance for the maintenance of a wife or such child, father or mother, at such monthly rate as such magistrate thinks fit.[126] However, she loses that right 'if she is living in adultery, or if, without any sufficient reason, she refuses to live with her husband, or if they are living separately by mutual consent.'[127] Child maintenance can also be awarded under this legislation.[128] Although a secular law, Muslims were excluded in 1986 on the basis that it is contrary to sharia law.[129]

Finally, the *DV Act*, arguably the most efficient mechanism, provides for maintenance payable to (qualifying) victims of domestic violence (of any religion) on the basis of 'adequate, fair and reasonable and consistent with the standard of living to which the aggrieved person is accustomed.'[130]

Applying women's human rights

Frustrating or denying women access to spousal and/or child maintenance is a form of economic regulation which contributes to and reinforces women's economic dependency.[131] Indeed, spousal and child maintenance are inadequate under all the available legislative frameworks. The *CEDAW* Committee states in GR 21(21) 'the responsibilities that women have in bearing and raising children affect their ability to access education, employment opportunities and other activities related to their personal development.'[132] Additionally, after divorce, women are more likely to retain the custody and day-to-day care of children, further disadvantaging them in relation to their ability to earn.[133] Article 16(1)(d) of *CEDAW* specifically states that in all matters relating to children, including in relation to child maintenance, the interests of the child shall be paramount in accord with article 3(1) and article 9 of the *CRC*. The *CEDAW* Committee further states in GR 21(19) that after separation and divorce, 'many fathers fail to share the responsibility of care, protection and maintenance of their children' and has urged state parties to 'put in place adequate legislative measures, including the review and amendment of existing laws, to guarantee that women obtain child support.'[134] Women's human rights principles, therefore, support a framework in which maintenance, both spousal and child, is easy to obtain upon separation and divorce, based on equality and need and universally available to women of all religions.

We suggest that the different laws for spousal and child maintenance are confusing and inadequate – maintenance is difficult to obtain and poorly paid. We argue that uniform legislation should ensure spousal maintenance is available to women immediately upon any separation, whether formalised by judicial decree or not. Maintenance should be payable on the basis of clear and fair criteria, based on the actualities of women's lives, such as commitments, income and earning capacity.[135] Statistics across India indicate that women are at a financial disadvantage after divorce and typically experience a decline in their standard of living, while men experience an increase.[136] Indeed, many women face poverty after the end of marriage for a range of reasons. First, there is no comprehensive welfare programme in India, and therefore women parenting alone must either earn money or receive support from family or their ex-husbands.[137] Second, women often have the day-to-day care of children of the marriage after its breakdown and therefore have little opportunity for generating a paid income as they do not have access to childcare.[138] Additionally, many families organise their lives during marriage on the basis that the wife forgoes employment opportunities or career advancements to focus on raising children and providing domestic support to the family, while the husband works for financial gain. The result is that the wife is at a huge financial disadvantage after separation in terms of future employment opportunities and earning potential.[139] The denial of financial support to women reinforces that gendered division of labour. To achieve substantive equality, the assessment of spousal maintenance after divorce should, therefore, fully account for the historical and ongoing disadvantages that women face in supporting themselves and their children.[140]

We argue that uniform legislation should also ensure that the parent not providing the day-to-day care of the child (often the father) is required by legislation to pay child maintenance to the person providing day-to-day care of the child in order to meet the needs of the child. Research suggests that child maintenance is positively associated with a number of child well-being indicators, such as health, educational achievement and social and psychological development.[141] However, many children are left in the care of a parent (usually the mother) without adequate support in both developed and developing countries.[142] In many countries, child maintenance is provided informally, if at all; however, the *CEDAW* Committee has urged state parties to 'put in place adequate legislative measures, including the review and amendment of existing laws, to guarantee that women obtain child maintenance.'[143] The payment of child maintenance after divorce should be based on based on the needs of the child and the earning capacity of both parties. This ensures that fathers take responsibility for the costs of child rearing and at the same time recognises the reduced earning power of many mothers and the costs that women bear in the raising of children.

Marital property division regime

Defining marital property division regime

Marital property division regime refers to the way in which property acquired during the course of a marriage is distributed at its dissolution. A legislative framework that ensures that property is divided equally and fairly when the marriage ends is critical to women's economic independence and to ensure that they are able to leave violent or failing marriages.[144] There is, however, no legislative marital property division regime in India (except in Goa),[145] which means that the division of property at divorce is determined according to title or legal ownership of property. The husband and wife are entitled to their separate property in their individual capacity, and any property owned jointly will be divided equally. Women, however, rarely have separate property and often do not own property jointly with their husbands.[146]

Applying women's human rights

In GR 21(32) the *CEDAW* Committee states that in relation to the division of marital property 'financial and non-financial contributions should be accorded the same weight'. Each party's contribution to a marriage 'whether in running the home or funding it' should be given equal recognition without any reference to the 'economic value' of the contribution. The Committee explains that non-financial contributions during a marriage, such as raising children, caring for elderly relatives and discharging household duties, 'enable a husband to earn an income and increase the assets of the marital relationship'. The failure to establish a marital property division framework in any of the personal laws leaves women, who often do not legally own property or make financial contributions to the purchase and upkeep of marital property, significantly disadvantaged.[147] In GR 29, the Committee recommends that state parties introduce 'equality within the property regimes available to couples' and 'the right to choose the property regime'. The Committee also emphasises that women must fully understand the consequences of each property division regime.[148]

The legislative framework that currently exists (a full separation of property regime) could be argued to represent formal equality. If a woman has the title to the marital home, then she will receive it in its entirety after the marriage, in the same way as a male title holder. If she owns property in her own right, either from before the marriage or purchased during the marriage, she will be entitled to retain ownership of that property after divorce.[149] However, women overwhelmingly do not have title to land or ownership of property within marriage yet, as research indicates, invariably contribute in non-financial ways to many marriages.[150] We argue that a legislative marital property division framework should be enacted, to ensure that women's non-financial contributions to a marriage are recognised. This is a substantive equality measure which recognises that women are disproportionately disadvantaged by the current formal equality framework.

There are three regimes of marital property division that meet the *CEDAW* Committee's recommendations and which can deliver a more favourable, substantive equality outcome for women. All three regimes prevent the exclusion of the woman on the basis that she does not legally own property or has not made a financial contribution to the marital property. The first is the partial community of property, where some property is separate (typically property owned before the marriage and gifts and inheritance received during the marriage), but all other property is considered joint, regardless of legal title, and is equally divided at the end of the marriage. Although favoured by some feminist commentators because it enables property owned separately and gifts to remain the property of the woman throughout marriage and after divorcing,[151] it is not, in our view the best model in the Indian context. Women often do not inherit even when they have an entitlement, and although *stridhan* is intended to be a gift to the bride by her parents, it is typically managed by the husband and his family.[152]

The second regime is full community of property, where all property is joint including anything owned prior to the marriage and is equally divided at the end of the marriage. This model, in our view, has the capacity to provide the most financial security for women in the Indian context. Regardless of title and control over property and resources, women are automatically presumed entitled to half at the end of the marriage.[153] Although we recommend this model, we understand that it would be strongly resisted.

The third regime is a separation of property regime, in which property is separately owned during and after marriage; however, either spouse can argue that they are entitled to a portion of the other spouse's property based on their non-financial contributions during the marriage.[154] This is the least desirable of the three models, in our view, because it requires a non-financially contributing spouse to prove their non-financial contributions and to convince the judge. The court's assessment of the respective contributions of each of the spouses is highly subjective and is likely to disadvantage the female spouse in the Indian context if her primary contribution is non-financial.[155]

All three property division regimes are further complicated in the Indian context by joint family homes and joint family agricultural property in rural areas. However, an amount can be calculated based on half the husband's interest in the property, which he must then pay to his ex-wife. Although we favour the full community of property model, all three regimes recognise domestic work as productive work and recognise marriage as an economic partnership.[156]

Inheritance

Defining inheritance

Inheritance is the practice of passing on property, titles, rights and obligations on the death of a person. Importantly, inheritance is a primary means through which wealth is transferred within a family, within a society and between generations. Inheritance law is important to gender equality in India, a predominately rural country, because it determines access to land and the opportunity for productive activities.[157] If women are discriminated against in inheritance laws, their economic empowerment is significantly restricted.[158] Discrimination against women in inheritance, in the laws relating to both wills and testacy, continues in India, justified by stereotypes about the roles that women and men should play within the family and the community and assumptions that women will marry and leave their natal families to become dependent members of their husbands' families.[159]

A will is the legal instrument that permits a person, the testator, to make decisions on how her or his estate will be managed and distributed after her or his death. The *Indian Succession Act* 1925 (*Indian Succession Act*) governs the rules relating to wills made by all persons, except Muslims. For Hindus, the rules relating to wills in the *Indian Succession Act* apply to individual property (anything acquired by an individual during his or his lifetime) and to his or her share in the joint family property (property and assets held jointly by the Hindu undivided family). The testator, female or male, has full testamentary freedom to dispose of her or his individual property as she or he deems fit.[160] A married woman is expressly granted testamentary capacity over her own property.[161] There are no provisions, however, preventing a deceased husband from excluding his wife, a possibility that is prohibited in other world jurisdictions to protect the economic security of female spouses. The following rules apply to a will: it must contain a legal declaration of the testator's intention; it must relate to the disposition of the testator's personal property; it must be in writing (subject to the prescribed exceptions); it must be signed or marked by the testator or by some other person in his or her presence and at his or her direction and it must be attested by at least two witnesses.[162]

The requirements for a valid Muslim will are derived from sharia law. A Muslim will can be made orally or in writing and does not require any signature or attestation. A Muslim cannot by a will dispose more than of one third of her or his estate unless the beneficiaries (as determined by sharia law) consent to it.[163] If a Muslim is married under the *Special Marriage Act*, however, the requirements of a will are then governed by the *Indian Succession Act*.[164]

Intestate legislation determines what happens to a person's property after death when there is no will. Most persons do not leave a will, and therefore intestate legislation must protect the rights of women.[165] Intestate succession in India is governed by the different personal laws.

The *Hindu Succession Act* 1956 (*Hindu Succession Act*) governs intestate inheritance for Hindus, Sikhs, Jains and Buddhist, Lingayat and followers of Arya and Prarthana and Brahmo Samaj. The rules of disposition are formally unequal providing different rules for female and male intestates. The separate property of a male devolves upon class I heirs – sons, daughters, widow and mother in equal parts. If a son or a daughter predeceases the intestate, his widow (not the daughter's widower), his or her children and grandchildren (excluding the son's daughter's son and the daughter's son's son) are also entitled to the share in the property which the class I heirs would have received. If he is unmarried, the property devolves in full to his mother.[166] The property of a female intestate devolves in the first instance to sons, daughters and widower in equal parts. The mother is not included because married women have no responsibility to their natal mother. If she is unmarried, then her self-acquired property devolves to her parents in equal parts.[167]

The *Indian Succession Act* governs intestate inheritance for those who are not Muslim, Hindu, Muhammadan, Buddhist, Sikh or Jain.[168] The rules are the same for males and females. For Parsis, property is devolved equally between children and remaining spouse. One-half the share of a child goes to parents whether they are male or female.[169] For others, the property devolves at one third to the remaining spouse, and the remainder is equally shared by lineal descendants.[170] If there are no lineal descendants, then one half will go to the remaining spouse, and the other half will be shared equally by eligible (non-lineal) kin.[171]

Finally, sharia law governs intestate inheritance for Muslims. Usually, females get half the share of males.[172] The justification for this difference is that the female at marriage receives *mehr* and maintenance from her husband while males have only inheritance to rely upon. Also, males have the duty of maintaining their wives and children.[173]

The *Hindu Succession Act* also governs ancestral joint family property, a form of property ownership that is recognised only by Hindus. It is undivided joint family property, both movable and immovable, which belongs equally to every member (who are known as coparceners).[174] Ancestral land devolves through a process of survivorship or birthright so that with every birth or death in the family, the share of every other surviving coparcener is either diminished or enlarged.[175] For example, if a coparcenary consists of a father and his two sons, the birth of a new son would result in each share being reduced from one third to one quarter. Ancestral property can be increased when a coparcener merges her or his self-acquired property with the joint family property. Ancestral property can only be sold with the permission of all coparceners. If there is only one coparcener left, then it can be disposed of as that person wishes.[176] Ancestral joint family property can be divided (called partition). Upon division, each divided property gets a new title as each owner gives up her or his interest in the property in favour of the other owners. The new owner is the absolute owner and can dispose of the property at her or his free will. This means she or he can sell, transfer, exchange or gift the property.[177]

Although ancestral property historically was granted only to male members of the joint family upon birth, an amendment to the *Hindu Succession Act* in 2005 extended it to include daughters, along with the sons, as coparceners.[178]

Applying women's human rights

We suggest that the different laws for inheritance are confusing and discriminatory. The *CEDAW* Committee has noted that serious discrimination against women occurs when the law and practice concerning inheritance do not treat females equally with males[179] and urges state parties to take appropriate measures to eliminate all forms of discrimination against women with respect to inheritance.[180]

Uniform legislation applying to all persons regardless of religion should guarantee that both women and men, irrespective of marital status, have capacity and freedom to make a will (testamentary freedom). The legislation should also ensure that women receive fair and equal treatment by imposing some restrictions on testamentary freedom.[181] Possible approaches include prohibiting a spouse from bequeathing the marital home to anyone other than their spouse;[182] requiring that a will must provide maintenance for a spouse and dependents based on their needs and earning capacity and on the basis of equality;[183] prohibiting a testator from granting parenting responsibility to a chosen party and determining parenting responsibilities on the basis of the best interests of the child.[184]

Uniform intestate legislation applying to all persons regardless of religion should place the surviving spouse at the top of the list, who should receive a significant fixed share of the estate prioritising their care and financial security.[185] If there are multiple spouses, then they should inherit equally.[186] Children should be next on the list of succession, and all children, female and male, should be treated equally whether born within or outside marriage and whether adopted, natural or step-children.[187]

The extension of birthright to daughters under the *Hindu Succession Act* in 2005 has led to an increase in daughters' inheritance,[188] although it remains difficult in many situations for them to exercise their right.[189] There is evidence that the reforms are linked to the growth of nuclear family structures, replacing the joint family structure with positive outcomes for women's autonomy.[190] This is because the extra bargaining power from inheritance is placed in women's hands and loosens the ties with the ancestral family.[191]

While we support the extension of birthright to daughters, we nevertheless recommend that birthright be abolished. When property has multiple owners, the number of whom increase at every birth, it is difficult to manage the property meaningfully. Hindu joint family property owners also receive a special concession in payment of income tax. There is no justifiable reason for one religious community to have a form of inheritance that receives special concessions in tax.

Conclusion

This chapter focussed on women's right to equality in marriage and family relations. Although law represents only a first step toward equality in the family for women, in our view, Indian feminists must continue to push for widespread legal reform.[192] In this chapter, we have illustrated that marriage and family remain powerful sites for the control, subordination and marginalisation of women. The Indian state is committed to a policy of secularism in the public sphere but supports religious laws in the private sphere, even when they conflict with constitutional guarantees. We support the introduction of a uniform civil code which reflects the norms of *CEDAW* and establishes minimum standards to apply to all marriages and family relations in all communities in India. This must include minimum standards in the formation of marriage, the recognition of live-in relationships, reform of matrimonial remedies including the abolishment of the action for restitution of conjugal rights and the introduction of no-fault divorce. Importantly, to ensure the economic independence of women, appropriate spousal and child maintenance must be payable, and a marital property division regime after divorce that recognizes women's non-economic contributions must be introduced. Inheritance rules must be equal, and women must be encouraged to enforce their rights. The connection between women's subordination in the private sphere institutions of marriage and family and their lack of economic independence and voice in the public sphere of political institutions and the workplace is plain.

Notes

1 *Hindu Marriage Act* 1955; *Special Marriage Act* 1954; *Indian Christian Divorce Act* 1869; *Parsi Marriage and Divorce Act* 1936; *Indian Christian Marriage Act* 1872; *Special Marriage Act* 1954.

2 Flavia Agnes, *Family Law. Family Law and Constitutional Claims*, Vol. 1 (Oxford University Press, 2011) 7; Sally Engle Merry, *Human Rights: Gender Violence: Translating International Law into Local Justice* (Oxford University Press, 2006) 109–110.

3 There is a significant body of feminist literature on the debate between plural personal laws and a uniform civil code. See, for example, Manisha Desai, 'Legal Pluralism versus a Uniform Civil Code' in Kenneth Cuno and Manisha Desais (eds.), *Family, Gender and Law Globalising Middle East and South Asia* (Syracuse University Press, 2009); Varun Srinivasan, 'Need for a United or Unified Code? Understanding the Implications of the Uniform Civil Code' (2016). https://papers.ssrn.com/sol3/papers.cfm?abstract_id=2757592 Accessed 17/4/19; Partha Ghosh, *The Politics of Personal Law in South Asia: Identity, Nationalism and the Uniform Civil Code* (Routledge, 2018); Vasudha Dhagamwar, *Towards the Uniform Civil Code* (Indian Law Institute, 2015); Nivedita Menon, 'A Uniform Civil Code in India: The State of the Debate in 2014' (2014) 40(2) *Feminist Studies* 480–486.

4 *CEDAW* Committee, General Recommendation 21, *Equality in Marriage and Family Relations* 1994, 13th Session (UN Doc A/49/38).

5 *CEDAW* Committee, General Recommendation 29, *Economic Consequences of Marriage, Family Relations and their Dissolution* 2013 (UN Doc CEDAW/C/GC/29).

6 *Convention on the Rights of the Child* 1990, art 16.

7 *CRC* Committee, 'The Role of the Child' at [190] CRC/C/34.

8 Srinivasan, n 3, 4.

9 Mahendra Pal Singh, 'On Uniform Civil Code, Legal Pluralism and the Constitution of India' (2014) 5 *Journal of Indian Law and Society* 5–12, 7, 8; Ratna Kapur, 'The Two Faces of Secularism and Women's Rights in India' in Courtney Howland (ed.), *Religion, Fundamentalism and the Human Rights of Women* (MacMillan Press, 1999) 143–153, 147. Kapur argues that the debate around the uniform code must be viewed in the context of targeting of the Muslim minority. See also Flavia Agnes, *Law and Gender Inequality: The Politics of Women's Rights in India* (Oxford University Press, 2011) 193.

10 Premchand Dommaraju Chaudery, 'Divorce and Separation in India' (2016) 42(2) *Population and Development Review* 195, 195, 237.

11 Ibid 195.

12 Bitto Rani, 'Sharia Courts as Informal Justice Institution in India' (2014) 1(9) *International Journal of Humanities, Social Sciences and Education* 129–139, 134.

13 *Prohibition of Child Marriages Act* 2006, s 1(2), 2(a).

14 Ibid s 3.

15 *Mrs Tahra Begum v. State of Delhi and Ors* (2012) W.P. (CRL) 446/2012.
16 General Recommendation 21, n 4, at [36].
17 See Jaya Sagade, *Child Marriage in India: Socio-Legal and Human Rights Dimensions* (Oxford University Press, 2005) 175–192, which discusses in detail the adverse consequences of child marriage.
18 WHO, *Gender and Health*, 2003 at 2. www.who.int/gender/documents/en/HIV_AIDS.pdf Accessed 17/4/19 See also UN CESCR General Comment 14, *The Right to Health*, 2000 E/C/12?2004/CESCR) at [22].
19 General Recommendation 21, n 4, at [38].
20 Velina Valcheva, *Child Marriage in India: Implementing Universal Human Rights in a Culturally Diverse World* (Grin Publishing, 2017).
21 Sagade, n 17, 142.
22 Concluding Comments of the *CEDAW* Committee India (2007) 37th Session at [56] (UN Doc CEDAW/C/IND/CO3).
23 *Prohibition of Child Marriages Act* 2006, s 13.
24 Lal Suresh, 'Child Marriage in India: Factors and Problems' (2015) *International Journal of Science and Research* 2995–2997.
25 Core Committee led by Justice Shivraj V. Patil, *Report on the Prevention of Child Marriages in the State of Karnataka*, Vol. 2, 2011. www.concernedforworkingchildren.org/wp-content/uploads/Report-on-prevention-of-child-marriages-in-Karnataka-Vol-1.pdf Accessed 17/4/19.
26 Ibid.
27 Ibid.
28 *Independent Thought v. Union of India* Writ Petition No 382 of 2013. See also Arima Pankaj, 'Independent Thought vs. Union of India: An Evaluation of the Judgement and Its Repercussion in the Field of Marital Laws' (2017) 22(11) *Journal of Humanities and Social Science* 79–85.
29 *Independent Thought*, n 28, J. Madan and B. Lokur at [40], [43], [44], [60] and J. Deepak Gupta at [33].
30 *Independent Thought*, n 28, J. Deepak Gupta at [67].
31 Raksha Pande, 'I Arranged my Own Marriage: Arranged Marriages and Post-Colonial Feminism' (2015) 22(2) *Gender, Place and Culture* 172–187.
32 *Hindu Marriage Act* 1955, s 5(ii)(a).
33 Aisha Siddiqa and Ruby Ruby, 'Status of Women in Islam and the Present Indian Scenario' (2018) 3(1) *Journal of Islamic Studies in Indonesia and Southeast Asia* 1–12, 4.
34 Ibid.
35 Beijing Declaration and Platform for Action, Fourth World Conference on Women, 15 September 1995, (A/CONF.177/20) and (A/CONF.177/20/Add.1) at [274(e)].
36 Jennifer Roest, *Child Marriage and Early Child-Bearing in India* (Young Lives, 2016) 21. www.younglives.org.uk/sites/www.younglives.org.uk/files/YL-PolicyPaper-10-Sep16.pdf Accessed 17/4/19.
37 Susan Ross, 'Polygyny as a Violation of Women's Right to Equality in Marriage: An Historical, Comparative and International Overview' (2002) 24 *Delhi Law Review* 375–384.
38 Lisa Kelly, 'Polygyny and HIV/AIDS: A Health and Human Rights Approach' (2006) 31 *Journal for Juridical Science* 1–38; Alean Al-Krenawi, 'Women from Polygamous and Monogamous Marriages in an Out-Patient Clinic' (2001) 38 *Transcultural Psychiatry* 187–199.
39 Alean Al-Krenawi, John Graham and Vered Slonim-Nevo, 'Mental Health Aspects of Arab-Israeli Adolescents from Polygamous versus Monogamous Families' (2002) 142 *Journal of Social Psychology* 446–460; Salman Elbedour, William Bart and Joel Hektner, 'The Effect of Polygamous Marital Structure on Behavioural, Emotional and Academic Adjustment in Children: A Comprehensive Review of the Literature' (2002) 5 *Clinical Child and Family Psychology Review* 255–271.
40 Radhika Coomaraswamy, *Cultural Practices in the Family That Are Violent towards Women* UN ESCOR, 2002, (UN Doc E/CN4/20002/83) at [63].
41 *Penal Code* 1860, s 494.

42 *Hindu Marriage Act* 1955, s 11; *Special Marriage Act* 1954, s 24(i); *Divorce Act* 1869, s 19(4); *Parsi Marriage and Divorce Act* 1936, s 4.
43 Vrinda Narain, *Reclaiming the Nation: Muslim Women and the Law in India* (University of Toronto Press, 2008).
44 *Penal Code* 1860, s 494.
45 *Khurshed Ahmad Khan v. State of Uttar Pradesh* Civil Appeal No 1662 of 2015 (SC).
46 General Recommendation 21, n 4, at [14].
47 UN HRC, General Comment No 28. *Equality of Rights between Men and Women* (Article 3), 1994, 68th Session at para [14] (UN Doc. A/47/38).
48 Narain, n 43, 93.
49 David Phillips, Carla AbouZahr, Alan Lopez, Lene Mikkelsen, Donald de Savigny, Rogelio Lozano, Janet Wilmoth and Philip Setel, 'Are Well Functioning Civil Registration and Vital Statistics Systems Associated with Better Health Outcomes?' (2015) 386(10001) *The Lancet* 1386–1394.
50 Elisa Scolaro, 'Child Marriage Legislation in the Asia-Pacific Region' (2015) 13(3) *Review of Faith & International Affairs* 23–31, 29.
51 General Recommendation 29, n 5, at [25].
52 General Recommendation 21, n 4, at [39].
53 Sagade, n 17, 89.
54 See, for example, Uttar Pradesh *Marriage Registration Guidelines* 2017.
55 Concluding Comments of the CEDAW Committee: India (2007) 37th Session at para [59] (UN Doc CEDAW/C/IND/CO3); see also General Recommendation 21, n 4, at [39].
56 General Recommendation 21, n 4, at [39].
57 Law Commission of India, *Compulsory Registration of Marriages* 2017, 10. http://lawcommissionofindia.nic.in/reports/Report270.pdf Accessed 17/4/19.
58 Ibid.
59 Ibid. The Report recommends a maximum of 100 IR.
60 Sagade, n 17, 89.
61 Fritzi-Marie Titzmann, 'Contesting the Norm? Live-in Relationships in Indian Media Discourses' (2017) 16 *South Asia Multidisciplinary Academic Journal* 1–23.
62 *State v. Zarzoliani* (2012) SC NO: 32/2010. Judge Surinder S. Rathi declared live-in relationships to be 'immoral' and an 'infamous product of Western culture'. 'Living-in is just a fad,' he said, 'visible only in urban areas.'
63 Robert Wintemute, 'From "Sex Rights" to "Love Rights": Partnership Rights as Human Rights' in Suzanne Goldberg (ed.), *Sexuality and Equality Law* (Routledge, 2017) 85–134.
64 *Protection of Women from Domestic Violence Act* 2005.
65 *Dhannulal & Ors v. Ganeshram and Anr* (April 2015).
66 Ibid 15.
67 *Antony v. Siyath* 2008 (4) KLT 1002; 2009 ACJ 2272; *SPS Balasubramanyam v. Sruttayan* 1994 AIR 133.
68 General Recommendation 21, n 4, at [18].
69 Concluding Observations of the *CEDAW* Committee: Nauru (2017) 68th Session. CEDAW/C/NRU/CO/1-2) at [45(d)].
70 For an overview of these arguments, see Robert Wintemute, *The Legal Recognition of Same-Sex Relationships: A Study of National, International and European Law* (Hart Publishing, 2001) 751–758.
71 The form and scope of protections varies considerably globally. Many countries have extended marriage laws to include same-sex relationships. (The Netherlands was the first in 2001.) As of 2018, same-sex marriage is recognised by law (nationwide or in some parts) in Argentina, Australia, Austria, Belgium, Brazil, Canada, Colombia, Denmark, Finland, France, Germany, Iceland, Ireland, Luxembourg, Malta, Mexico, the Netherlands, New Zealand, Norway, Portugal, South Africa, Spain, Sweden, the

United Kingdom, the United States and Uruguay. Additionally, Armenia, Estonia and Israel recognize the marriages of same-sex couples validly entered into in other countries. Same-sex marriage will be recognised by law in Costa Rica and Taiwan in 2020. Other countries have civil union laws which give same-sex persons similar rights and responsibilities to those granted through marriage.

72 UN Secretary-General, 'Confront Prejudice, Speak Out against Violence, Secretary-General Says at Event on Ending Sanctions Based on Sexual Orientation, Gender Identity' (Press Release, SG/SM/13311, 10 December 2010); Human Rights Council, *Human Rights, Sexual Orientation and Gender Identity* 14 July 2011 (UN Doc A/HRC/RES/17/19). In 2012, the UN Human Rights Office released its first major work on LGBTI human rights, a report entitled *Born Free and Equal*, which was followed by the 2013–2014 awareness-raising campaign on LGBTI rights under the same name.

73 Human Rights Council, *Protection against Violence and Discrimination Based on Sexual Orientation and Gender Identity* (adopted 30 June 2016) (A/HRC/RES/32/2).

74 Pratiksha Baxi, Shirin M. Rai and Shaheen Sardar Ali, 'Legacies of Common Law: "Crimes of Honour" in India and Pakistan' (2006) 27(7) *Third World Quarterly* 1239–1253.

75 Flavia Agnes, 'Reforms as If Women Mattered: A Critique of the Proposed Christian Marriage Bill' (2015) Issue 119 *Manushi*, 23–27, 27.

76 Brenda Hale, 'Equality and Autonomy in Family Law' (2011) 33(1) *Journal of Social Welfare and Family Law* 3–14, 5.

77 UK Law Reform Commission, *Proposal for the Abolition of the Matrimonial Remedy of Restitution of Conjugal Rights* 1969, 1. www.gov.uk/government/uploads/system/uploads/attachment_data/file/228673/0369.pdf Accessed 17/4/19.

78 *Parliamentary Debates on the Special Marriage Bill* (10 December 1954).

79 *T. Sareetha v. T. Venkata Subbaiah* (1983) AIR AP 356.

80 *Saroj Rani v. Sudarshan Kumar Chadha* (1983) AIR P H 59.

81 Ibid.

82 *T. Sareetha v. T. Venkata Subbaiah*, n 79, at [18].

83 Ibid at [20]. See also Mala Htun and Laurel Weldon, *Sex Equality in Family Law: Historical Legacies, Feminist Activism, and Religious Power in 70 Countries* (World Bank, 2012) 18; Anuradha Saibaba Rajesh, 'Women in India: Abysmal Protection, Peripheral Rights and Subservient Citizenship' (2010) 16 *New England Journal of International and Comparative Law* 111–143, 112.

84 Jaya Sagade, *Law of Maintenance: An Empirical Study* (Indian Law Society, 1996) 138–147, where the author found that 75 percent of actions were brought by husbands.

85 Raj Kumari Agarwala, 'Restitution of Conjugal Rights under Hindu Law: A Plea for the Abolition of the Remedy' (2016) 12 *Journal of the Indian Law Institute* 257–268; Padma Anagol, 'Rebellious Wives and Dysfunctional Marriages: Indian Women's Discourses and Participation in the Debates over Restitution of Conjugal Rights and the Child Marriage Controversy in the 1880s and 1890s' in Sumit Sarkar and Tanika Sarkar (eds.), *Women and Social Reform in Modern India: A Reader* (Indiana University Press, 2008) 282–312.

86 Census 2011, C2 Marital Status by Age and Sex. http://censusindia.gov.in/ Accessed 17/4/19.

87 Ibid.

88 Ibid.

89 Premchand Dommaraju and Gavin Jones, 'Divorce Trends in Asia' (2011) 39(6) *Asian Journal of Social Science* 725–750, 749; Premchand Dommaraju, 'Divorce and Separation in India' (2016) 42(2) *Population and Development Review* 195–223, 196.

90 *Hindu Marriage Act* 1955, s 13; *Divorce Act* 1869, s 10; *Special Marriage Act* 1954, s 27, s 28.

91 *Hindu Marriage Act* 1955, s 131A.

92 Dommaraju, 'Divorce and Separation in India', n 89, 199.

93 Ibid.
94 Gopika Solanki, *Adjudication in Religious Family Laws: Cultural Accommodation, Legal Pluralism, and Gender Equality in India* (Cambridge University Press, 2011) 121.
95 *Hindu Marriage Act* 1955, s 2(2); *Special Marriage Act* 1954, s 4.
96 Geetha Ravindra, 'Panchayats Mediation, Lok Adalat People's Court Conciliation, and Institutionalization of ADR' in Stephanie P. Stobbe (ed.), *Conflict Resolution in Asia: Mediation and Other Cultural Models* (Lexington Books, 2018) 219; Ella Verver, *Colonialism and the Functions of Village Panchayats in Maharashtra, India* (BS thesis, Leiden University College, 2016).
97 Werner Menski, 'Ancient and Modern Boundary: Crossings between Personal Laws and Civil Law in Composite India' in Joel A. Nichols (ed.), *Marriage and Divorce in a Multicultural Context: Multi-Tiered Marriage and the Boundaries of Civil Law and Religion* (Cambridge University Press, 2012) 219–252.
98 Sylvia Vatuk, 'The Application of Muslim Personal Law in India: A System of Legal Pluralism in Action' in Elisa Giunchi (ed.), *Adjudicating Family Law in Muslim Courts* (Routledge, 2013) 48–69.
99 Furqan Ahmad, 'Understanding the Islamic Law of Divorce' (2003) 45(3/4) *Journal of the Indian Law Institute* 484–508.
100 Ibid 488.
101 Ibid 488, 489.
102 Ibid 488, 492.
103 Ahmad Nehaluddin, 'A Critical Appraisal of "Triple Divorce" in Islamic Law' (2009) 23(1) *International Journal of Law, Policy and the Family* 53–61.
104 *Shayara Bano v. Union of India and Others* (22 August 2017) Writ Petition (C) No 118 of 2016.
105 Cyra Choudhury, '(Mis)appropriated Liberty: Identity, Gender Justice, and Muslim Personal Law Reform in India' (2008) 17(1) *Columbia Journal of Gender & Law* 45–110, 73.
106 Ibid.
107 *Dissolution of Muslim Marriages Act* 1939, s 2.
108 Vinitha Johnson, 'A Note on the Operation of the Dissolution of Muslim Marriages Act, 1939' (2011) 52(2) *Journal of Divorce & Remarriage* 94–108.
109 Choudhury, n 105, 73.
110 Katherine Lemons, 'When Marriage Breaks Down How Do Contracts Matter? Marriage Contracts and Divorce in Contemporary North India' in Ravinder Kaur and Rajni Palriwala (eds.), *Marrying in South Asia: Shifting Concepts, Changing Practices in a Globalising World* (Orient Blackswan, 2013) 371–388.
111 See Ziba Mir-Hossein, Karl Vogt, Lena Larsen and Christian Moe (eds.), *Gender and Equality in Muslim Family Law: Justice and Ethics in the Islamic Legal Tradition* (IB Tauris, 2013) for a critique of sharia law on divorce from a selection of Muslim authors.
112 Heather Brook, 'S/he Done Me Wrong: Adversarial Versus "No-Fault" Divorce' in *Conjugal Rites* (Palgrave MacMillan, 2007) 121–151, 123.
113 Ibid.
114 Shurlee Swain and Danielle Thornton, 'Fault, Gender Politics and Family Law Reform' (2011) 57(2) *Australian Journal of Politics and History* 207–220, 211; Karin Carmit Yefet, 'Constitution and Female-Initiated Divorce in Pakistan: Western Liberalism in Islamic Garb' (2011) 34 *Harvard Journal of Law and Gender* 553–617, 580.
115 Brenda Hale, 'Equality and Autonomy in Family Law' (2011) 33(1) *Journal of Social Welfare and Family Law* 3–14.
116 Srimati Basu, 'Judges of Normality: Mediating Marriage in the Family Courts of Kolkata, India' (2012) 37(2) *Signs: Journal of Women in Culture and Society* 469–492, 470, 480.
117 Jian Wang, 'To Divorce or Not to Divorce: A Critical Discourse Analysis of Court-Ordered Divorce Mediation in China' (2013) 27(1) *International Journal of Law, Policy and the Family* 74–96.
118 Esita Sur, 'Triple Talaq Bill in India: Muslim Women as Political Subjects or Victims?' (2018) 5(3) *Space and Culture, India* 5–12.

119 *Muslim Women (Protection of Rights on Divorce) Act* 1986, s 3(a).
120 Ibid.
121 *Hindu Marriage Act* 1955, s 27.
122 *Hindu Adoption and Maintenance Act* 1956, s 18(3).
123 Ibid s 18(2).
124 *Indian Divorce Act* 1869, s 36.
125 *Special Marriage Act* 1954, s 37.
126 *Code of Criminal Procedure* 1973, s 125.
127 Ibid.
128 Ibid.
129 *Muslim Women's (Protection of Rights on Divorce) Act* 1986, s 5. If a husband and wife both agree to the use of s 125 of the *Code of Criminal Procedure* 1973, then it can be applied.
130 *Protection of Women from Domestic Violence Act* 2005, s 20(1)(d).
131 Kapur and Cossman, n 1, 133, 139.
132 General Recommendation 21, n 4.
133 Anisa Shaikh, 'Juridical Referendum on Child Custody and Guardianship Laws' (January 11, 2016). https://ssrn.com/abstract=2713766 or http://dx.doi.org/10.2139/ssrn.2713766 Accessed 17/4/19.
134 General Recommendation 21, n 4.
135 Liat Kulik, 'Developments in Spousal Power Relations: Are We Moving toward Equality?' (2011) 47(7) *Marriage and Family Review* 419–435.
136 Kirti Singh, *Separated and Divorced Women in India: Economic Rights and Entitlements* (Sage Publications, 2013).
137 Beth Goldblatt, *Developing the Right to Social Security: A Gender Perspective* (Routledge, New York, 2016) 153. Formal social security covers 8 percent of the workforce, and there are no benefits for persons parenting alone.
138 Singh, n 136.
139 Ibid.
140 Marianne Dainton, 'Equity, Equality, and Self-Interest in Marital Maintenance' (2017) 65(3) *Communication Quarterly* 247–267.
141 Mario Biggeri and Santosh Mehrotra, 'Child Poverty as Capability Deprivation: How to Choose Domains of Child Well-Being and Poverty' in Mario Biggeri, Jerome Ballet and Flavio Comim (eds.), *Children and the Capability Approach* (Palgrave MacMillan, 2011) 46–75.
142 Laura Cuesta and Daniel Meyer, 'The Role of Child Support in the Economic Wellbeing of Custodial Mother Families in Less Developed Countries: The Case of Colombia' (2014) 28(1) *International Journal of Law, Policy and the Family* 60–76.
143 Concluding Comments of the *CEDAW* Committee: Cook Islands (2007) 39th Session, at para [41] (UN Doc CEDAW/C/COK/CO/1).
144 Matthias Doepke, Michele Tertilt and Alessandra Voena, 'The Economics and Politics of Women's Rights' (2012) 4(1) *Annual Review of Economics* 339–372; Carmen Deere et al., 'Property Rights and the Gender Distribution of Wealth in Ecuador, Ghana and India' (2013) 11(2) *The Journal of Economic Inequality* 249–265.
145 *Goa Daman and Diu Administration Act* 1962. See Manohar S. Usgaocar, *Family Laws of Goa, Daman and Diu* (Vela Associates, 2013).
146 Aarushi Bhatnagar, 'Marital Property Law: A Prerequisite for Progressive Divorce Reforms in India' (May 10, 2018), 5. https://ssrn.com/abstract=3201944 or http://dx.doi.org/10.2139/ssrn.3201944 Accessed 17/4/19.
147 Bhatnagar, n 146, 8, 9.
148 General Recommendation 29, n 5, at [47].
149 The exception is gifts received during the marriage, which are equally shared by both spouses. *Hindu Marriage Act* 1955, s 27.
150 Swati Dutta, 'The Extent of Female Unpaid Work in India: A Case of Rural Agricultural Households' (2016) 31(2) *Asia-Pacific Population Journal* 75–90; Laishram Ladusingh, 'Rural-Urban and Gender Differences in Time Spent in Unpaid Household

Work in India' in Martin Hyde, Holendro Chungkham and Laishram Ladusingh (eds.), *Work and Health in India* (Policy Press, 2017) 87–107; Mohammed Zakaria Siddiqui, Kuntala Lahiri-Dutt, Stewart Lockie and Bill Pritchard, 'Reconsidering Women's Work in Rural India: Analysis of NSSO Data, 2004–05 and 2011–12' (2017) 52(1) *Economic and Political Weekly* 45–52.

151 Carmen Diana Deere et al., n 144, 250.

152 Bikash Bhattacharya, 'Gender Inequality in the Right of Inheritance' in N. Chakrabarti and Shachi Chakrabarti (eds.), *Gender Justice* (R. Cambray and Co. Pvt. Ltd, 2006) 65–80, 68.

153 Vijender Kumar, 'Matrimonial Property Law in India: Need of the Hour' (2015) 57(4) *Journal of the Indian Law Institute* 499–522, 519.

154 Ibid 500.

155 Ibid 502.

156 Rob Langham, *Good Women Do Not Inherit Land: Politics of Land and Gender in India* (Routledge, 2017) 16, 17.

157 Sulagna Mookerjee, *Gender-Neutral Inheritance Laws: Family Structure and Women's Status in India Policy Research Working Paper* (World Bank, 2017) 2.

158 Ibid.

159 Debarati Halder and Jaishankar Karuppannan, 'Property Rights of Hindu Women: A Feminist Review of Succession Laws of Ancient, Medieval and Modern India' (2008–2009) 24(2) *Journal of Law and Medicine* 663–687, 685, 686.

160 *Indian Succession Act* 1882, s 59.

161 Ibid.

162 Lexis Nexis, *Halsbury's Laws of India: Wills and Succession*, Vol. 38 (LexisNexis, 2013).

163 Malcolm Voyce, Selda Dagistanli, Adam Possamai, Joshua Roose, Bryan Turner and Lisa Worthington, 'Islamic Inheritance and Sharia Wills: The Recognition of Muslim Inheritance Traditions in Australia' (2016) *Muslim Integration: Pluralism and Multiculturalism in New Zealand and Australia* 211–228.

164 *Special Marriage Act* 1954, s 21.

165 Archana Mishra, 'Vicissitudes of Women's Inheritance Right England Canada and India at the Dawn of 21st Century' (2016) 58 *Journal of the Indian Law Institute* 481–508, 492.

166 *Hindu Succession Act* 1956, s 8 read with Schedule I.

167 Ibid s 15.

168 *Indian Succession Act* 1925, s 29.

169 Ibid Chapter III.

170 Ibid Chapter II.

171 Ibid s 46, s 47.

172 Vrinda Narain, 'Muslim Women's Equality in India: Applying a Human Rights Framework' (2013) 35 *Human Rights Quarterly* 91–115.

173 Ibid.

174 Shivani Singhal, 'Women as Coparceners: Ramifications of the Amendment in the Hindu Succession Act' (2006) 30(2) *Cochin University Law Review* 238–257, 240.

175 *Hindu Succession Act* 1956, s 6.

176 Ibid.

177 *Hindu Succession Amendment Act* 2005.

178 *Hindu Succession Act* 1956, s 6.

179 General Recommendation 21, n 4, at [34].

180 Ibid.

181 The *CEDAW* Committee states in General Recommendation 29, n 5, at [52], that states parties are obligated to adopt laws relating to the making of wills that provide equal rights to women and men as testators, heirs and beneficiaries.

182 Daphna Hacker, 'The Gendered Dimensions of Inheritance: Empirical Food for Legal Thought' (2010) 7(2) *Journal of Empirical Legal Studies* 322–354, 346.

183 Ibid 346.
184 Ahmed Fekry Ibrahim, 'The Best Interests of the Child in Pre-Modern Islamic Juristic Discourse and Practice' (2015) 63(4) *American Journal of Comparative Law* 859–891, 864.
185 Klaus Deininger, Aparajita Goyal and Hari Nagarajan, *Inheritance Law Reform and Women's Access to Capital: Evidence from India's Hindu Succession Act* Policy Research Working Paper 5338 (World Bank, 2010).
186 The *CEDAW* Committee in General Recommendation 21(34), n 4, directs state party to implement the Economic and Social Council Resolution (884) which requires state party to ensure that 'men and women in the same degree of relationship to a deceased are entitled to equal shares in the estate and to equal rank in the order of succession.'
187 See, for example, UN Women, *Inheritance Laws for an Overview of Good Practice in Inheritance Legislation*. www.endvawnow.org/en/articles/1679-inheritance-laws.html Accessed 17/4/19.
188 Klaus Deininger, Aparajita Goyal and Hari Nagarajan, 'Women's Inheritance Rights and Intergenerational Transmission of Resources in India' (2013) 48 *Journal of Human Resources* 114–141, 137.
189 Langham, n 156, 16, 17.
190 Sulagna Mookerjee, *Gender-Neutral Inheritance Laws: Family Structure and Women's Status in India* Policy Research Working Paper (World Bank, 2017) 16, 19, 21.
191 Ibid 4.
192 Gopika Solanki, 'Beyond the Limitations of the Impasse: Feminism, Multiculturalism, and Legal Reforms in Religious Family Laws in India' (2013) 40(1) *Politikon* 83–111.

7

RIGHT TO POLITICAL REPRESENTATION AND PARTICIPATION

Introduction

This chapter focusses on women's right to equal political representation and participation in elected public office. India is a decentralised federation with a central government (the Union), 36 subnational state and territory governments and a three-tier local governance system known as the panchayat raj. It is a parliamentary democracy, with a strong multiparty political system.[1] Women have become increasingly active and influential in political life, marked by increased participation in voting since 2012,[2] political representation at the panchayat levels[3] and an increased input into decision-making and policy formulation.[4] The chapter assesses the extent to which women's human rights principles, particularly those articulated in article 7 of *CEDAW*, GR 23 of the *CEDAW* Committee on public and political life and women's human rights theories, particularly theories of public and private and principles of equality and non-discrimination, have been or could be utilised to advance the political representation and participation of women in three key areas. First, women's participation as voters, second, women's representation in elected public office at all levels of governance extending from the Union government to local panchayats where day-to-day administration occurs and, third, women's participation in decision-making, policy formulation and lawmaking once elected to public office. The full political representation and participation of women is a fundamental prerequisite for gender equality and genuine democracy.

The chapter begins in 7.2 by considering, in general terms, the obligations placed on India by article 7 of *CEDAW*, GR 23 and other international instruments to advance women's political representation and participation. Section 7.3 maps women's participation as voters. It explores the factors which influence and constrain women's ability to exercise their right to vote and reduce or increase the independence of the vote cast, particularly across lines of class, religion and caste. Section 7.4 maps women's (numerical) representation in elected public office at all levels of governance – Union, state and local. It sets out three solutions which we argue could increase women's representation, including electoral reform, political party reform and gender reservations at the Union and state levels. As an illustration, we showcase the introduction of reservations at the local panchayat level as an example of positive law reform based on women's human rights principles. Section 7.5 examines the extent to which women participate in decision-making, policy formulation and lawmaking once in public office. While harder to measure, research indicates that women are less likely to participate in decision-making and often hold and are given portfolios that involve less responsibility and lack training and skills in leadership.[5] We argue that enhanced participation could be achieved through creating gender-sensitive parliaments, training women members in various aspects of political office and providing child-care support and elderly care and support for household duties. Finally, section 7.6 examines women's representation in informal bodies of governance, such as caste panchayats and tribal councils, on which women have very low or non-existent representation, concluding that, in this context, women's political representation and participation is very weak. We argue, however, that literacy, education, training and strengthening women's political representation and participation at other levels of governance will eventually increase representation and participation in these communities.

Political representation and participation: obligations of human rights law

This section examines, in general terms, the obligations to advance women's political representation and participation created by key international conventions in the human rights framework, ratified and acceded to by India. According to the *Universal Declaration of Human Rights* 1948, everyone has the right to take part in the governance of her or his country.[6] The UN *Convention on the Political Rights of Women*, adopted on 31 March 1953 and acceded to by India in 1961, has three main components.[7] Article 1 states women are entitled to vote in all elections on equal terms with men, without any discrimination; article 2 states women shall be eligible for election to all publicly elected bodies established by national law on equal terms with men, without any discrimination and article 3 states women shall be entitled to hold public office and to exercise all public functions established by national law on equal terms with men. The *ICCPR* and the *ICESCR* provide general agreements on the right to equality between men and women in public and political life.[8]

Article 7 of *CEDAW* and GR 23 represent, however, the most developed statements on women's political representation and participation. The *CEDAW* Committee notes that *CEDAW* places 'special' importance on the participation of women in public life, emphasising that the 'just and effective organisation of society demands the inclusion and participation of all its members.'[9]

Article 7(a) of *CEDAW* obligates state parties to ensure that women have 'on equal terms with men the right to vote in all elections and public referenda.' The right to vote must be enjoyed both '*de jure* and *de facto*'.[10] The *CEDAW* Committee in GR 23 outlines some of the obstacles that women face in exercising their right to vote and in particular their right to vote for the person of their choice. Those obstacles include less access to information regarding candidates and party-political platforms, illiteracy, lack of knowledge and understanding of political systems and the impact of particular policies on their lives and their domestic burden and financial limitations, which may hinder them from following electoral campaigns and casting a vote on election day.[11] Moreover, traditions and cultural stereotypes of men's and women's roles in society may discourage women from exercising their right to vote, and important men in their lives may influence the votes they cast, particularly in relation to female candidates.[12] In GR 23(15), the *CEDAW* Committee states that 'while removal of *de jure* barriers is necessary, it is not enough to achieve full compliance with article 7'.[13] Put simply, this means that giving women the right to vote does not fully satisfy India's international obligations. Instead, India must work towards the removal of barriers that deny women full, informed and independent participation in the voting process.[14]

Article 7(a) of *CEDAW* states that state parties must ensure that women have the right to be eligible, on equal terms with men, for election to all publicly elected bodies, and article 7(b) obligates state parties to ensure that women have the right to hold public office. Together, these provisions mean that a right to run for election must be accompanied by measures that ensure women do, in practice, achieve equal representation in public office. This means that state parties must work towards the removal of barriers that prevent the equal representation of women at all levels of governance. Accordingly, the *CEDAW* Committee has recommended that state parties introduce temporary special measures in accordance with article 4(1) of *CEDAW* and GR 23 and GR 5 on temporary special measures as a means of achieving equal representation at all levels of governance. Temporary special measures can be utilised to implement gender reservations and to set candidate quotas in political parties.[15] Other temporary special measures recommended by the Committee to accelerate women's political participation include financial support for women for building campaign strategies and campaigning [16] and training to develop leadership and negotiation skills for women.[17]

Article 7(b) of *CEDAW* requires state parties to ensure that women, on equal terms with men, participate in the formulation and implementation of government policy and perform all public functions at all levels of government. This requires not just equal representation, but also equal participation once elected into public office. In GR 23(8), the *CEDAW* Committee notes that women are often excluded from top-ranking positions in the cabinet and in the civil service.

Once elected, women are rarely appointed to posts or given responsibilities in economic policy, political affairs, defence, conflict resolution or constitutional interpretation and determination.[18]

Women's participation as voters

Defining women's right to vote

Universal franchise (also known as universal suffrage) is the right of all adults, women and men, to vote in elections for seats in public office.[19] Women's right to vote is essential to achieving gender equality because 'the just and effective organisation of society demands the inclusion and participation of all its members,'[20] because women should participate in choosing those who will make the laws they are expected to obey and because research indicates female suffrage shifts public spending towards programs that benefit women. The right to vote, however, is a formal equality measure. It does not address barriers that prevent women from exercising their votes freely and in accord with their own informed political preferences. Universal franchise in elections to the Lok Sabha (Lower House or House of the People) and state parliaments was introduced across India through article 326 of the *Constitution of India* 1950 (Constitution). Article 326 provides 'elections to the House of the People and to the Legislative Assembly of every state shall be on the basis of adult suffrage; that is to say, every person who is a citizen of India and who is not less than 18 . . . shall be entitled to be registered as a voter at any such election.' Members of Rajya Sabha (the Upper House or the Council of States) are not elected by universal adult suffrage; rather, they are elected by the legislative assemblies of the various states. Given the low representation of women in the legislative assemblies, their right to vote for members of the Rajya Sabha is significantly limited. The Union Territories are governed by the Union Parliament, and there are no elections, except for Delhi and Pondicherry, where women have an equal right to vote. The panchayat raj system, establishing three levels of elected governance bodies within each state and union territory (except Delhi), was introduced by constitutional amendment in 1992 for all states and territories (except Delhi) having a population of over two million. From its inception, it adopted universal adult franchise. Additionally, the Supreme Court has held that the voter has the right to know the full particulars of a political candidate, including education, any criminal history and property owned.[21]

Applying women's human rights

Women have an equal right to vote in the election of seats to public office at all levels of governance as guaranteed by the Constitution. In the 2014 national election, voter participation was 66.38 percent (the highest since Independence), and female turnout was 65.6 percent, compared to a 67.09 percent turnout for men.[22] In the states, voter participation was similar. In some states, women's turnout marginally exceeded the turnout of men. In some states, male turnout decreased while female turnout increased.[23] Although women are voting in (almost) equal numbers as men, we view article 7(a) of *CEDAW*, which obligates state parties to ensure that women have 'on equal terms with men the right to vote in all elections and public referenda', as requiring more than numerical equality. It requires measures to ensure that all women exercise their right to vote, that women's votes are informed and that women are voting in accord with their own views and perspectives and without coercion or persuasion from others in their lives (such as husbands, brothers and fathers).[24]

We view compulsory voting as a means of increasing women's participation in voting. Gallego explains, 'Compulsory voting is the only institution that, by itself, can achieve near-universal voter turnout rates . . . [as a result, it is a way] to achieve equality in participation by getting voting participation close to its ceiling'.[25] This is a challenging goal in the Indian context for both legal and practical reasons. In *PUCL v. Union of India*, the court held that article 19 of the Constitution (the right to free expression) protects a right not to vote.[26] Mandatory voting, therefore, may be contrary to the Constitution. From a practical perspective, mandatory voting would pose further challenges. India has a huge population with widespread illiteracy, poverty and many people living transient lives. Compulsory voting would, consequently, place a huge monitoring burden on the election commission. Additionally, the election process does not currently provide for absentee voting. Physical presence at the voting booth is required, and, consequently, it can be difficult for voters living outside their constituency to vote. Penalising them in such circumstances would be unpopular.[27] Compulsory voting may also, according to some, increase the ability of goondas and those with power in society to coerce persons to vote in a particular way.[28] However, despite these challenges, we support it as an important goal, in accord with women's human rights standards, to work towards for the following reasons. Mandatory voting would raise women's participation in the voting process.[29] It would create opportunities and motivations for women to acquire or be exposed to political information and might result in higher rates of female engagement with the electoral process and its main actors, particularly political parties.[30]

There are other measures, in accord with women's human rights principles, which can be adopted to ensure that women cast informed votes. A number of platforms have emerged, particularly electronic, in local language which have rapidly increased access to information on voting and the political process. This is creating greater awareness of candidates and what they stand for and educating women about their political and electoral rights. Indeed, the proportion of women with no media exposure to the political process has dropped from 65 percent in 2009 to 39 percent in 2014. Coupled with a rise in literacy through increasing educational access and opportunity amongst women, the easier and more rapid spread of information can enhance informed voting amongst women. Additionally, supporting the electoral commission to ensure free, fair and violence-free elections can make it safer for women to vote.[31] While research indicates many women are influenced in their voting choices by men in their lives, providing women with rights and autonomy in all aspects of their lives is a fruitful strategy, in our view, for encouraging independent, informed voting.[32]

Women's representation in elected public office

Defining women's representation in elected public office

Representative democracy means a political system where members of the public are elected to represent the population. India is the largest representative democracy in the world. The three levels of governance have multiple elected public office positions that women can potentially hold. The Union has an elected president and an elected vice-president. The Rajya Sabha (the Upper House or the Council of States) has 250 members and is constituted through indirect election by state and territorial legislatures using single transferable votes. Additionally, the president can appoint up to 12 members for their contributions to art, literature, science and social services. Members of the Rajya Sabha sit for staggered six-year terms, with one third of members retiring every two years. The Lok Sabha (the Lower House or the House of the People) has a maximum of 552 members, constituted by direct election of up to 530 members to represent the states, up to 20 members to represent the Union Territories and not more than 2 members of the Anglo-Indian community to be nominated by the president, if, in her or his opinion, that community is not adequately represented. Members of the Lok Sabha sit for five years.

At the subnational level, the 29 states each have their own parliament. There is a bicameral legislature (the Vidhan Sabha and the Vidhan Parishad) in seven states[33] and a unicameral legislature (Vidhan Sabha) in the rest of the states. In total, there are over 4,120 representative seats in the states. Only Delhi and Pondicherry of the seven Union Territories have an elected parliament; the remaining are governed by the Union Parliament.

The lowest level of governance is the panchayat raj system (rule by village committee), which was formalised in 1992 through two constitutional amendments (the 73rd and 74th), based on the vision of Mahatma Gandhi, to devolve the highly centralised governance model by granting much greater local autonomy.[34] Although the panchayats have no law-making capacity, the intent was to create greater participation in local government by people and more effective implementation of rural development programmes.[35] The states were given one year to pass conformity acts either by amending existing laws or by passing entirely new laws in line with the 73rd amendment.

The three-tier panchayat raj system has elected governance bodies at the village, intermediate (block) and district levels. Direct elections for panchayats at all three levels are mandatory every five years. The village panchayats are at the base of the governance structure and are responsible for provision of public services in health, education, drinking water and roads, setting rates and local taxes, administration, formulation and implementation of local development plans and the selection of beneficiaries of central government–sponsored social and economic programmes. The intermediate (taluk or block) panchayat provides the link between the district and the village panchayats while the district panchayat is at the top of the tier, providing the link between the state government and the panchayats. There are direct elections to the panchayats at each level every five years. In total, there are approximately 13 lakh elected public office positions in panchayat raj institutions across the country.[36]

Applying women's human rights

In accord with article 7(a) of *CEDAW*, the Constitution gives women the right, on equal terms with men, to stand for election to all publicly elected positions, including the presidency.[37] However, as the *CEDAW* Committee explains in GR 23(16), state parties have an obligation to close the gap between the right to representation and the reality of women's representation. Equal representation of women in public office in both houses of the Union Parliament, in state parliaments and at the local level in districts and villages where day-to-day administration occurs is an important component of advancing women's human rights for the following reasons. First, it marks genuine substantive equality for women in accord with the general mandate of *CEDAW* and article 7. Second, research demonstrates that if women's participation in public office reaches 30 to 35 percent (generally termed 'critical mass'), there is often a significant impact on the outcomes of political and public processes, leading to policy shifts and legislative outputs that favour women's interests.[38] The priorities of women, research has indicated, are not just their own, but they are connected with children and community. Women are more willing to support the interests of other sectoral groups; to promote public goods and services such as clean water, improved schools, health and sanitation; to hold leaders to account and to support policies that assist children, the sick and the elderly.[39] Third, women bring specific areas of expertise to politics, especially on social issues such as welfare, education and health care.[40] Fourth, research suggests that more women in public office may increase trust in politicians; lower corruption; enhance pride, self-respect and solidarity amongst women and lessen discrimination against future women politicians.[41] It expands the voter's choices at the ballot box and leads to more inclusive, legitimate and diverse parliaments.[42] Fifth, economic, political and social development are dependent on the utilisation of all available resources. Women represent half the talent potential, and having them in public office increases the talent pool.[43] Finally, the representation of women from scheduled tribes and castes in public office can lead to major reversals of traditional gender and caste roles. Villagers may see a scheduled caste woman on a ceremonial dais providing her opinion and signing off on panchayat decisions or walking through the village to inspect works. A villager from an elite caste may have to visit the home of the *sarpanch*. This represents a significant social change in the life of the village. It increases contact and communication between groups that would not have previously had conversations and contact based on both gender and caste.[44]

However, women do not occupy positions of public office in equal numbers with men, particularly at the Union and state levels. In the Union Parliament in 2019, there are 64 female members in the Lok Sabha and 27 female members in the Rajya Sabha, a total of 11 percent. This is below the global average of women members of parliaments (both houses combined), which is 24 percent.[45] There are no significant differences between percentages in lower and upper houses – 23.9 percent and 24 percent, respectively India is ranked 151 out of 193 countries worldwide, and within Asia, India is ranked a low 13 out of 18 countries for female representation in the central parliament.[46] The representation of women is even lower in state and territory parliaments. As of 2019, only 9 percent of the unicameral state assembly members are women. The states of Bihar, Haryana and Rajasthan have the highest share of women in their respective state assemblies at 14 percent each. There is, however, no female representation in the state assemblies of Mizoram, Nagaland and Pondicherry.[47] In the panchayat system, reservations of one third of seats for women have resulted in a much higher representation of women although the reservation is not always fulfilled. Indeed, overall, women hold 46 percent of panchayat seats.

The obligation of state parties to *CEDAW* to actively seek substantive equality means that measures to ensure actual equal representation of women are required. Reservations in the panchayat raj system provide an illustration of how women's human rights principles can be utilised to lead to positive law reform. Reservations are recommended by article 4(1) on temporary special measures of *CEDAW* and by the *CEDAW* Committee in GR 23(15) as a means of increasing women's political representation at all levels of governance.[48]

TABLE 7.1 Women's Representation in Elected Public Office: 2018

Level of government	*Position*	*Total*	*Women*	*Women as % of total*
National	Lok Sabha Parliamentarian	542	64	11.8%
	Rajya Sabha Parliamentarian	245	27	11%
	Total	787	91	11.4%
	Cabinet Minister	25	5	18.5%
State and Territory	Parliamentarian			9.%
State and Territory	Chief Ministers	36	3	8.3%
Panchayat	Members	2,950,128	1,355,425	46%

BOX 7.1 EXAMPLE: RESERVATIONS IN PANCHAYAT SYSTEM

In response to a growing and forceful women's movement, the Union Parliament established a separate department for women in 1989. Significant pressure was placed on parliament to respond to the very low representation of women in public office in rural areas, which was 4.5 percent. Subsequently, in 1992, when the 73rd amendment to the Constitution established the framework of a three-tiered panchayat system with regular elections throughout India, 33 percent of seats were reserved for women to be directly elected. When the reserved seats were first introduced, many were not filled. However, there are now a total of approximately 13 lakh elected public office positions in panchayat raj institutions across the country, and in 2019, women hold 46 percent of those positions. Five states have increased the proportion of reserved seats to 50 percent. Bihar was the first state to do so in 2006 and was followed by Chhattisgarh, Madhya Pradesh, Rajasthan and Himachal Pradesh. Sikkim has raised it to 40 percent. There is also a (randomly applied) reservation of one third of village council headships for women. Of the 28 states whose data on elected representatives in panchayat raj institutions is available, 14 states have equal representation of women and men. In 7 states, the share of women is more than 50 percent, including 59 percent in Jharkhand and 58 percent in Uttarakhand and Rajasthan. Only in 3 states – Jammu and Kashmir (29 percent), Daman and Diu (29 percent) and Punjab (30 percent) – is the representation of women less than one third.[49] The example of the panchayat reservations illustrates that equality in representation can be achieved through the use of gender reservations.

Source: Authors

We propose, as illustrative examples, three further strategies to increase the representation of women in public office based on women's human rights principles. The first is electoral reform, the second is political party reform and the third is extension of reservations to the Union and state and territory parliaments and enhancement of the reservation system at the panchayat level.

BOX 7.2 TYPES OF ELECTORAL SYSTEMS

Plurality electoral system

Also called 'first past the post', this system awards a seat to the individual candidate who receives the most votes in an election. The candidate does not require a majority (50 percent +) of the vote to win. India uses this for election to the Lok Sabha and state parliaments.

Majority electoral system

This system requires that candidates receive a majority of votes in order to win (50 percent plus one vote). If no candidate gets a majority of votes, then a second round of voting is held (often a week or so after the initial ballot), where typically only a select number of candidates from the first round participate. Austria, Finland, Portugal, Russia and other east European states, as well as presidential and National Assembly elections in France, use this system.

Source: Authors

BOX 7.3 PROPORTIONAL REPRESENTATION ELECTORAL SYSTEM

This is the general name for voting systems that align the percentage of elected candidates with the percentage of votes that they received in the election. There are a number of methods for achieving proportional representation:

Party List: Voters vote for parties rather than for individual candidates

- **closed party list system** is where voters vote for a particular party, and then the party decide which party members will actually serve as representatives.
- **open party list system** is where voters are given some degree of choice among individual candidates, in addition to voting for entire parties (Denmark, Finland, Italy, Luxembourg and Switzerland).

Single transferable vote: Individual voters rank candidates according to their firsts choice, second choice, third choice etc. Rather than simply voting for a single candidate, voters have the opportunity to express a range of preferences for several candidates on the ballot. In various forms, it is used widely in many countries, although only Ireland, Australia and Malta use it in national elections. India uses this system for election to the Rajya Sabha.

Source: Authors

Electoral system reform

Electoral systems consist of sets of rules that govern all aspects of the voting process: when elections occur, who is allowed to vote, who can stand as a candidate, how votes are marked and cast, how votes are counted, limits on campaign spending and other factors that can affect the outcome. Electoral systems are typically broadly defined by a country's constitution while electoral legislation sets out the required detail. Electoral commissions are usually established to conduct elections. Different types of elections can be used for different levels of public office.

Electoral systems have a direct impact on women's representation in elected public office. They determine who gains power, how power will be shared and the nature of representation in any system of governance.

A plurality 'first-past-the-post system' is generally considered the least favourable electoral system for women's representation. One candidate from each party contests each seat. If a man and a woman candidate compete for a party's nomination, a victory for the woman means a loss for the man. When nominating candidates for an election in single-member districts, political parties usually put up the 'most broadly acceptable' candidate, and that candidate is less likely to be a woman or visible minority.[50] Research also shows that an incumbent has a far greater chance of re-election, and, therefore, a 'first-past-the-post' system, where men already hold the majority of seats, is unlikely to yield successful challenges by women candidates.[51]

India has a 'first-past-the-post' plurality electoral system for the Lok Sabha and state parliaments which allows for the nomination of only one candidate per district, and political parties overwhelmingly choose male candidates. We support, instead, a proportional representation system for the Lok Sabha and state parliaments, in accord with research that consistently shows that such a system leads to greater representation of minority interests, a much higher representation of women in parliaments[52] and a much higher voter turnout.[53] Proportional representation can support greater representation of women because political parties can be encouraged (or directed) to craft either a balanced party list or a party list that alternates women and men, and because they do not have to choose individual candidates for specific seats. Therefore, the bias towards male candidates is removed, reflecting the wide range of interests and the social and demographical make-up of the wider society, appealing to a wider spectrum of voters' interests.[54]

India has a proportional representation system for the Rajya Sabha. However, the single transferable vote system utilised achieves proportional representation through ranked voting in each state. A voter has a single vote that is initially allocated to their most preferred candidate. If their candidate achieves one fourth of the total number of votes plus one, he or she is elected, and if not, any surplus vote is transferred to the second-choice candidate. There is no mechanism to ensure the equal representation of women. We recommend advocating for the introduction of some form of gender reservation for election to the Rajya Sabha and the introduction of a proportional representation system for the Lok Sabha. Another option recommended by the *CEDAW* Committee and possibly as effective is political party reform.

Political party reform

A political party is an organised group of people with similar political aims and opinions that seeks to influence public law and policy by the election of its candidates to public office. In most democratic countries, including India, most candidates are elected from political parties. Political parties are, therefore, major 'gatekeepers' in determining the candidates for election to public office.

India has a number of political parties that contest Union and state seats. In 2019, the Bharatiya Janata Party (BJP), a religious, right-leaning party, is the current ruling party, with approximately 31 percent of the vote at the last election. The Indian National Congress (Congress), a centrist party, is the main opposition party, with approximately 19 percent of the vote at the last election. Other parties include the Janata Party, a centrist party, and the Communist Party of India (CPM), a left-leaning party. There are numerous smaller parties.[55]

Neither the BJP nor the Congress offers significant numbers of women candidates for election – approximately 10 percent – directly correlating to the low numbers of women in the Union and state parliaments. While political parties often nominate women for unwinnable seats, both major parties did nominate women for winnable seats in the last election. Notably, however, those women were strong candidates, based on their previous political experience.[56] Strategic action is required to ensure that women's presence in the Union and state parliaments is increased and promoted by party organisations.[57] In general, the process of determining candidates is as follows: parties draw up an initial short list of two to five candidates from each constituency and then embark on information-gathering exercises, including third-party voter surveys, to assess candidate quality. The main candidate quality emphasised by all parties is the ability to win the election, termed 'winnability' in Indian politics. To this end, several metrics, including the candidate's name recognition within the constituency, service to the party, financial resources, caste identity and internal party support are considered relevant. Interestingly, research suggests that very few party leaders believe that women voters are more likely to vote for women candidates, although several expressed the view that women were less interested in politics than men and that a political career was not attractive to women.[58] We recommend three areas for the reform of political parties to facilitate greater representation of women.

First, more women must be encouraged and invited to join political parties. Some political parties have women's wings which have proven successful at attracting more women membership. The Mahila (Women's) Congress, established in 1983, is the women's wing of the Congress Party; BJP Mahila Morcha is the women's wing of the Bharatiya Janata Party and Shiv Sena, an Indian far-right regional political party based in Mumbai, also has a women's wing. We support the mandatory establishment of women's wings that work on strengthening political party electoral strategies, particularly by integrating into a party platform a specific commitment to gender equality or a policy perspective that aims to strengthen women's rights or better respond to their needs. Women's wings can be a powerful means of differentiating a party platform from those of others. It can also make the party more attractive to an increasing share of voters who believe that gender equality is important. In India, women make up more than 50 percent of the voting population, and with the growth of competitive party politics, parties have increasingly sought women's votes, often by appealing to their interests and addressing their concerns in party manifestos. Women's wings are a potentially powerful tool by which to reach out to female members of its electorate and increase female membership. The parties should recognise that women are often perceived as more credible on key social issues and use this as a way to expand their political platforms and party lists.[59]

Second, we support legislated candidate reservations as a concrete means to increase women's representation within political parties. Men are often viewed as aligned with public life and therefore more viable as candidates while women are viewed as being more suited to the private domestic realm of home and family.[60] Even when women possess the 'masculine' characteristics that are perceived as necessary to be a political candidate, they often are not encouraged to step forward even when they perform well at the panchayat level.[61] Women are also less likely to present themselves as candidates, often seeing themselves as lacking the skills necessary to perform well in politics. The division between the public and private clearly evidenced in the political party system must be challenged.

A candidate quota means that each political party must have a minimum percentage or number of women candidates. Financial penalties can be imposed on parties that fail to meet this obligation. In Spain, lists of candidates put forward for elections must have a balanced proportion of women and men so that candidates of either sex make up at least 40 per 100 of total membership.[62] This approach does not necessarily lead to more women in elected positions as they still must receive enough votes to win the seat. If India were to transition to a proportional representation approach of election to the Lok Sabha and state parliaments, we recommend a 'closed list' system (where voters select a political party list rather than an individual candidate), coupled with a 'zipper list' (where male and female candidates are alternated on the list), which can yield positive results for the election of women.[63] East Timor, for example, which requires that on electoral lists one out of every group of three candidates must be a woman, now has 38 percent women in the national parliament.[64]

A final reform strategy is to ensure that women candidates have access to sufficient funding and resources to support their campaigns for election. A key obstacle to increasing women's participation in political affairs is unequal access to party resources. Even after selection as candidates, women seeking election to public office can be constrained by lack of financial support and time for campaigning because of difficulties in finding childcare, balancing family and public life, lack of confidence about relevant skills and fewer connections to politically relevant networks.

Reserved seats in Union and state parliaments

Reserving seats for women in the Union and state parliaments is in accord with the recommendations of the *CEDAW* Committee and India's international obligations more generally. Indeed, the *CEDAW* Committee has urged India to enact the Women's Reservation Bill (108th amendment), which was introduced in the Union Parliament to reserve 33 percent of Lok Sabha and Vidhan Sabha seats for women. The proposal in the bill was to reserve the seats in rotation, which would be determined by drawing lots in such a way that a particular seat would be reserved only once in three consecutive general elections. While the Rajya Sabha passed the bill on 9 March 2010, the Lok Sabha never voted on the bill. The bill subsequently lapsed after the dissolution of the 15th Lok Sabha in 2014. Although the enactment of the bill and the reservation of seats for women are in accord with women's human rights principles, it was by the major political parties, which do not want to cede their power. Opponents argue that it would perpetuate the unequal status of women since they would not be perceived to be competing on merit; however, it is hard to sustain the argument that the current system of election is based on merit, given the lack of women representatives despite their evident capacity.[65] Others argue that at the local-level political bosses regularly compel their wives, sisters and daughters to contest reserved seats. National politicians would duplicate this strategy, and the women entering politics would be mere fronts for male power.[66]

We support the reservation of seats for women in the Union and state parliaments. We also support a reservation in the Rajya Sabha. There are different models of reserved seats other than that proposed in the Women's Reservation Bill that could be adopted. Seats can be reserved for women based on a geographic distribution. For example, in Afghanistan, 2 seats in the lower house are reserved for women in each of the 34 provinces of the country, resulting in 68 of the 249 total seats (27 percent).[67] Seats can be reserved to broadly represent women throughout the country. For example, in Bangladesh, of the 350 seats in parliament, 50 are reserved for women.[68] There are also diverse ways by which reserved seats can be filled. They may be selected by the political parties, depending on the proportion of seats won by each party. For example, in Bangladesh, the 50 total reserved seats are distributed between parties based on the proportion of seats they win in the parliament. Another approach is to fill the reserved seats with the women who received the highest number of votes. For example, in Samoa, 10 percent of seats are reserved for women, and if that quota is not met through the election process, the women candidates who received the most votes will become additional members.[69]

Women's participation in policy and lawmaking

Defining women's participation in policy and lawmaking

Equal participation in public office requires the active, independent and full participation of women in all aspects of the role, including policy formulation, lawmaking and other decision-making. Many factors limit the full and equal participation of women once they are in public office. First, caste and class restrict the role that women can play in decision-making once they enter public office because of the history of discrimination against women of low caste and class.[70] Second, a general view of women as lacking the skills seen as integral to the design and delivery of services may make it hard for them to be active in decision-making. It may also mean they are not entrusted with responsibility, included in the cabinet or placed on committees.[71] Third, the lack of exposure of women themselves to politics and the lack of any experience in exercising their political responsibilities may limit their capacity to engage in the process.[72] Fourth, low literacy levels, absence of education and limited or no exposure all may lead to a lack of confidence to volunteer for working groups or greater responsibility.[73]

Applying women's human rights principles

While achieving the equal representation of women in public office is important, it is insufficient to satisfy article 7(b) of *CEDAW*, which requires state parties to ensure that women, on equal terms with men, participate in the formulation and implementation of government policy and perform all public functions at all levels of government. Indeed, there is evidence that women, once elected into public office, often do not participate equally. For example, of the 25 cabinet ministers in the Union Parliament, only 7 are women holding portfolios. The portfolios they hold are External Affairs Overseas Indian Affairs, Human Resource Development, Minority Affairs, Women and Child Development, Food Processing Industries, State for Commerce and Industry (Independent Charge) and Finance Corporate Affairs and Water Resources, River Development and Ganga Rejuvenation. With exception of External Affairs Overseas Indian Affairs, these portfolios could be categorised as 'soft' and with lower levels of responsibility and prestige.[74] Women are often given 'soft' portfolios handling domestic and social issues, while men dominate 'hard' committees and are given 'hard' portfolios, such as economics and defence. With women already underrepresented in nearly all legislatures, this additional distortion leads to their stark absence from central areas of decision-making. Decisions about budgets or foreign policy affect both sexes but are made disproportionately by men.[75]

The gender reservation in the panchayat raj system, which has achieved a 46 percent representation of women, provides an illustrative example of how equal representation may not amount to equal participation. Following the introduction of reserved seats on the panchayats, 800,000 women were suddenly brought into politics, and many were unprepared for leadership.[76] Research reveals the elected women were less able to deal with local officials, to hold officials to account, to be transparent in the selection of beneficiaries and to take care of local problems.[77] They had a low attendance at meetings compared to men[78] and low levels of knowledge and understanding of national laws, panchayat laws, rural development programmes and social problems.[79] Over the period from the introduction of the reserved seats in 1996, however, that situation has dramatically shifted in some communities. Resonating with Fredman's theory of participative approaches to substantive equality, women serving as panchayat members have reported growing enhancement of their status amongst the community.[80] For example, 72 percent of female members of panchayats in Madhya Pradesh and 90 percent of female members in panchayats in Rajasthan report an increase in status.[81] As well as an increase in status, the contribution of women to the governance of their villages has dramatically increased over the time period as they have gained skills, experience, confidence and capacity.[82] Further, the increased representation of women in panchayats correlates positively and significantly with investments in primary school amenities and teacher quality and quantity,[83] and other research has found that women who sit on panchayats are significantly more likely to participate in politics in a variety of ways.[84] Gender reservations may, therefore, be best approached as a long-term strategy which takes time to increase the genuine participation of women.[85]

Making parliaments and panchayats 'gender sensitive' is an approach to enhancing women's political participation.[86] A gender-sensitive political body responds to the needs and interests of both men and women in its composition, structures, operations, methods and work.[87] The environment of political institutions is often not 'gender friendly' and deters many women from entering and, if they do, succeeding as members. It operates around a set of standardised rules, operating procedures and institutional facilities that may make it difficult for women members to function effectively, including late-night schedules and sitting times making it difficult for women who have domestic responsibilities, particularly when no childcare is provided to juggle family and domestic responsibilities.[88] Further, if the parliament is a long distance away (the Union Parliament, for example, sits in Delhi), this may be prohibitive for many women, particularly because travelling and staying alone is considered unsuitable and unsafe.[89]

A gender-sensitive parliament or panchayat is one in which there are no barriers – substantive, structural or cultural – to women's full participation and to equality between its men and women members and staff. It is not only a place where women can work, but also one where women want to work and contribute. A gender-sensitive parliament sets a positive example by promoting gender equality and women's empowerment within society, both nationally and internationally. Solutions could include sittings for shorter periods, no late-night sessions and the provision of childcare.

Other governance bodies

In both rural and urban settings, there are other governance bodies, some unregulated by the state, where women's representation is very low or non-existent. Two such bodies include the caste panchayats, which operate in both urban and rural areas, and councils, which operate in tribal communities, typically one in each village. Each caste has its own caste association, some more formal than others, consisting of elders from a rural village or an area in a larger urban center. The caste panchayats are informal, unelected and unregulated by the state.[90] They operate alongside and separate from the panchayat system established by law.[91] Although they do not have any official government recognition or authority, caste panchayats exert significant social influence within the community they represent. It is primarily a men's assembly where women are not able to participate, although there some evidence of an increasing women's presence in some areas.[92] Caste panchayats use customary rules (and sometimes their own discretion) to determine disputes and issues, decide what evidence is required and the quantum and mode of punishment which may deliver outcomes even further from international norms and outside any possible system of monitoring.[93]

Village councils in tribal communities do have authority in law to govern their communities in relation to personal laws in accord with customary law and traditional practices.[94] They do not have authority to govern in relation to other aspects of law, such as criminal law.[95] They vary throughout India and are largely undocumented; however, indications are that they do not operate within the formal law or international norms.[96] In Northeast India, for example, research indicates that despite the contribution of women to the economy, they do not find their space and voice in the traditional village councils.[97]

BOX 7.4 CASE STUDY: TRIBAL COMMUNITIES IN MANIPUR

We visited 16 tribal communities in Manipur in 2016 as part of a broader project on customary systems of law operating in tribal communities across India. In each of these communities, a council – sometimes elected, sometimes appointed by the chief, sometimes hereditary – operated to manage a range of governance issues in each community. There were no women represented on any of the village councils that we visited. In all the communities visited, the tribal council administered customary law and practices and made other governance decisions regarding life in the community, including family matters such as marriage, divorce and inheritance and criminal matters such as theft, violence and even murder. Several communities we visited had written codes of the customary law they administered. For example, the *Piate Customary Law and Practices* (2nd amendment 2013) is a written code of the customary law used in 12 ethnic groups in the Lamka region in the state of Manipur. It states in Section 28 that 'It is the duty of the Chief and his Village Council to look after the general welfare of the villagers, mode of earning their livelihood and the preservation of the village land in general. In particular, the Council must allocate sites for building dwelling houses and jhum field among the villagers, make and amend rules and laws for the administration of the village, and hear and adjudicate on cases and problems of those who violate the village rules in accordance with customary laws'. In these communities, formal law was rarely accessed, although the *Piate Code* states 'the parties are at liberty to file suits to the government courts of the village (panchayat) courts.' There was no evidence of connection to or with the formal panchayat system.

Source: Authors

Conclusion

This chapter has focussed on women's right to political representation and participation in elected public office. Although women have become increasingly active and influential in India's political life, the gendered division between public and private life continues to restrict women's participation in political life. Women continue to be located primarily in the domestic sphere, bearing the burden of their reproductive and family life roles, while being confronted with a view that they are unsuited to public life, sometimes amounting to active discouragement and without access to training, support, skills and resources. The introduction of gender reservations at the local panchayat level is, however, an example of positive law reform based on women's human rights principles, which can operate to transform gender relations. The increasing skill and confidence of elected women on panchayats over a period of time has showcased women's capacity to dismantle the divide between the private and the public and to take an active role in the governance of India.

Notes

1 Mudit Kapoor and Shamika Ravi, 'Women Voters in Indian Democracy: A Silent Revolution' (2014) 49(12) *Economic and Political Weekly* 63–67, 63, 64.
2 Election Commission of India, 'Electoral Roll Data: 2013'. https://eci.gov.in/ Accessed 17/4/19.
3 Ashok Kumar, 'Elected Tribal Women Representatives in Panchayati Raj Institutions in Karnataka: A Study of Mysore District' (2018) 2(7) *International Journal in Advances in Social Sciences and Humanities* 7–11.
4 P. Sindhuja and Kurunathan R. Murugan, 'A Gender Perspective on Role Performance of Elected Panchayat Leaders in India' (2018) 19(3) *Journal of International Women's Studies* 199–214.
5 Tiffany Barnes and Diana O'Brien, 'Defending the Realms: The Appointment of Women Defense Ministers Worldwide' (2018) 62(2) *American Journal of Political Science* 355–368; Amy Alewxander and Farida Jalaalzai, 'Symbolic Empowerment and Female Heads of States and Government: A Global, Multi-Level Analysis' in *Politics Groups and Identities* (Routledge, 2018) 1–20; Maria Escobar-Lemon and Michelle Taylor-Robinson, *Women in Presidential Cabinets: Power Players or Abundant Tokens?* (Oxford University Press, 2016).
6 *Universal Declaration of Human Rights* 1948, Article 2.
7 *Convention on the Political Rights of Women* 1953 (United Nations Treaty Series Vol 193).
8 See, for example, General Comments 25, 28, and 34 of the Human Rights Committee; General Comments 16 and 20 of the Economic, Social and Cultural Rights Committee.

In particular, article 25 of the ICCPR states: 'Every citizen shall have the right and the opportunity, without any of the distinctions mentioned in article 2 and without reasonable restrictions: a) To take part in the conduct of public affairs, directly or through freely chosen representatives; b) To vote and to be elected at genuine periodic elections which shall be by universal and equal suffrage and shall be held by secret ballot, guaranteeing the free expression of the will of the electors; c) To have access, on general terms of equality, to public service in his country'.

9 *CEDAW* Committee, General Recommendation 23: *Women in Public Life* 1997 (UN Doc A/52/38/REV.1) at [13].

10 General Recommendation 23, n 9, at [18].

11 Ibid at [20].

12 *CEDAW* Committee, General Recommendation 5: *Temporary Special Measures* 1988 (UN Doc A/43/38).

13 General Recommendation 23, n 9, at [15].

14 Tiffany Barnes and Diana Z. O'Brien, 'Defending the Realm: The Appointment of Female Defense Ministers Worldwide' (2018) 62(2) *American Journal of Political Science* 355–368, 356; Amy C. Alexander and Farida Jalalzai, 'Symbolic Empowerment and Female Heads of States and Government: A Global, Multilevel Analysis' (2018) (1) *Politics, Groups, and Identities*; Maria Escobar-Lemmon and Michelle M. Taylor-Robinson, *Women in Presidential Cabinets: Power Players or Abun-Dant Tokens?* (Oxford University Press, 2016).

15 Concluding Observations of the CEDAW Committee: Germany (2017) 66th Session at [32] (UN Doc CEDAW/C/DEU/CO/7-8); Bhutan (2016) 65th Session at [23] (UN Doc CEDAW/C/BTN/CO/8-9); Federated States of Micronesia (2017) 66th Session at [31] (UN Doc CEDAW/C/FSM/CO/1-3); Philippines (2016) 65th Session at [32] (UN Doc CEDAW/C/PHL/CO/7-8).

16 Concluding Observations of the CEDAW Committee: Argentina (2016) 65th Session at [27] (UN Doc CEDAW/C/ARG/CO/7); Aremenia (2016) 65th Session at [20] (UN Doc CEDAW/C/ARM/CO5-6).

17 Concluding Observations of the CEDAW Committee: Ukraine (2017) 66th Session at [33] (UN Doc CEDAW/C/UKR/CO/8); Rwanda (2017) 66th Session at [31] (UN Doc CEDAW/C/RWA/CO/7-9); Concluding Observations of the CEDAW Committee: Jordan (2017) 66th Session at [38] (UN Doc CEDAW/C/JOR/CO/6).

18 General Recommendation 23, n 9, at [30].

19 Suffrage has been achieved in most countries worldwide. Exceptions include Lebanon (partial), Brunei (no one can vote) and the Vatican City.

20 General Recommendation 23, n 9, at [13].

21 *Union of India v. Association for Democratic Reforms and Another* (2001) Civil Appeal No 7178 of 2001.

22 Electoral Commission of India. https://eci.gov.in/files/category/97-general-election-2014/ Accessed 18/4/19.

23 Ibid.

24 Françoise Gaspard, 'Unfinished Battles: Political and Public Life' in Hanna Beate Schöpp-Schilling and Cees Flinterman (eds.), *The Circle of Empowerment: Twenty-Five Years of the UN Committee on the Elimination of Discrimination against Women* (Feminist Press at the City University of New York, 2007) 145–153, 148.

25 Aina Gallego, *Unequal Political Participation Worldwide* (Cambridge University Press, 2015) 50–51; Abdurashid Solijonov, *Voter Turnout Trends around the World* (IDEA, 2016) 37. www.idea.int/sites/default/files/publications/voter-turnout-trends-around-the-world.pdf Accessed 17/4/19; Abby Córdova and Gabriela Rangel, 'Addressing the Gender Gap: The Effect of Compulsory Voting on Women's Electoral Engagement' (2017) 50(2) *Comparative Political Studies* 264–290.

26 *People's Union of Civil Liberties v. India* (2003) Writ Petition (civil) 490 of 2002 SC.

27 Gopal K. Kadekodi and Shiddalingaswami V. Hangodimath, 'Does Development Motivate More to Vote?' (2015) 50(18) *Economic and Political Weekly* 47–57, 52.

28 Ahmed Usman, Shabbir Hussain and Muhammad Usman, 'Caste and Character of Candidates, Political Patronage and Voting Behavior in India' (2017) 3(2) *Journal of Indian Studies* 89–94, 92.
29 Abby Córdova and Gabriela Rangel, 'Addressing the Gender Gap: The Effect of Compulsory Voting on Women's Electoral Engagement' (2017) 50(2) *Comparative Political Studies* 264–290.
30 Sarah Birch, *Full Participation. A Comparative Study of Compulsory Voting* (Manchester University Press, 2016).
31 Praveen Rai, 'Electoral Participation of Women in India: Key Determinants and Barriers' (2011) 46(3) *Economic and Political Weekly* 47–55, 51.
32 Sanjay Jumar and Pranav Gupta, 'Changing Patterns of Women's Turnout in Indian Elections' (2015) 3(1) *Studies in Indian Politics* 7–18, 11.
33 The seven Union Territories are Delhi, Pondicherry, Daman and Diu, Dacra and Nagar, Chandigarh, Lakshadweep and Andaman and Nicobar Islands.
34 Mangesh Nadkarni, N. Sivanna and Lavanya Suresh, *Decentralised Democracy in India: Gandhi's Vision and Reality* (Routledge, 2017)1–4.
35 Ibid.
36 Yatindra Singh Sisodia, *Functioning of Panchayat Raj System* (Rawat Publications, 2005).
37 *Constitution of India* 1950, art 58 (1): No person shall be eligible for election as President unless he – (a) is a citizen of India, (b) has completed the age of thirty-five years, and (c) is qualified for election as a member of the House of the People.
38 The *CEDAW* Committee in General Recommendation 23(16) nominates 30 to 35 percent as the critical point of representation and the Beijing Conference set a benchmark of 30 percent. See the discussion on critical mass in Diana O'Brien and Johanna Rickne, 'Gender Quotas and Women's Political Leadership' (2016) 110(1) *American Political Science Review* 112–126, 113.
39 Klaus Deininger, Songqing Jin, Hari Nagarajan and Fang Xia, 'Does Female Reservation Affect Long-Term Political Outcomes? Evidence from Rural India' (2015) 51(1) *Journal of Development Studies* 32, 33–49, 39, 40; Louise Edwards and Mina Roces, *Women's Suffrage in Asia: Gender, Nationalism and Democracy* (Routledge, Oxford, 2004) 1.
40 Irma Clots-Figueras, 'Women in Politics: Evidence from the Indian States' (2011) 95(7–8) *Journal of Public Economics* 664–690.
41 Anne Marie Goetz, 'Political Cleaners: Women as the New Anti-Corruption Force?' (2007) 38(1) *Development and Change* 87–105.
42 Deininger et al., n 40, 32, 34.
43 Pamela Paxton and Melanie Hughes, *Women, Politics, and Power: A Global Perspective* (CQ Press, 2015) 16.
44 Simon Chauchard, 'Can Descriptive Representation Change Beliefs about a Stigmatized Group? Evidence from Rural India' (2014) 108(2) *American Political Science Review* 1–20, 3, 7.
45 As at September 2018 Women in National Parliaments. http://archive.ipu.org/wmn-e/arc/classif010918.htm Accessed 17/4/19.
46 Ibid.
47 Ministry of Panchayat Raj, *Women and Men in India*, 2016. www.mospi.gov.in/sites/default/files/reports_and_publication/statistical_publication/social_statistics/WM16 Chapter5.pdf Accessed 17/4/19.
48 Concluding Observations of the CEDAW Committee: Germany (2017) 66th Session at [32] (UN Doc CEDAW/C/DEU/CO/7-8); Bhutan (2016) 65th Session at [23] (UN Doc CEDAW/C/BTN/CO/8-9).
49 Ministry of Panchayat Raj, n 47.
50 Katrine Beauregard, 'Gender, Political Participation and Electoral Systems: A Cross-National Analysis' (2014) 53(3) *European Journal of Political Research* 617–634.
51 Leslie Swhwindt, Michael Malecki and Brian Crisp, 'Candidate Gender and Electoral Success in Single Transferable Vote Systems' (2010) 40(3) *British Journal of Political Science* 693–709, 696.

52 Jennifer Curtin, 'Women and Proportional Representation in Australia and New Zealand' (2003) 22(1) *Policy and Society* 48–68, 52.
53 Tracy-Ann Johnson-Myers, *The Mixed Member Proportional System: Providing Greater Representation for Women? A Case Study of the New Zealand Experience* (Springer, 2017).
54 Pippa Norris, 'The Impact of Electoral Reform on Women's Political Representation' (2006) 41(2) *Acta Politica* 197–213.
55 Smaller parties include the Bahujan Samaj Party, which won 4 percent vote share but did not win any parliament seats. Note that in May 2019, there are national elections which will change the party landscape.
56 Carole Spary, 'Women Candidates and Party Nomination Trends in India: Evidence from the 2009 General Election' (2014) 52(1) *Commonwealth and Comparative Politics* 109–138, 119.
57 Jennifer Curtin, 'Women and Proportional Representation in Australia and New Zealand' (2003) 22(1) *Policy and Society* 48–68.
58 Sonia Bhalotra, Irma Clots-Figueras and Lakshmi Iyer, *Path-Breakers: How Does Women's Political Participation Respond to Electoral Success?* IZA Discussion Paper No 7771 2013. https://ssrn.com/abstract=23632727 Accessed 17/4/19.
59 Amrita Basu, *Women, Political Parties and Social Movements in South Asia*, UNRISD Occasional Paper, No 5, 2005.
60 Mona Lena Krook and Pippa Norris, 'Beyond Quotas: Strategies to Promote Gender Equality in Elected Office' (2014) 62(1) *Political Studies* 2–20, 4.
61 Spary, n 56, 132.
62 *Organic Law on Regime of General Elections*, art 44(1).
63 Blanca Delgado-Márquez, Adolfo López-Carmona and Victoriano Ramírez-González, 'Ensuring Parliamentary Gender Equality through a New Zipper Method: An Application to Finland' (2014) 116(2) *Social Indicators Research* 475–492.
64 *Law on the Elections of the National Parliament* 2006, art 12(3).
65 Shirin Rai, 'Democratic Institutions, Political Representation and Women's Empowerment: The Quota Debate in India' (1999) 6(3) *Democratization* 84–99, 94.
66 Mala Htun, 'Is Gender like Ethnicity? The Political Representation of Identity Groups' (2004) 2(3) *Perspectives on Politics* 439–458, 448.
67 *Constitution of Afghanistan* 2004, art 84.
68 *Constitution of Bangladesh* 1972, art 65 (3A).
69 *Constitution of the Independent State of Samoa* 1960, art 44, as amended by the *Constitution Amendment Act* 2013.
70 Nethra Palaniswamy, Ramya Parthasarathy and Vijayendra Rao, 'Unheard Voices: The Challenge of Inducing Women's Civic Speech' (2019) 115 *World Development* 64–77, 68.
71 Srilatha Batliwala, 'Transforming of Political Culture: Mahila Samakhya Experience' (1996) 31(21) *Economic and Political Weekly* 1248–1251, 1248.
72 Farzana Afridi, Vegard Iversen and M. R. Sharan, 'Women Political Leaders, Corruption, and Learning: Evidence from a Large Public Program in India' (2017) 66(1) *Economic Development and Cultural Change* 1–30, 27.
73 Anuradha Kumari, Sourabh Dubey and Udham Gautam, 'What Hinders the Elected Women Village Panchayat Members in Their Role Performance?' (2016) 11(1) *Journal of Community Mobilization and Sustainable Development* 61–65.
74 Rainbow Murray and Réjane Sénac, 'Explaining Gender Gaps in Legislative Committees' (2018) 39(3) *Journal of Women, Politics and Policy* 310–335; Praveen Rai, 'Women's Participation in Electoral Politics in India: Silent Feminisation' (2017) 37(1) *South Asia Research* 58–77, 73.
75 Ibid 311; Kamala Liyanage, 'Gender Inclusive Governance: Representation of Women in National and Provincial Political Bodies in Sri Lanka' in Nizam Ahmed (ed.), *Women in Governing Institutions in South Asia: Parliament, Civil Service and Local Government* (Palgrave MacMillan, 2018) 117–137.
76 Poornima Vyasulu and Vinod Vyasulu, 'Women in Panchayati Raj: Grass Roots Democracy in Malgudi' (1999) 34(52) *Economic and Political Weekly* 3677–3686.

77 Aarti Garg, 'Empowerment of Elected Women Representatives in Panchayati Raj Institutions: A Case Study of Moradabad Division' (2017) 5(4) *Voice of Research* 46–50, 50.
78 Shahadat Hussain, 'Evaluate the Participation Level of Elected Women Representatives (EWRs) in Panchayati Raj Institutions and Challenges Faced by Them: A Study of Kadwa Block in Katihar of Bihar' (2015) 4(1) *Social Work Chronicle* 60–75, 66. Hussain, however, found that elected Muslim women rarely attended meetings, and this has not changed since the introduction of the gender reservation.
79 Shashi Kaul and Shradha Sahni, 'Study on the Participation of Women in Panchayati Raj Institution' (2009) 3(1) *Studies on Home and Community Science* 29–38.
80 Nirmala Buch, *Women's Experience in New Panchayats: The Emerging Leadership of Rural Women* Occasional Paper No 35, 2012, 1–25, 20–24; Pamela Singla, *Women's Participation in Panchayati Raj: Nature and Effectiveness, a Northern India Perspective* (Rawat Publications, 2007); Arati Behera and Smita Nayak, 'Revisiting Women Empowerment in Rural Local Governing Institutions: India's Tryst with Gender Just Local Governance' (2018) 7(7) *Global Journal for Research Analysis* 21–25, 22.
81 Ibid Buch.
82 P. Raghu, 'A Study on the Women Empowerment through Self Help Groups in Ezhilur Panchayat, Tiruvarur District' (2017) 1(4) *International Journal of Current Humanities and Social Science Researches* 28–32; Sanchita Hazra, 'Women Participation in Panchayat Raj in West Bengal: An Appraisal' (2017) 62(2) *Economic Affairs* 347–351, 350.
83 Nirmala Buch, *From Oppression to Assertion: Women and Panchayats in India* (Routledge, 2013) 97.
84 Ibid.
85 Devin Joshi and Timothy Rakkee, 'Long-Term Impacts of Parliamentary Gender Quotas in a Single-Party System: Symbolic Co-option or Delayed Integration?' (2018) *International Political Science Review* 1–17.
86 Sonia Palmieri, *Gender Sensitive Parliaments: A Global Review of Good Practice* (Interparliamentary Union, 2011).
87 Ibid.
88 Devin Joshi and Kara Kingma, 'The Uneven Representation of Women in Asian Parliaments: Explaining Variation across the Region' (2013) 12(4) *African and Asian Studies* 352–372.
89 Rituparna Bhattacharyya, 'Street Violence against Women in India: Mapping Prevention Strategies' (2016) 10(3) *Asian Social Work and Policy Review* 311–325; Aparna Parikh, 'Politics of Presence: Women's Safety and Respectability at Night in Mumbai, India' (2018) 25(5) *Gender, Place and Culture* 695–710.
90 Ratika Thakur, Anil Sinha and R. Pathak, 'Khap Panchayats in Transition with Contemporary Times: An Anthropological Evaluation' (2015) 15(1) *South Asian Anthropologist* 9–14, 10.
91 Ramesh Kumar, 'Emerging Conflicts between Panchayati Raj Institutions and Khap Panchayats in Haryana' in E. Venkatesu (ed.) *Democratic Decentralization in India: Experiences, Issues and Challenges* (Routledge, 2016) 188–233.
92 Vasuda Nagaraj, 'Local and Customary Forums: Adapting and Innovating Rules of Formal Law' (2010)17(3) *Indian Journal of Gender Studies* 429–450, 432.
93 Ibid.
94 Kanato Chophy and Avitoli G Zhimo, 'Naga Tribal Councils: A. Formidable Political Force' (2018) 53(32) *Economic and Political Weekly* 18–21, 19.
95 Ibid.
96 Matthias Kötter, Röder Tilmann, Gunnar Schuppert and Rüdiger Wolfrum, *Non-State Justice Institutions and the Law. Decision-Making at the Interface of Tradition, Religion and the State* (Palgrave MacMillan, 2015).
97 Rosemary Dzuvichu, 'Gender and Livestock in Nagaland' in Govind Kelkar and Maitreyi Krishnaraj (eds.), *Women, Land and Power in Asia* (Routledge, 2013) 175–177.

8

RIGHT TO ECONOMIC EMPOWERMENT

Introduction

This chapter focusses on women's right to economic empowerment. It examines both the organised economic sector, which includes employment that is subject to income tax and formal business structures, and the unorganised economic sector which includes informal employment that is not subject to income tax and informal businesses (small and large) that are not licenced or incorporated. India placed a low 142 out of 145 countries in the 2018 global gender gap report for economic participation and opportunities,[1] with an overall labour force participation rate for women of only 24 percent.[2] The economic empowerment of women, as well as meeting state obligations under international instruments to achieve gender equality, would also benefit the Indian economy;[3] reduce poverty, inequality and social exclusion[4] and increase the health and education of children.[5] The chapter assesses the extent to which women's human rights principles, particularly those articulated in article 11 of *CEDAW*, and women's human rights theories have been or could be utilised to advance the economic empowerment of women through, first, examination of women's rights in employment in the organised economic sector, second, women's participation in India's five formal business structures and, third, women's participation in the unorganised economic sector, overwhelmingly the most significant source of women's independent income. We examine the challenges faced by women in all three economic sectors as workers and entrepreneurs and identify strategies for women to generate and maintain independent income streams.

The chapter begins in 8.2 by outlining, in general terms, the obligations placed on India through its accession or ratification of international instruments to advance women's economic empowerment. Section 8.3 examines women's participation in employment in the organised sector, focussing on equal pay for work of equal value; maternity, paternity and parental leave and sexual harassment and protective employment legislation as examples to showcase the role of women's human rights principles and theories in advancing women's economic empowerment. Section 8.4 focusses on women in formal business structures. We argue that while participating in formal business structures can enhance women's economic empowerment, many challenges face women in this sector, particularly in relation to licensing, incorporation and access to finance. Section 8.5 focusses on the unorganised economic sector where most women are located. We argue that while the organised sector is the most effective location for women's economic empowerment, it is unrealistic to recommend moving women into that sector in large numbers. Instead we argue for the expansion of the rights and protections afforded to women in the organised sector into the unorganised sector.

Economic empowerment: obligations of human rights law

This section examines the obligations, in general terms, to advance women's economic empowerment created by the key international instruments in the human rights framework to which India is a party. The *ICCPR* provides general agreements on the right to equality before the law and the equal protection of the law. The *ICESCR*, however, provides a number of specific agreements relevant to the economic empowerment of women. Article 7 requires state parties to ensure all workers receive 'fair wages and equal remuneration for work of equal value without distinction of any kind, in particular women being guaranteed conditions of work not inferior to those enjoyed by men, with equal pay for equal work'; to provide 'safe and healthy working conditions' and to ensure 'equal opportunity for everyone to be promoted in his employment to an appropriate higher level, subject to no considerations other than those of seniority and competence.' Article 9 requires state parties to 'recognise the right of everyone to social security.' India has ratified six of eight core International Labour Organisation (ILO) Conventions, including the *Equal Remuneration for Men and Women Workers for Work of Equal Value*,[6] and the *Discrimination (Employment and Occupation) Convention*.[7] India has not ratified the *Domestic Workers Convention*,[8] an important convention protecting the rights of domestic workers.

In article 11, however, *CEDAW* contains the most detailed obligations in relation to women's economic empowerment, although it has a primary focus of women's employment in the organised sector. We examine the obligations of article 11 on equal pay for work of equal value, maternity, paternity and parental leave, sexual harassment and protective legislation in detail in the following sections. In brief, however, article 11(1) of *CEDAW* obligates state parties to take all appropriate measures to eliminate discrimination against women in the field of employment in order to ensure that women have, on a basis of equality with men, access to the same rights, opportunities, choices and benefits. Discrimination against women in employment, particularly in relation to their reproductive and child-rearing roles, continues to hinder women in India from achieving equality in employment. The importance of incorporating anti-discrimination provisions in employment legislation was highlighted in the BPA, which calls upon 'governments, employers, employees, trade unions and women's organisations to prohibit direct and indirect discrimination on grounds of sex, marital or family status, in relation to access to employment, conditions of employment, including training, promotion, health and safety, as well as termination of employment and social security of workers'.[9] In addition to a prohibition on discrimination, adequate sanctions and remedies for breaches are required to ensure the effectiveness of such provisions. Temporary special measures are specifically recommended by the *CEDAW* Committee in GR 5 on temporary special measures and 25 on temporary special measures for the advancement of women in employment and other income-producing activities.[10]

Article 11(1)(a) of *CEDAW* obligates state parties to ensure 'the application of the same criteria for selection in matters of employment.' Discriminatory advertising or the application of different criteria for job selection (such as marital status) can perpetuate sex-role stereotypes or hinder women from achieving equality in the field of employment. For example, many job advertisements in Indian media openly request applications from a 'beautiful, mature female', or a female with a 'smart, bold and good personality'.[11] Article 11(1)(c) of *CEDAW* obligates state parties to take all appropriate measures to ensure that women, on an equal basis with men, have the right and the opportunity to 'receive vocational training and retraining, including apprenticeships, advanced vocational training and recurrent training'.

Article 11(2)(c) of *CEDAW* obligates state parties 'to encourage the provision of the necessary supporting social services to enable parents to combine family obligations with work responsibilities and participation in public life, through promoting the establishment and development of a network of childcare facilities.' Also highlighting the importance of the provision of childcare, the Beijing Platform recommends that governments provide 'high quality, flexible and affordable childcare services which take into account the needs of working men and women'.[12] The provision of universally available, reliable and affordable child care is linked to gender equality, because without it, women are unable to work or to access educational opportunities due to their continuing role as caregivers of children. Research comparing countries with publicly funded universal childcare with those that have not has indicated greater gender equality has been achieved in the former.[13] This is indicated by lower poverty rates amongst single mothers,[14] a smaller disparity between men and women in the amount of time spent on paid work and housework,[15] higher rates of women's employment and child care usage[16] and a smaller gap between the pay rates of men and women.[17]

While article 11 of *CEDAW* provides clear standards of women's human rights in the area of formal paid employment in the organised sector, it does not provide guidance on women's economic empowerment through business ventures. The United Nations Guiding Principles on Business and Human Rights do, however, provide some helpful standards.[18] Although they are focussed primarily on making businesses accountable for how they conduct their business rather than the economic empowerment of women, the principles can be read and understood in the context of women's lives. There is also little guidance in the human rights framework on how to increase women's rights in the unorganised sector, other than moving them to the organised sector, which is unrealistic in the Indian context.

Employment in the organised sector

This section considers women's employment in the organised sector. Employment is defined for the purposes of this section as when there is an agreement between an employer and an employee that the employee will provide certain services for remuneration. Employment in the organised sector means employment with regular ongoing wages recognised as income sources and on which income taxes must be paid. Most women with an independent income stream are not in the organised sector. Indeed, only 13.4 percent of employed women are in the organised sector, with the public sector as the largest employer, employing 70 percent of those women.[19] Women's employment has been declining as the growing mechanisation in agriculture replaces many of the activities that women were typically employed in, such as threshing and winnowing. The increasing demand for skilled labour in the manufacturing sectors is also excluding women, who are uncompetitive because of lower education levels.[20] Women are much less likely than men to work as employers or to occupy the senior positions in organisations and institutions.[21] Women, because of the gendered division of labour, bear a double burden as they continue to be responsible for domestic work in the home and are unable to sustain the working hours and responsibility of higher-paying work.[22] The following subsections use selected illustrative examples – equal pay for work of equal value; maternity, paternity and parental leave; sexual harassment and protective legislation – to explore the rights of women in the organised economic sector.

Equal pay for work of equal value

Defining equal pay for work of equal value

Equal pay means that women and men are paid the same wages for the same work. For example, if a woman and a man are employed as shop assistants doing the same job, equal pay means they are both paid at the same rate. Differentiation in the rate of pay for women undertaking the same jobs as men can be traced to the notion of the 'family wage' (or the 'living wage'), which was enshrined in legislation in many countries early in the twentieth century, including India.[23] Family wage legislation fixed men's wages above women's on the basis that men were typically the breadwinners, and therefore, since wages were a payment for reproductive as well as productive labour, men should be paid to support a wife and children.[24] If women worked, their income was considered supplementary to the main income of the male breadwinner and therefore justifiably less than a man's wage. The family wage, which supported a gendered division of labour, is no longer considered appropriate in a modern employment law framework, and accordingly a provision was included in the *Constitution of India* 1950 (Constitution) in article 39(d) of the Directive Principles of State Policy which requires the state to 'direct the policy towards securing that there is equal pay for equal work for both men and women.' This general provision in the Constitution was strengthened by the *Equal Remuneration Act* 1976 (*Equal Renumeration Act*), which provides that: 'No employer shall pay to any worker, employed by him in an establishment or employment, remuneration, whether payable in cash or in kind, at rates less favourable than those at which remuneration is paid by him to the workers of the opposite sex in such establishment or employment for performing the same work or work of a similar nature.'[25] Penal provisions with a penalty for violating the equal pay provision of a fine between 10,000 and 20,000 IR, imprisonment for three months to one year or both supports the equal pay mandate. For second and subsequent offences, imprisonment can extend to two years.

Equal pay for work of equal value, however, requires more than equal pay; rather, it means equating the rate of pay with the value of the work in terms of skill, effort and responsibility.[26] For example, the skills required for a servant doing gardening and small jobs outside the house (an occupation typically undertaken by men) could be argued to be similar to the skills required by a domestic servant doing cooking, cleaning and laundry inside the house (an occupation typically undertaken by women). Equal pay for work of equal value would mean that they are paid at the same rate, despite the different tasks of the two jobs. The interpretation of the phrase 'equal pay for equal work' in the Constitution and equal pay for 'work of a similar nature' in the *Equal Remuneration Act* have not, however, been interpreted in the Supreme Court as embracing a requirement for equal pay for work of equal value.[27] The court has approached the provision as requiring only that if a man and a woman are employed to do the same work, they must be paid the same rate. They have not interpreted the words 'of a similar nature' as requiring a comparison between the skills of work typically performed by women with the skills of work typically performed by men.[28]

Applying women's human rights

Women continue to earn less than men,[29] regardless of education and work experience,[30] with a significant national gender pay gap (the difference between men's and women's average wages) of 27 percent.[31] The gender pay gap reduces women's income stream and economic independence and is caused by legislative, social and cultural barriers. Employers avoid the equal pay mandate of the *Equal Renumeration Act* by dividing the kind of tasks performed between men and women,[32] but the failure of the court to interpret the Constitution and the *Equal Remuneration Act* as requiring equal pay for work of equal value also perpetuates the gender pay gap. Women are predominantly employed in industries and sectors where jobs are undervalued (often due to sex-role stereotyping) and attract lower rates of pay that do not reflect the level of skill required.[33] The misallocation of talent in the labour market, where high-ability women are in low-skilled, low-return occupations, hinders women's economic empowerment and is a significant hindrance to economic growth. In order to implement the requirement for equal treatment with respect of work of equal value,[34] we recommend that a mechanism be legislatively adopted to facilitate the comparison of the value of jobs in which women presently are predominant with those jobs that men presently predominate.[35] Such a mechanism could compare 'required level of education, skills, effort, working conditions and responsibility', and jobs similarly ranked would attract the same level of pay.[36] For example, in agriculture, weeding and transplanting (tasks performed exclusively by women) are classified as unskilled, while ploughing, sowing and harvesting (tasks performed exclusively by men) are classified as skilled and attract higher wages, although similar levels of skill and experience are required for both activities.[37] The introduction of a mechanism that properly and systematically provides equal pay for work of equal value is important to further the economic empowerment of women.

Maternity, paternity and parental leave

Defining maternity, paternity and parental leave

Maternity leave provides leave to a woman from her place of employment during pregnancy and the birthing process, recognising the biological reproductive function of women. Paternity leave provides leave to a father during and after the birth to assist the mother during childbirth and to care for the child after birth. Paternity leave specifically encourages fathers to take responsibility for the childbirth process and caring for a newborn.[38] Parental leave provides leave for either or both parents to enable them to care for the child during its first year of life (or longer). Parental leave recognises the dual and equal responsibility of both parents to care for children and, importantly, signifies that parenting is work.[39] Both paternity and parental leave encourage fathers to care for young children while parental leave encourages mothers to continue their careers in employment after childbirth. Maternity, paternity and parental leave can be paid or unpaid and must be coupled with a guarantee that the person's job will be retained until her or his return to work.

Maternity leave was introduced in 1961, providing 12 weeks of leave to women on full pay.[40] In 2017, the *Maternity Benefit Amendment Act* increased paid leave time to 26 weeks for the first two children.[41] For further children, the entitlement remains at 12 weeks.[42] The legislation is applicable to factories, mines, plantations, government establishments, shops and establishments with more than ten employees.[43] There is no legislative provision for paternity leave for private sector workers (although some businesses provide it despite the lack of legislative mandate); however, Union government civil servants are entitled to paternity leave for a period of 15 days before or up to six months from the date of delivery of the child.[44] If paternity leave is not taken within six months of the birth of the child, it lapses.[45] Workers on paternity leave are paid at a rate equal to the pay drawn immediately before the leave.[46] There are no legislative provisions requiring any employer, public or private, to provide parental leave.

Applying women's human rights

The state has an obligation to mandate that public and private employers provide maternity, paternity and parental leave. Article 11(2)(b) of *CEDAW* requires state parties to introduce maternity leave 'with pay or with comparable social benefits.' While *CEDAW* does not stipulate a rate of pay for maternity leave,[47] nor does it explicitly designate a specified period of leave, the ILO recommends a minimum of 18 weeks maternity leave in both the public and private sectors.[48] Article 11(2)(a) of *CEDAW* requires state parties to ensure that women cannot be dismissed on the grounds of pregnancy during maternity leave. The Beijing Platform also recommends that governments 'eliminate discriminatory practices by employers on the basis of women's reproductive roles and functions, including refusal of employment and dismissal of women due to pregnancy and breast-feeding responsibilities'[49]

In our view, the provisions of maternity leave, paternity leave and parental leave in the organised sector are essential for women's economic empowerment and acknowledge the unique contribution of women to India through the birthing process. The different forms of leave have different roles and functions. Maternity leave accommodates women's real biological needs in relation to the birthing process. Paid maternity leave of sufficient duration enables women to give birth, to recover from the birthing process and to breastfeed the newborn child. A survey of 1,000 working women in New Delhi found that only 18 to 34 percent of women continued to work after having a child.[50] This survey found most employers failed to provide adequate maternity and child-care support to employees, and this resulted in women resigning or taking unpaid leave as the only viable options.[51] This failure perpetuates an assumption that families are primarily supported by male earners and that women can afford to take unpaid leave because their incomes are not essential to their livelihood.[52] Accordingly, we recommend that maternity leave should be extended to all workplaces and not limited to those with ten employees or more. Opportunities for temporary workers and part-time workers are also created by maternity leave provisions.

Importantly, paternity leave and parental leave both have vital roles to play in deconstructing the gendered division of labour. Much of the variation in labour supply patterns between men and women is not related to the biological act of childbirth but to the ways in which the family and employment regimes treat mothers. Indeed, research shows that the birth of a child is a crucial moment in the crystallisation of gendered parental roles.[53] It establishes and shapes emotional ties with the child, develops gendered patterns of sharing care between women and men and influences the way care responsibilities are allocated within the family.[54] An increase in the use of paternity or parental leave by men will, therefore, have a positive impact on gender equality, while a failure to provide paid paternity and parental leave reinforces the male breadwinner model and the gendered division of labour. We argue that men's involvement in caring for children is essential for eliminating differentiated gender roles and must be supported in employment legislation. We recommend paternity and parental leave be introduced across all workplaces, public and private, accompanied by a guarantee of security to the mother's and/or the father's employment or conditions of work.

Sexual harassment

Defining sexual harassment

The *CEDAW* Committee in GR 19(18) on violence against women defines sexual harassment as 'unwelcome sexually determined behaviour such as physical contact and advances, sexually coloured remarks, showing pornography and sexual demands whether by words or actions.'[55] The Committee also states that 'sexual harassment and intimidation at work' is a form of gender-specific violence[56] and is 'discriminatory when the woman has reasonable grounds to believe that her objection would disadvantage her in connection with her employment, including recruitment or promotion or when it creates a hostile work environment'.[57] The BPA identifies sexual harassment as both a form of violence against women[58] and a barrier to their equality[59] stating 'the experience of sexual harassment is an affront to a worker's dignity and prevents women from making a contribution commensurate with their abilities.'[60] Sexual harassment in the workplace, primarily directed against women, who frequently occupy a less influential place in the labour market and are therefore vulnerable, is widespread throughout Indian workplaces as revealed in survey results.[61] For example, a survey by the Indian National Bar Association of 6,047 participants from IT, media, education, legal, medical and agriculture sectors in 2016 found that 38 percent of women workers had faced sexual harassment in their workplace,[62] 68.9 percent of whom stated they had not made a complaint due to fear, embarrassment and lack of confidence.[63] Sexual harassment is also widespread in public spaces, including on the footpaths and on public transport.[64] In Delhi, for example, a survey conducted in 2013 revealed 95 percent of women aged 16 through 49 felt unsafe in public spaces.[65] This is significant because if women are exposed to sexual harassment when they travel to work and home from work, this will have a (largely invisible) impact on their ability to participate in paid employment.

The effects of sexual harassment are economic and social at both the individual and structural levels. At the individual level, sexual harassment causes financial challenges to victims, such as lost wages, unpaid leave, and the denial of career opportunities and job loss.[66] It also causes a range of psychological and physical effects (especially if the sexual harassment is ongoing and where it is perpetrated by a supervisor, involves sexual coercion or occurs in a male-dominated setting) including anxiety, depression, low confidence and self-esteem, headaches and sleeplessness.[67] At the structural level, sexual harassment creates a hostile working environment which jeopardises safety,[68] imposes costs on organisations[69] and reduces the quality of work life for all employees.[70] It has a direct additional impact on employers because of absenteeism, low productivity, employee turnover, low morale and legal costs stemming from sexual harassment.[71] Taken together, the negative effects of sexual harassment seriously impair equality in employment and, in effect, deny women equal opportunities in the workplace.[72]

Applying women's human rights

The *CEDAW* Committee calls on state parties to condemn sexual harassment and to pursue a policy to eliminate it.[73] The strategy adopted in the Indian context by feminist advocates resulted in legal protection from sexual harassment, providing an excellent example of the application of women's human rights principles to achieve positive reform.

A campaign against the sexual harassment of women started in India in the 1970s.[74] Several women's rights organisations staged protests with little response from the state.[75] At this time, while the *Penal Code* 1860 criminalised acts which 'insulted and outraged the modesty' of a woman, there was no effective legal protection from sexual harassment.[76] The campaign against sexual harassment of women gained further momentum in the 1990s, after the gang rape of a social worker who was an employee of the state government of Rajasthan. The victim had complained to the local authorities about the harassment she experienced from men belonging to the upper caste while she was trying to stop a child marriage. The authorities ignored her complaints of harassment, which subsequently culminated in her gang rape by the upper-caste men in the presence of her husband, who was tied to a tree. In a public interest litigation action brought by women's rights organisations before the Supreme Court, they argued, using *CEDAW*, that women had a right to legal protection from sexual harassment in their place of employment.[77] Convinced by the arguments of the feminist advocates and taking note of the international obligations of India through its accession to *CEDAW*, the Supreme Court interpreted article 14 of the Constitution as requiring sexual harassment protection in both public and private places of employment. The court issued detailed guidelines that prescribed measures to be taken by employers to deal with complaints of sexual harassment, including setting up an internal complaints committee.[78] Although the guidelines were not enshrined in legislation, they were upheld in subsequent cases.[79] The implementation of the guidelines remained limited, however, as internal complaints committees were not established by many employers, and where committees were established, they rarely acted.[80]

Along with changes in the criminal law, a civil law, the *Sexual Harassment of Women at Workplace (Prevention, Prohibition and Redressal) Act* 2013 (*Sexual Harassment Act*) was eventually enacted specifically to protect women from sexual harassment and to replace the Vishaka Guidelines. The *Sexual Harassment Act* makes it unlawful to sexually harass women in the workplace. It is an example (like the *Protection of Women from Domestic Violence Act 2005*) of legislation which reflects women's human rights principles. It contains a comprehensive legislative framework prohibiting sexual harassment and providing appropriate remedies to ensure that sexually harassing behaviour is stopped and that its victims are adequately compensated for their financial loss and emotional injury. Such laws can operate as deterrents to potential harassers, while encouraging employers to introduce preventive policies.[81] Although the legal framework is comprehensive, implementation to date is slow and does not yet have community support.[82]

Protective employment legislation

Defining protective employment legislation

Protective legislation is legislation that treats women differently on the basis that they need special protection from perceived dangers they are exposed to through their employment. Typically, protective legislation restricts women from undertaking certain types of employment or working certain hours. There are a number of examples of protective legislation in India's employment laws. For example, the *Factories Act* 1948 provides that 'no woman shall be required or allowed to work in any factory except between the hours 6 A.M. and 7 P.M'. While there is some flexibility, no variation 'shall authorise the employment of any woman between the hours of 10 P.M. and 5 A.M.'[83] Another example is the *Bidi and Cigar Workers Act* 1966, which provides that no woman is allowed to work in any industrial premises except between 6 a.m. and 7 p.m.[84] While protective legislation is often presented as a substantive equality measure, it is based, however, not on biological differences but on socially constructed differences and therefore constitutes direct discrimination.

Applying women's human rights

Article 11(1)(c) of *CEDAW* obligates state parties to ensure that women have, on a basis of equality with men, the right to a free choice of profession and employment. Legislation banning women from working in certain occupations, such as manual labour; from working in mines; from working at night and from working overtime restricts women's employment,[85] contributes to lower incomes for women[86] and denies them the autonomy to control their working and economic lives.[87] While these laws were historically grounded in early ILO Conventions[88] and justified on the basis that they 'protected' women, they are now considered in the human rights discourse to be 'discriminatory, paternalistic and as stereotyping women.'[89] As Kapur puts it, protective legislation adopts an 'essentialist understanding of gender difference assuming that women are naturally weaker than man'. [90]Additionally, article 11(3) of *CEDAW* explicitly states that any 'protective legislation' should be reviewed periodically in the light of scientific and technological knowledge and should be revised, repealed or extended as necessary. Therefore, any legislation that restricts women's employment choices, unless supported by scientific evidence that provides a substantiated reason for the restriction, is discriminatory. An example of lawful protective legislation is ensuring that pregnant or breastfeeding women are not obliged to perform work which has been determined by the competent authority to be prejudicial to the health of the mother, the fetus or the child.[91]

We recommend that any employment provisions that apply only to women should be scrutinised carefully to determine whether it is a positive response to a verified biological danger or a negative discriminatory measure preventing her from participating equally in paid employment. For example, preventing a woman from working a night shift in a factory purports to protect her from the danger of being out at night and the physical exertion that a night shift would entail. A restriction on night work is likely to discourage employers from employing women, particularly in industries such as the garment industry, which requires night workers to complete an order.[92] The restriction is not based on any scientific knowledge that women are at risk if they work at night; rather, it is reflective of discriminatory stereotypes which assume that women should be at home during the night tending to their children and their homes or, alternately, that women are at risk during the night from attacks by male offenders. In the aftermath of the Delhi gang rape, a survey of 2,500 women across a number of Indian cities found that 82 percent of women reported leaving work early or before dark to ensure their safety. While assault may constitute a genuine safety risk, solutions should focus on how to prevent men from violating women, not restricting women from exercising the right to choose a profession. If there is a safety issue with traveling to and from work at night, then the state should be required to develop infrastructure to ensure adequate and safe means of public transport. All discriminatory 'protective' provisions should be removed from the legislation.

Women in business

Defining women in business

There are five formal business structures in India, as illustrated in the next table, with varying degrees of complexity in terms of establishment, monitoring and compliance. Most women who do become entrepreneurs do so in the unorganised sector and do not, and often cannot, formalise their business. Yet formal business structures provide many incentives and benefits for increasing women's economic empowerment. The benefits of business over other income stream options include greater flexibility in terms of working hours, pace of work and proximity of the job to home.[93] The advantages to women in formalising their businesses are social and fiscal.[94] In particular, formalisation can lead to increased income earning potential, financial inclusion, expanded networking and advertising opportunities, access to training and support such as financial literacy training and enhanced market opportunities, both domestic and international.[95] Importantly, it can lead to greater access to loans, grants and credit because banks require formalisation for lending, and grants from government and donor agencies typically require a formal business structure.[96] Further, formalisation provides access to employment and social protection laws and to public goods and services, such as electricity and a clean water supply.[97] Finally, formal businesses can enforce rights and contracts in court and issue receipts for transactions, expanding the customer base.[98]

A sole proprietorship is the simplest business structure. It is a business run by one person who retains all the profits but who is also fully responsible for any losses. A sole proprietor is taxed at the same rate as an individual employee. A bank account is all that is technically required to establish a sole proprietorship. However, to open a bank account, a sole proprietor must register a business name, unless the business name is the person's own name. For example, if the sole proprietor's name is Agarwal and the business is called 'Agarwal Beautician', then there is no requirement to register a business name. A permanent account number, a unique ten-digit alphanumeric identity allotted to each taxpayer by the income tax department under the supervision of the Central Board of Direct Taxes, is also required to open a business bank account and to facilitate the payment of taxes. Finally, there are different licences or registration requirements, depending on the nature of the business. For example, if the new business is a restaurant, hotel or a shop, it must be registered and a fee paid.[99] A restaurant may additionally require a food safety licence, a certificate of environmental clearance and a health trade licence.

A partnership is a business structure where two or more individuals agree on the level of risks they share and the pool of resources they contribute. Like a sole proprietorship, a partnership is easy to form since no complex business formalities are required. Indeed, the requirements are the same as for a sole proprietorship. Additionally, although optional, a partnership deed may be drawn up which sets

TABLE 8.1 Categories of Formal Business Structure

Type of Business	*Key Features*	*Main Requirements*
Sole Proprietorship	A one-person company, where the business and the owner are the same. The owner bears all the risks and liabilities	• Register business name if not own name • Business licence required (different licences for different industries with different fees) • Tax registration (PAN) • Bank account
Partnership	An arrangement between two or more individuals on the level of risks they share, liability sharing and the pool of resources they contribute.	• Register business name • Business licence required (different licence for different industries with different fees.) • Tax registration (PAN) • Bank account. • Register partnership (not mandatory)
Limited Liability Partnership	A partnership where each partner is protected from personal liability.	• Obtain digital signature for the partners • Apply for the director identification number • Register partnership name • Apply to Registrar of Companies for certificate of incorporation • File for a PAN • File LLP agreements • Open a bank account
Private Limited	A voluntary association of two or more people (limited to fifty), who have limited liabilities; the transfer of shares is limited to its members and excludes the public.	• Incorporation • Bank account • Tax registration (PAN) • Obtain a PAN • Register with Employees Provident Fund
Public Limited	An association of seven or more individuals, who can raise capital by selling shares to the general public, who have limited liabilities	• Incorporation • Bank account • Tax registration (PAN) • Register with Employees Provident Fund

out the respective rights and obligations of the partnership, including the duration of the partnership, the capital contribution by each partner and the profit-sharing ratio among the partners. The partnership deed should be filed with the Registrar of Firms to protect all partners, which will, once satisfied it meets all requirements, record it in the Register of Firms and issue a certificate of registration.[100]

A limited liability partnership is a business structure where each partner is protected from personal liability, except to the extent of their capital contribution, allowing individual partners to be shielded from joint liability created by another partner's wrongful business decisions or misconduct.[101] There is no requirement of minimum capital, and while at least two members are required initially, there is no limit on the maximum number of partners.[102] The registration process requires digital signatures for the partners, tax registration, a bank account, a director identification number and name approval. Once approved, the Registrar of Companies issues a certificate of incorporation.[103]

A company is a more complex business structure which can be public or private. A private company is a voluntary association of between two and two hundred people.[104] A public company is a voluntary association of seven or more people, but there is no maximum number of members.[105] Incorporation, both public and private, offers advantages over a sole proprietorship or partnership. A company is vested with corporate personality and becomes a legal person with liability. A company can therefore sue and be sued in its own name, but no individual member is liable for the actions of the company. Shares can be easily transferred. However, while a public company can transfer shares to any member of the public, a private company can only transfer shares to other members. No members, not even all the members collectively, can claim ownership of any of the company's assets. Moreover, the members of a company do not have the right to participate in the day-to-day management of the business of the company. Instead, decision-making in a company is vested in a board of directors, and all policy decisions are taken at the board level on a majority basis.[106] As a company is an independent legal person, its existence is not affected by the death, retirement or insolvency of any of its members.

To incorporate a business and form a company, public or private, the business must be registered in accordance with the *Companies Act* 2013. To obtain registration, an application must be filed to the registrar, including, amongst other information, the memorandum and articles of the company, a declaration that all the requirements of the legislation have been complied with and an affidavit from each of the subscribers and first directors that they not been found guilty of any fraud or misfeasance.[107] If the registrar is satisfied that all requirements are met, the name of the company is entered in the Register of Companies, and a certificate of incorporation is issued.[108]

Applying women's human rights

Establishing a formal business structure or formalising an informal business can be advantageous to entrepreneurs. All formal businesses, for example, can register, electronically, as a micro, small or medium enterprise under the *Micro Small and Medium Enterprises Act* 2006 and receive benefits from both the Union and the state governments.[109] Benefits include easier access to bank loans (priority sector lending), lower rates of interest, access to the excise exemption scheme and exemption under direct tax laws. State and Union Territories' governments also have developed their own package of facilities and incentives for businesses registered under the act. Some of the benefits provided include development of specialised industrial estates, tax subsidies, power tariff subsidies and capital investment subsidies.[110]

There are 8.05 million businesses in India managed by women;[111] however, most of those businesses are in the unorganised sector.[112] Of businesses which are formalised only 14 percent are run by women entrepreneurs. Only 1 percent of businesses are incorporated, and only 2.8 percent of incorporated businesses are run by women.[113] Women entrepreneurs who have formalised their businesses are most active in the services, such as wearing apparel; education; health and other personal services, such as beauty treatment, hairdressing, cleaning, textile cleaning and household maintenance, which have low capital requirements.[114] Male entrepreneurs, by contrast, are dispersed in more diverse activities.[115] While both men and women face challenges in formalising, operating and growing their businesses, women face significant gendered challenges.

First, finances are required to start up a business, to formalise a business and to grow a business.[116] Women entrepreneurs experience greater difficulties than men in accessing bank loans and other sources of capital.[117] In order to be granted a loan from a formal lending institution such as a bank, a person must have collateral that can be secured as a guarantee if the loan is not paid back. The collateral most readily accepted by banks and other formal lending institutions is land, land leases or an already-operating and successful business. If other collateral is accepted, on average, collateral equivalent to 215 percent of the loan amount is required. Women are unlikely to be able to meet these requirements. In rural areas, according to the latest Human Development Survey, 83 percent of agricultural land is inherited by male family members and less than 2 percent by female family members.[118] A regionwide examination of the data indicates that women own 28 percent of land in the hills and 8 percent in the east and west regions.[119] Women do not inherit property in urban areas due to unequal inheritance laws, and even if the laws are equal, such as for Hindus, women do not enforce their rights because of social norms.[120] Additionally, property purchased during marriage is typically in the name of the husband.[121] As well as requiring collateral, financial institutions are more likely to lend money to individuals and enterprises with a high and predictable income. Indeed, most formal financial products remain high end, limited to urban, rich educated males employed in the organised sector.[122] As well as requiring collateral and income stability, the complicated procedure of bank loans may deter many women who aspire to be entrepreneurs. A typical small business loan requires up to 27 steps for the bank and nine meetings with the client to ensure compliance with formal finance documentation and creditworthiness requirements. As a result, the largest source of credit in India is friends and family (20 percent), compared to bank credit (8 percent). Women, however, are less likely to get family support because of gendered perceptions of their ability to run a business and the expectation that they should be focussed on their domestic responsibilities.[123] Women who cannot source capital from formal lending institutions or family and friends are more likely to borrow from a moneylender who charges exorbitant rates. Indeed, few enterprises run by women are financed by money from a formal financial institution.[124]

We recommend improvements to secured transactions law to better enable women to access finance. Secured transactions legislation can ease access to finance for women by enabling personal property, including tangible and intangible property, such as jewellery, livestock, vehicles, household assets and other movable assets, to be pledged as collateral. The *Securitisation and Reconstruction of Financial Assets and Enforcement of Security Interest Act* 2002 was recently amended to broaden the scope of movable property that can be used as collateral, as well as enhancing enforcement provisions, providing lenders with greater security to encourage them to promote the use of movable property as a security for loans.[125] While positive, further changes could expand the definition of movable assets.

Second, an adequate level of literacy is required to navigate the procedures of formalisation, such as filling out forms, opening bank accounts and registering for a tax number. Once a business if formalised or a company is incorporated, there are formal compliance requirements which also require adequate literacy. Proper bookkeeping must be maintained and taxes paid. A company must keep financial records[126] and produce an annual financial statement,[127] which must be lodged with the registrar.[128]

Third, many women lack financial literacy – the education and understanding of knowing how money is made, spent and saved, as well as the skills and ability to use financial resources to make decisions. They may not, as a consequence, be confident about handling money, managing accounts and doing the banking.[129] A bank account is required for all business structures, which requires a deposit and identity documents. Borrowers must also be able to travel to the bank. There is a strong link between women's financial inclusion and their performance as entrepreneurs in developing countries.[130]

Fourth, women are likely to have less access to the markets and business networks that men rely on to expand their business. Indeed, research suggests that male clients may question women's expertise and capacity to run a business because of both their family responsibilities and their perceived inexperience in the business world.[131]

Fifth, social norms locate women in the private sphere of home rather than the market, and although in poorer families, the need to increase the family income enables women to operate small businesses in the unorganised sectors, managing a business in a formal capacity challenges the gendered division of labour more directly.[132]

Finally, formalising a business means paying income taxes, compliance with labour and environmental regulations and the possibility of government officials demanding bribes.[133]

Women in the unorganised sector

Defining the unorganised sector

The unorganised sector is the part of an economy that is not taxed or monitored by the state. Unlike the organised sector, activities in the unorganised sector are not included in the gross national product and gross domestic product of a country. It is also the sector which is not entitled to and does not receive the protections of the organised economy.[134] In India, a significant proportion of economic activity occurs in the unorganised economic sector as opportunities for salaried employment are scarce, particularly in impoverished rural areas.[135] Although exact figures are hard to obtain, estimates are that 92 to 94 percent of workers nationwide are in the unorganised sector, of which women comprise 32 percent (approximately 118 million women).[136] The participation rate in the unorganised sector is higher among rural women (27 percent) than urban women (10 percent).[137] Women work as piece rate workers, self-employed workers in informal enterprises, in family businesses, as casual workers without fixed employers and sub-contract workers at home. They do arduous work as domestic servants (usually lower-caste and lower-class women), as part-time helpers in households, in tanneries (setting, parting and drying), in match and beedi industries, as rag pickers, block printers, coolies, beauticians, construction labourers and garment workers.[138] Street vendors, of whom 40 percent are women and 30 percent are the sole earning members in their families, are the most varied category. It includes women engaged in selling commodities such as broomsticks, cane baskets, utensils, petty cosmetics, bangles, vegetables and tea and snacks in roadside tea stalls.[139]

Many women work in agriculture, and, although the significance of the roles played by women as workers is well established, their rights to agricultural property remain minimal. According to the latest census of 2011, only 13.5 percent of land holdings are in the names of women even though 65 percent of women rely on agriculture as their primary source of income.[140] The lack of titled land prevents women working in agriculture from accessing a number of benefits, including institutional credit and federal agricultural benefits.[141]

Women workers in the unorganised sector face gender discrimination and low wages that are often insufficient to meet minimum living standards; have hazardous working conditions; have no basic services such as first aid, drinking water and sanitation at the work sites and earn dramatically less than men.[142] They are excluded from employment legislation protections[143] and do not receive paid leave, pensions, bonuses, medical support, health insurance, maternity leave benefits, compensation after accidents or the right to raise and lodge grievances.[144] Most have no fixed working hours. For example, beauticians set their own working hours, vendors may stay open until 10 p.m. at night, garment workers and domestic workers have set workloads rather than set hours and rag pickers work until their bags are full. Many workers leave their dwellings at about 6 a.m. and come back home at 9 p.m.[145] Instead of police protection, many workers in the unorganised sector pay bribes to police in order to conduct their business. For example, a project that researched women train hawkers in Mumbai, who buy beauty and make-up items, decorative accessories, stationary, brushes, toiletries, cutlery and food and sell them on the trains, making a profit of two or three rupees on each item, found that because their activity was unlawful, in order to operate, the women had to pay the police regular bribes to prevent arrest.[146]

Applying women's human rights

The organised sector provides legislative protection for women employees and business owners. However, employment in the organised sector is reducing not growing, and most women working in paid employment or running informal businesses will remain in the unorganised sector. We argue, therefore, that increasing legal rights for women in the unorganised sector is the most important focus for women's economic empowerment.[147] The challenge, therefore, is to replicate the positive aspects of the organised sector in the unorganised sector including recognition, regularity and adequacy of wages, social protection, police protection and voice in public affairs and in relation to the issues that concern them. Three illustrative examples of measures that could increase women's rights in the unorganised sector are first, a national minimum wage, second, legislation that regulates the employment of temporary workers to ensure they receive the same protections as workers in the organised sector and, finally, using special provision to create targeted opportunities for women in the unorganised sector.

National minimum wage

The 'law of one price', the central organising principle for labour economists' approach to wage determination, assumes that, in a competitive unregulated labour market, workers with similar skill levels and who are employed in similar jobs will receive the same wage.[148] The introduction of a national statutory minimum wage, the lowest amount a worker can be legally paid for her or his work regardless of the industry, is contrary to that theoretical position. India does not have a national minimum wage. Rather, each state sets minimum wage rates for particular occupational categories, regardless of whether the jobs are in the organised or unorganised sector, with the end result that there are more than 1,000 different minimum wage rates across India.[149]

A national minimum wage, however, has proven to significantly increase women's incomes in other countries, particularly women in lower pay brackets, and to reduce the gender pay gap overall.[150] It is much more effective than the form of industry-specific minimum wage approach that India currently employs.[151] This is because women are overwhelmingly employed in the lowest-paying industries. They are limited in their job choice because their family responsibilities often mean they are only able to take jobs within a certain geographical area or with certain working hours because they are less educated and because they experience discrimination in many aspects of employment.[152]

Employers will not pay a living wage in the absence of a legislated requirement. A minimum wage creates a basic income regardless of the industry or the job and may reduce disparities between male- and female-dominated sectors and workplaces and thereby contribute to the narrowing of the gender pay gap. The higher the minimum wage, the greater the economic independence of women and the corresponding reduction of women's dependence.[153]

However, research also suggests that while a minimum wage will raise the relative average earnings of women in the organised sector, it is less clear that the same positive effect will flow to women working in the unorganised sector.[154] While we recommend the introduction of a national uniform minimum 'living' wage, most women workers are in the unorganised economy and, therefore, enforcement mechanisms must support such a measure. We recognise enforcement would be challenging due to the huge numbers and remote locations of workers in this sector but recommend sanctions, regular inspections and compliance incentives. Ensuring that workers receive, upon complaint, any outstanding amounts due to them, is another effective measure to encourage compliance.[155]

Protecting temporary workers

Many women are employed as temporary workers. Most of the benefits and protections of labour law, however, are offered to permanent, but not temporary, workers. For example, the *Factories Act* 1948 provides that a factory that employs more than 30 permanent women workers must have a creche.[156] Maternity benefits must also be paid to permanent, but not temporary, women workers.[157] To avoid the mandate to provide a creche and to pay maternity leave, many factories employ women on a temporary basis, enabling them to avoid providing protections offered to permanent workers.[158] Removing the legislative distinction between permanent and temporary workers would be an important measure towards the protection of temporary workers. Additionally, there are considerable economic benefits to protecting temporary workers (who are often women) and offering them greater stability as they are likely to be more productive if their children are cared for and they have guaranteed maternity leave.[159] India's temporary workforce is governed by the *Contract Labour (Regulation and Abolition) Act* 1970. A recent case held that the principle of 'equal pay for equal work' in the Constitution and the *Equal Renumeration Act* did apply to temporary workers, provided they had similar duties and responsibilities to regular employees holding similar positions. The court held that, otherwise, it would be 'an act of exploitative enslavement, emerging out of a domineering position' and 'oppressive, suppressive and coercive, as it compels involuntary subjugation.'[160] A similar argument could be used to extend other protections to temporary workers, including maternity leave, anti-discrimination provisions and protection against dismissal.

Special provision example

The Mahatma Gandhi National Rural Employment Scheme, established by the *Mahatma Gandhi National Rural Employment Guarantee Act* 2005, provides an example of a special provision designed to provide access to the organised sector for rural workers, either unemployed or working in the unorganised sector. Organised and funded by the Union but implemented at the state level, the scheme guarantees every rural household 100 days of unskilled manual work at a set wage.[161] Women's economic empowerment is a specific goal of the scheme, with a third of the workdays reserved for women.[162] To facilitate female participation, the jobs should be no more than five kilometers from home,[163] and if there are five or more children under six accompanying the women workers, one of the women will be paid to care for the children instead of doing the manual labour.[164] Women are also involved in monitoring progress through a one-third reservation for women on the Central Council, which monitors the scheme.[165] The scheme initially included 200 districts, but it reached all districts by 2008.[166] The scheme is underscored by the recognition that special provisions are necessary to secure an independent income stream for women who are disproportionately affected by the multiple dimensions of poverty and vulnerability.[167]

We view the scheme as demonstrating a transformative approach to achieving gender equality. The scheme guarantees employment as a right, and the gender reservation specifically guarantees employment as a women's human right.[168] It gives women an opportunity to work and to become more confident outside the home.[169] It provides women with an independent income, which is paid at the same rate as men and must be paid into a bank account in their own name.[170] It provides work experience for women, increasing their opportunities to gain other work outside the scheme. It also challenges and potentially breaks the social norms that compel women to focus on unpaid work in the home rather than paid work outside the home.[171]

There are limitations to the scheme, which could be strengthened by the application of women's human rights principles. While challenging the gendered division of labour by requiring the prioritisation of work for at least one third of women, the scheme offers work without reducing women's domestic responsibilities. Many women who participate in the scheme are still expected to perform all the domestic work in the home.[172] Offering a bonus payment to workers who have domestic responsibilities would recognise that unpaid work in the home is work. Additionally, childcare is targeted at women workers (rather than all workers) also reaffirming the gendered division of labour and women's responsibility for children.[173] More flexible working hours in recognition of women's domestic and care responsibilities and the option of different types of work according to gendered life-cycle vulnerabilities such as pregnancy could assist in strengthening the scheme. Training could enable women to participate in the skilled work offered under the scheme. Although money is paid into the worker's bank account, studies have shown that women are pressured to give their earnings to the household head (either father-in-law or mother-in-law),[174] and information and training might provide women with a greater capacity to control their own incomes. Finally, there are also examples of corruption, for which strong provisions should be introduced.[175]

Conclusion

This chapter has focussed on women's right to economic empowerment. Increasing women's control of resources and independent income, even small and temporary increases, in turn can increase their bargaining power in households. Most women are located in the unorganised economic sector, either working as temporary workers or running small, informal businesses and are significantly disadvantaged. They do not receive the protections of labor law, police protection and health and safety protection. By contrast, women in the organised sector receive much greater protections and opportunities. Women's human rights principles, particularly those articulated in article 11 of *CEDAW*, can be utilised to increase women's independent income stream. We have provided examples of judicial decision-making, reformed legislation and the use of special measures to illustrate how women's human rights can be utilised to increase the economic empowerment of women. However, women continue to face considerable challenges in all economic sectors as workers and entrepreneurs.

Notes

1 World Economic Forum, *Global Gender Gap Report*, 2018. www.weforum.org/reports/the-global-gender-gap-report-2018 Accessed 17/4/19.
2 Ibid.
3 Amit Singh Khokhar and Bharat Singh, 'Status of Women Entrepreneurship in India' (2016) 4(5) *Asian Journal of Multidisciplinary Studies* 199–204, 199.
4 Esther Duflo, 'Women Empowerment and Economic Development' (2012) 50(4) *Journal of Economic Literature* 1051–1079.
5 Research indicates that women spend their income on nutrition, health and education for their family. Therefore, increasing women's income correlates with increasing the well-being and socio-economic status of the whole community. Farzana Afridi, Abhiroop Mukhopadhyay and Soham Sahoo, 'Female Labor Force Participation and Child Education in India: Evidence from the National Rural Employment Guarantee Scheme' (2016) 5(1) *IZA Journal of Labor and Development* 1–27, 2.
6 ILO, *Convention Concerning Equal Remuneration for Men and Women Workers for Work of Equal Value* 1951 (No 100) 34th Session (*entry into force* 23 May 1953).
7 ILO, *Discrimination (Employment and Occupation) Convention* 1958 (No 111) (*entry into force* 5 September 2013).

8 ILO, *Convention Concerning Decent Work for Domestic Workers* 2011 (No 189) (*entry into force* 5 September 2013).
9 Beijing Declaration and Platform for Action, *Fourth World Conference on Women*, 15 September 1995 (A/CONF.177/20) at [178(c)].
10 *CEDAW* Committee, General Recommendation 25: *Temporary Special Measures* 2008 (UN Doc HRI/Gen/1/Rev.9); *CEDAW* Committee, General Recommendation 5: *Temporary Special Measures* 1988 (UN Doc HRI/Gen/1/Rev.9).
11 Rahul Anand, 'Gender Stereotyping in Indian Recruitment Advertisements: A Content Analysis' (2013) 8(4) *International Journal of Business Governance and Ethics* 306–322, 316.
12 Beijing Platform, n 9, at [173].
13 Nicole Telford, 'Can Canadian Women Have It All? How Limited Access to Affordable Child Care Restricts Freedom and Choice' (2016) 8(1) *Canadian Journal of Family and Youth/Le Journal Canadien de Famille et de la Jeunesse* 153–172, 164, 168.
14 Michael Kottelenberg and Steven Lehrer, 'Targeted or Universal Coverage? Assessing Heterogeneity in the Effects of Universal Child Care' (2017) 35(3) *Journal of Labor Economics* 609–653, 647.
15 Ibid.
16 Ibid.
17 Piritta Sorsa, *Raising the Economic Participation of Women in India: A New Growth Engine?* OECD Economics Department Working Paper No 1185 (OECD Publishing, Paris, 2015) 19; Tarjei Havnes and Magne Mogstad, 'Is Universal Child Care Levelling the Playing Field?' (2015) 127 *Journal of Public Economics* 100–114.
18 Special Representative of the Secretary-General of the United Nations, *Guiding Principles on Business and Human Rights: Implementing the United Nations 'Protect, Respect and Remedy' Framework* (Office of the High Commissioner, 2011). www.ohchr.org/Documents/Publications/GuidingPrinciplesBusinessHR_EN.pdf Accessed 17/4/19.
19 Maarten Klaveren, Kea Tijdens, Hughie Williams, Melanie Ramos and Nuria Martín, *An Overview of Women's Work and Employment in India* AIAS Working Papers 90, 2010, 57. www.researchgate.net/publication/254390834_An_overview_of_women%27s_work_and_employment_in_India Accessed 17/4/19.
20 Santosh Mehrotra and Jajati Parida, 'Why Is the Labour Force Participation of Women Declining in India?' (2017) 98 *World Development* 360–380, 363.
21 Pawan Budhwar, Debi Saini and Jyotsna Bhatnagar, 'Women in Management in the New Economic Environment: The Case of India' (2005) 11(2) *Asia Pacific Business Review* 179–193, 180.
22 Kamini Dashora, 'Problems Faced by Working Women in India' (2013) 2(8) *International Journal of Advanced Research in Management and Social Sciences* 82–94, 83.
23 Dhara Gill and Bennett Matthews, 'Changes in the Breadwinner Role: Punjabi Families in Transition' (1995) *Journal of Comparative Family Studies* 255–263, 257.
24 Nancy Fraser, 'After the Family Wage: Gender Equity and the Welfare State' (1994) 22(4) *Political Theory* 591–618, 592.
25 *Equal Remuneration Act* 1976, s 4.
26 *CEDAW* Committee, General Recommendation 13, *Equal Treatment in Respect of Work of Equal Value* 1989 (UN Doc A/44/38).
27 *MacKinnon MacKenzie & Co. Ltd v. Audrey D'Costa & Anr* (1987) SCR (2) 659.
28 *Randhir Singh v. Union of India (1982).*
29 *Global Gender Gap Report* 2018 n 1.
30 Ibid.
31 Ibid.
32 Rashmi Tiwari and Shivani Tiwaris, 'Women Employment in Unorganised Sector in India: An Empirical Analysis' (2016) 35(4) *Journal of Rural Development* 645–664, 657.
33 Rohini Pande, Charity Troyer Moore and Erin Fletcher, *Women and Work in India: Descriptive Evidence and a Review of Potential Policies.* No 339 (Centre for International Development at Harvard University, 2017) 11.

34 See for example *CEDAW* Committee, General Recommendation 13: *Equal Treatment in Respect of Work of Equal Value* 1989 (UN Doc A/44/38), which supports the introduction of such a mechanism; ILO, Convention No 100 *Concerning Equal Remuneration for Men and Women Workers for Work of Equal Value* 1951 34th Session (*entry into force* 23 May 1953).
35 Ibid General Recommendation 13 at [2].
36 Charlotte Doyle, *The Revival of Pay Equity in New Zealand: The Pursuit of a Social Goal Through Law Reform* Victoria University of Wellington Legal Research Paper, Paper No 47, 2017. https://ssrn.com/abstract=3024456 Accessed 17/4/19.
37 KPMG and Federation of Indian Chambers of Commerce and Industry, *Labour in Indian Agriculture: A Growing Challenge*, 2015, 23. http://ficci.in/spdocument/20550/FICCI-agri-Report%2009-03-2015.pdf Accessed 17/4/19; Tiwari and Tiwari, above n 32, 645, 652.
38 Erin Rehel, 'When Dad Stays Home Too: Paternity Leave, Gender, and Parenting' (2014) 28(1) *Gender and Society* 110–132, 111; Thomas Johansson, 'Fatherhood in Transition: Paternity Leave and Changing Masculinities' (2011) 11(3) *Journal of Family Communication* 165–180, 176.
39 Ann-Zofie Duvander and Mats Johansson, 'What Are the Effects of Reforms Promoting Fathers' Parental Leave Use?' (2012) 22(3) *Journal of European Social Policy* 319–330, 320.
40 *Maternity Benefit Act* 1961, s 5.
41 Maternity *Benefit Amendment Act* 2017, s 3.
42 Ibid.
43 *Maternity Benefit Act* 1961, s 2.
44 *Central Civil Services (Leave) Rules* 1972, Rule 43-A and 43-AA.
45 Ibid Rule 43-A (5).
46 *Central Civil Services (Leave) Rules*, n 44.
47 The *CEDAW* Committee noted in its 'Views' in relation to a communication pursuant to the Optional Protocol (*Dung Thi Thuy Nguyen v. The Netherlands* Communication No/3/2004, 2006, 36th Session, UN Doc CEDAW/C/36/D/3/2004) that article 11(2)(b) does not use the term 'full pay' or 'full compensation for loss of income' in relation to maternity leave, 'leaving state parties with a margin of discretion.'
48 *Convention Concerning the Revision of the Maternity Protection Convention* (Revised) 1952 (*entry into force* 7 February 2002) article 4(1). India has not, however, ratified this convention.
49 Beijing Platform, n 9, at [178].
50 Madyu Tyagi, *Working Women in Industries* (Horizon Books, 2016) 136.
51 Ibid.
52 Mimi Abramovitz, *Regulating the Lives of Women: Social Welfare Policy from Colonial Times to the Present* (Routledge, 2017) 2.
53 Erin Rehel, 'When Dad Stays Home Too: Paternity Leave, Gender, and Parenting' (2014) 28(1) *Gender and Society* 110–132, 111.
54 Carmen Castro-García and Maria Pazos-Moran, 'Parental Leave Policy and Gender Equality in Europe' (2016) 22(3) *Feminist Economics* 51–73.
55 *CEDAW* Committee, General Recommendation 19: *Violence against Women* 1992, 11th Session (GR 19) (UN Doc A/47/38).
56 Ibid at [19(17)].
57 Ibid.
58 Beijing Platform, n 9, at [37].
59 Beijing Platform, n 9, at [38].
60 Ibid at [39].
61 Indian Bar Association, *Sexual Harassment at Workplace* (Prabhat Books, 2017). www.indianbarassociation.org/wp-content/uploads/2017/07/Garima-1INBAs-Book.pdf Accessed 17/4/19.
62 Ibid 12.

63 Ibid 16.
64 Mangai Natarajan, 'Rapid Assessment of "Eve Teasing" (Sexual Harassment) of Young Women during the Commute to College in India' (2016) 5(1) *Crime Science* 1–11, 5, 6.
65 Dakshita Sangwan and Amit Thakre, 'Sexual Harassment at the Workplace in Public and Private Sectors in India: A Study at National Capital Region of Delhi' (2018) 13(1) *International Journal of Criminal Justice Sciences* 29–41.
66 Heather McLaughlin, Christopher Uggen and Amy Blackstone, 'The Economic and Career Effects of Sexual Harassment on Working Women' (2017) 31(3) *Gender and Society* 333–358, 351, 352.
67 James Campbell Quick and M. McFadyen, 'Sexual Harassment: Have We Made Any Progress?' (2017) 22(3) *Journal of Occupational Health Psychology* 286–298, 292; Dakshita Sangwan and Amit Thakre, 'Sexual Harassment at the Workplace in Public and Private Sectors in India: A Study at National Capital Region of Delhi' (2018) 13(1) *International Journal of Criminal Justice Sciences* 29–42, 41.
68 Girija Borker, *Safety First: Perceived Risk of Street Harassment and Educational Choices of Women* (Girija Borker, 2017). https://girijaborker.files.wordpress.com/2017/11/borker_jmp.pdf Accessed 17/4/19. In a study of 4,000 students at Delhi University, Borker found that women are willing to choose a college in the bottom half of the quality distribution over a college in the top quintile, or a more expensive college, for a route that is perceived to be safer.
69 Paula McDonald, 'Workplace Sexual Harassment 30 Years On: A Review of the Literature' (2012) *International Journal of Management Reviews* 1–17, 4.
70 Ibid.
71 Bhavna Verma and Amit Chandra, 'Sexual Harassment at Work Place: How Far Have We Travelled' (2015) 8(2) *Gyanodaya* 45–52.
72 Beijing Platform, n 9, at [39].
73 General Recommendation 19(17), n 55.
74 Geetanjali Gangoli, *Indian Feminisms: Law, Patriarchies and Violence in India* (Routledge, 2016).
75 Ibid.
76 *Penal Code* 1860, s 354; Daphne Barak-Erez and Jayna Kothari, 'When Sexual Harassment Law Goes East: Feminism, Legal Transplantation, and Social Change' (2011) *Stanford Journal of International Law* 175–199, 178.
77 *Vishaka v. State of Rajasthan* (1997) 6 SCC 241.
78 Ibid.
79 *Apparel Export Promotion Council v. AK Chopra* (1999) 1 SCC 759. See also *Medha Kotwal Lele v. Union of India* (2013) 1 SCC 297, where the Supreme Court specifically criticised the non-observation of the Vishaka guidelines at [1].
80 Barnali Maity, 'Vishaka Guidelines: Protecting Women's Dignity at Workplace' (2016) 7(4) *Research Journal of Humanities and Social Sciences* 229–237, 235.
81 Sanjeeva Rao, 'Prevention of Sexual Harassment at Workplace: An Analysis of Recent Legislative Initiatives in India' (2016) 6(1) *IUP Law Review* 30–41; Trishala Singh, 'Prevention of Sexual Harassment of Women in the Workplace: Seeking Gender Equality at Work in India' (2016) 18(1) *Journal of International Women's Studies* 104–113.
82 Sangwan and Thakre, n 67, 42.
83 *Factories Act* 1948, s 66(1).
84 *Bidi and Cigar Workers (Conditions of Work) Act* 1966, s 25.
85 Faustina Pereira, *The Fractured Scales: The Search for a Uniform Personal Code* (Popular Prakashan, Mumbai, 2002) 9.
86 Faiza Ali, 'A Comparative Study of EEO in Pakistan, India and Bangladesh' in Mustafa F. Özbilgin and Jawad Syed (eds.), *Managing Gender Diversity in Asia: A Research Companion* (Edward Elgar Publishing, 2010) 32–53.
87 Angela John, *By the Sweat of Their Brow: Women Workers at Victorian Coal Mines* (Routledge, 2013).

88 ILO Convention No 89 *Concerning the Nightwork of Women in Industry* 1948 (*entry into force* 27 February 1951); ILO Convention No 49 *Concerning the Employment of Women in Underground Work of All Kinds* 1935 (*entry into force* 30 May 1937).
89 Fereda Banda, *Laws That Discriminate against Women* (Office of the High Commissioner for Human Rights-Women's Rights and Gender Unit, 2008) 110. https://eprints.soas.ac.uk/21222/1/laws_that_discriminate_against_women.pdf Accessed 17/4/19.
90 Ratna Kapur, 'Challenging the Liberal Subject' in Maitrayee Mukhopadhyay and Navsharan Singh (eds.), *Gender, Justice, Citizenship Development* (International Development Research Centre 2007) 116–170, 118.
91 ILO Convention No 183 *Maternity Protection Convention* 2000 (*entry into force* 7 February 2002).
92 Paramjyoti Sharma, 'Women, Labour Laws and Employment: Gap between Theory and Practice' (2016) 2(12) *International Journal of Humanities and Social Science Research* 77–81, 79.
93 Arnaud Daymard, *Determinants of Female Entrepreneurship in India* Working Paper No 1191 (OECD Economics Department, 2015) 6.
94 Anjula Gurtoo and Colin Williams, 'Women Entrepreneurs in the Indian Informal Sector: Marginalisation Dynamics or Institutional Rational Choice?' (2011) 3(1) *International Journal of Gender and Entrepreneurship* 6–22, 14.
95 Carla Marques, Carmem Leal, João Ferreira and Vanessa Ratten, 'The Formal-Informal Dilemma for Women Micro-Entrepreneurs: Evidence from Brazil' (2018) *Journal of Enterprising Communities: People and Places in the Global Economy* 1–22, 4.
96 Ibid.
97 Ibid.
98 Carla Marques, Carmem Leal and Gina Santos, 'Why Do Some Women Micro-Entrepreneurs Decide to Formalise Their Businesses?' (2017) 30(2) *International Journal of Entrepreneurship and Small Business* 241–258, 253.
99 See, for example, *Delhi Shops and Establishments Act* 1954, s 5.
100 See the *Indian Partnership Act* 1932, which governs partnerships.
101 *Limited Liability Partnership Act* 2008, s 3, s 27.
102 Ibid s 7.
103 *Limited Liability Partnership Act* 2008, s 7(6), s 11.
104 *Companies Act* 2013, s 2(68), s 3(a).
105 Ibid s 3(b).
106 Ibid chapter VII and chapter XII.
107 Ibid s 7.
108 Ibid s 7(2).
109 A micro enterprise is where investment in plant and machinery does not exceed IR 25 lakh, a small enterprise is where the investment in plant and machinery is more than INR 25 lakh but does not exceed IR 5 crore and a medium enterprise is where the investment in plant and machinery is more than IR 5 crore but does not exceed IR 10 crore.
110 Aastha Khatri, Sangeeta Sharma and Adya Tiwari, 'Entrepreneurship Development Through SHG: A Weapon for Economic Empowerment of Rural Women' (2018) 5(3) *International Journal of Advances in Agricultural Science and Technology* 58–63, 59; Munish Kapila, Anju Singla and M. L. Gupta, 'Impact of Microcredit on Women Empowerment in India: An Empirical Study of Punjab State' (2016) 2 *Proceedings of the World Congress on Engineering* 1–6, 4, 5.
111 All India Report of Sixth Economic Census, 'Highlights of Sixth Economic Census', 2016, iv. http://mospi.nic.in/all-india-report-sixth-economic-census Accessed 17/4/19.
112 Ibid.
113 Arnaud Daymard, *Determinants of Female of Female Entrepreneurship in India* Working Paper 1191, 2015, 11. www.oecd.org/officialdocuments/publicdisplaydocumentpdf/?cote=ECO/WKP(2015)9&docLanguage=En Accessed 17/4/19.

114 Amit Singh Khokhar and Bharat Singh, 'Status of Women Entrepreneurship in India' (2016) 4(5) *Asian Journal of Multidisciplinary Studies* 199–204, 203.
115 Daymard, n 115, 13.
116 Ambreena Manji, 'Eliminating Poverty? "Financial Inclusion", Access to Land, and Gender Equality in International Development' (2010) 73(6) *Modern Law Review* 985–1004.
117 Viswanath Venkatesh, Jason Shaw, Tracy Ann Sykes, Samuel Fosso Wamba and Mary Macharia, 'Networks, Technology and Entrepreneurship. A Field Quasi-Experiment Among Women in Rural India' (2017) 60(5) *Academy of Management Journal* 1709–1741, 1711.
118 Sonalde Desai and Reeve Vanneman, *India Human Development Survey-II (IHDS-II)* (Inter-University Consortium for Political and Social Research, 2011–12).
119 Ibid.
120 Klaus Deininger, Aparajita Goyal and Hari Nagarajan, *Inheritance Law Reform and Women's Access to Capital: Evidence from India's Hindu Succession Act* World Bank Policy Research Working Paper No 5338, 2010. https://ssrn.com/abstract=1625154; Harold Valera, Takashi Yamaro, Ranjitha Puskur, Prakashan, Ishika Gupta, Pheobe Ricarte and Rohini Mohan, *Women's Land Title Ownership and Empowerment: Evidence from India* (Asian Development Bank, 2018) 3. www.adb.org/sites/default/files/publication/453696/ewp-559-women-land-title-ownership-empowerment.pdf Accessed 17/4/19.
121 Carmen Deere, Abena D. Oduro, Hema Swaminathan and Cheryl Doss, 'Property Rights and the Gender Distribution of Wealth in Ecuador, Ghana and India' (2013) 11(2) *Journal of Economic Inequality* 249–265, 257.
122 Yuko Nikaido, Jesim Pais and Mandira Sarma, 'What Hinders and What Enhances Small Enterprises' Access to Formal Credit in India?' (2015) 5(1) *Review of Development Finance* 43–52.
123 Navjot Sandhu, Javed Hussain and Harry Matlay. 'Barriers to Finance Experienced by Female Owner/Managers of Marginal Farms in India' (2012) 19(4) *Journal of Small Business and Enterprise Development* 640–655.
124 Hina Shah, *Creating an Enabling Environment for Women's Entrepreneurship in India* Development Papers 1304, 2013, 12. See also Navjot Sandhu, Javed Hussain and Harry Matlay, 'Barriers to Finance Experienced by Female Owner/Managers of Marginal Farms in India' (2012) 19(4) *Journal of Small Business and Enterprise Development* 640–655, 643, which finds that only 6 percent of the overall agriculture credit goes to women.
125 *Enforcement of Security Interest and Recovery of Debt Laws and Miscellaneous Provision (Amendment Act)* 2016.
126 *Companies Act* 2013, s 128.
127 Ibid s 129.
128 Ibid s 137.
129 Andrea Hasler and Annamaria Lusardi, *The Gender Gap in Financial Literacy: A Global Perspective* (Global Financial Literacy Excellence Centre, 2017). http://gflec.org/wp-content/uploads/2017/07/The-Gender-Gap-in-Financial-Literacy-A-Global-Perspective-Report.pdf?x87657 Accessed 17/4/19.
130 Organisation for Economic Co-operation and Development (OECD), Closing the Gender Gap: Act Now (OECD, 2012) 18, 19. www.oecd.org/gender/closingthegap.htm Accessed 17/4/19; Erica Field, Seema Jayachandran and Rohini Pande, 'Do Traditional Institutions Constrain Female Entrepreneurship? A Field Experiment on Business Training in India' (2012) 100(2) *American Economic Review* 125–129, 128.
131 Natalie Sappleton, 'Gender Congruency Theory, Experience of Discrimination and Access to Finance' in Kate Lewis, Colette Henry, Elizabeth Gatewood and John Watson (eds.), *Women's Entrepreneurship in the 21st Century: An International Multi-Level Research Analysis* (Edward Elgar Cheltenham, 2014) 50–73, 54.

132 Daya Ram, Monika Singh, K. P. Chaudhary and L. Jayarani, 'Entrepreneurship Behaviour of Women Entrepreneurs in Imphal of Manipur' (2016) 13 (2) *Indian Research Journal of Extension Education* 31–35, 31.
133 Luis Dau and Alvaro Cuervo-Cazurra, 'To Formalize or Not to Formalize: Entrepreneurship and Pro-Market Institutions' (2014) 29(5) *Journal of Business Venturing* 668–686.
134 Naila Kabeer, Ratna Sudarshan and Kirsty Milward (eds.), *Organizing Women Workers in the Informal Economy: Beyond the Weapons of the Weak* (Zed Books Ltd., 2013); Pandi Devi, 'Socio-Economic Conditions of Women in Unorganised Sector in Tenkasi Taluk of Tirunelveldi District, Tamil Nadu' (2018) 8(2) *Indian Journal of Applied Research* 39–40, 39; Mummidi Thanuja and Seema Pereira, 'The Socio-Economic Problems Faced by Women Working in the Unorganised Sector' (2017) 6(9) *Indian Journal of Research* 497–498, 497.
135 Ibid Thanuja and Pereira.
136 Diptirekha Mohapatra, 'Female Workers in the Unorganised Sector in India' *International Conference on Studies in Humanities and Social Sciences*, 2015, 1–4. http://icehm.org/upload/6334ED715042.pdf Accessed 17/4/19.
137 Ibid.
138 Ibid.
139 Colin Williams and Anjula Gurtoo, 'Evaluating Women Entrepreneurs in the Informal Sector: Some Evidence from India' (2011) 16(3) *Journal of Developmental Entrepreneurship* 351–369, 355.
140 Mondira Dutta, *Capturing Women's Work* (Pentagon Press, 2010) 27–29; Itishree Pattnaik, Kuntala Lahiri-Dutt, Stewart Lockie and Bill Pritchard, 'The Feminization of Agriculture or the Feminization of Agrarian Distress? Tracking the Trajectory of Women in Agriculture in India' (2018) 23(1) *Journal of the Asia Pacific Economy* 138–155, 136, 146.
141 Ritu Dewan, 'Contextualising and Visibilising Gender and Work in Rural India: Economic Contribution of Women in Agriculture' (2016) 71(1) *Indian Journal of Agricultural Economics* 49–58.
142 Naila Kabeer, Ratna Sudarshan and Kirsty Milward (eds.), *Organizing Women Workers in the Informal Economy: Beyond the Weapons of the Weak* (Zed Books Ltd., 2013).
143 Kamala Kanta, 'Women Workers in Informal Sector in India: Understanding the Occupational Vulnerability' (2012) 2(21) *Mohapatra International Journal of Humanities and Social Science* 197–207, 202.
144 Ibid.
145 Ibid 203.
146 Delfi Chinnappan, 'Formalising the Quandary of the Informal Sector: A Study of the Female Hawkers in the Local Trains of Mumbai' (2016) 2(1) *The Rights* 1–9, 3.
147 Mondira Dutta, *Capturing Women's Work* (Pentagon Press, 2010) 170.
148 Milton Friedman, *Price Theory* (Routledge, 2017).
149 Nidhiya Menon and Yana van der Meulen Rodgers, 'The Impact of the Minimum Wage on Male and Female Employment and Earnings in India' (2017) 34(1) *Asian Development Review* 28–64, 29.
150 Mary Hallward-Driemeier, Bob Rijkers and Andrew Waxman, *Can Minimum Wages Close the Gender Wage Gap? Evidence from Indonesia* (The World Bank, 2015) 3, 4; Christina Boll, Hendrik Hüning, Julian Leppin and Johannes Puckelwald, 'Potential Effects of a Statutory Minimum Wage on the Gender Pay Gap: A Simulation-Based Study for Germany' (SOEP Papers on Multidisciplinary Panel Data Research at DIW Berlin, 2015).
151 Uma Rani, Patrick Belser, Martin Olez and Setareh Ranjbar, 'Minimum Wage Coverage and Compliance in Developing Countries' (2013) 152(3–4) *International Labor Review* 381–410, 402.
152 Jill Rubery and Damian Grimshaw, 'Gender and the Minimum Wage' in Sangheon Lee and Deirdre McCann (eds.), *Regulating for Decent Work: Advances in Labour Studies* (Palgrave MacMillan, 2011) 226–254.

153 Ibid 233.
154 Uma Rani, 'Minimum Wage Policies and Their Effects in Developing Countries: A Comparative Perspective' (2017) 60(1) *The Indian Journal of Labour Economics* 33–55.
155 Rani, Belser Olez and Ranjbar, n 148, 398.
156 *Factories Act* 1948, s 48.
157 *Maternity Benefit Act* 1961.
158 Rahu Sapkal, 'Labour Law, Enforcement and the Rise of Temporary Contract Workers: Empirical Evidence from India's Organised Manufacturing Sector' (2016) 42(1) *European Journal of Law and Economics* 157–182, 158, 177.
159 Paramjyoti Sharma, 'Women, Labour Laws and Employment: Gap between Theory and Practice' (2016) 2(12) *International Journal of Humanities and Social Science Research*, 77, 79.
160 *State of Punjab and Ors. v. Jagjit Singh and Ors* (2016) Civil Appeal No 213 of 2013 at [57].
161 *Mahatma Gandhi National Rural Employment Guarantee Act* 2005, s 3(1) and (2).
162 Ibid schedule II, 15.
163 Ibid schedule II, 18.
164 Ibid schedule II, 24.
165 *National Rural Employment Guarantee (Central Council) Rules* 2006, s 3(2).
166 Nidhi Vij, 'Empowering the Marginalized: Mahatma Gandhi National Rural Employment Guarantee Act in India' (2013) 23(1) *Human Affairs* 91–104, 96.
167 Sangeeta Krishna, 'Analysis of Gandhian Economic Philosophy MNREGA and Inclusion of Rural Poor (Women)' (2015) 3(3) *International Journal of Scientific and Innovative Research Studies* 65–75, 67, 69.
168 Rebecca Holmes and Nicola Jones, *Gender Inequality, Risk and Vulnerability in the Rural Economy: Refocusing the Public Works Agenda to Take Account of Economic and Social Risks* (Agricultural Development Economics Division, 2011) 35; Dinesh Das, 'Examining India's Mahatma Gandhi National Rural Employment Guarantee Act (MGNREGA) Its Impact and Women's Participation' (2012) 2(6) *International Journal of Social Science Tomorrow* 209–218, 210.
169 Arora Vinita, Luxmi Rani Kulshreshtha and Vrajaindra Upadhyay, 'Mahatma Gandhi National Rural Employment Guarantee Scheme: A Unique Scheme for Indian Rural Women' (2013) 3(2) *International Journal of Economic Practices and Theories* 108–114, 109, 111.
170 Beth Goldblatt, *Developing the Right to Social Security: A Gender Perspective* 2016 (Routledge, 2016) 171–179; Sony Pellissery and Sumit Kumar Jalan, 'Towards Transformative Social Protection: A Gendered Analysis of the Employment Guarantee Act of India (MGNREGA)' (2011) 19(2) *Gender and Development* 283–294, 288.
171 Goldblatt, n 170, 174.
172 Neha Tiwari and Rajshree Upadhyay, 'Constraints Faced by the Women Beneficiaries under Mahatma Gandhi National Rural Employment Guarantee Act (MGNREGA)' (2012) 6(2) *Studies on Home and Community Science* 99–102, 100, 101.
173 Manisha Nair, Proochista Ariana and Premila Webster, 'Impact of Mothers' Employment on Infant Feeding and Care: A Qualitative Study of the Experiences of Mothers Employed through the Mahatma Gandhi National Rural Employment Guarantee Act' (2014) 4(4) *BMJ Open* 1–8, 6.
174 Ibid 5.
175 L Chaarlas and J Velmurugan, 'Mahatma Gandhi National Rural Employment Guarantee Act, 2005 (MGNREGA): Issues and Challenges' (2012) 2(6) *International Journal of Physical and Social Sciences* 253–261, 258.

9

CONCLUSION

Looking forward

Women's human rights principles and theories provide an explanatory framework for understanding discrimination against women, a standard-setting resource and a tool for achieving gender equality and advancing women's rights in India. *CEDAW*'s transformative approach to equality, in particular, provides standards through which to examine domestic legal frameworks and assess the extent to which women's human rights standards are reflected. At the same time, women's human rights theories provide a framework to examine the human rights framework and its translation into domestic law from a critical, feminist standpoint. The ultimate goal of women's human rights principles and theories is to reduce and ultimately end the inequality, marginalisation and subordination of women, rural and urban, of all castes, classes and religions, throughout their life-cycle. Gender equality means that women and men have equal rights, opportunities, responsibilities and access to resources, as well as the full enjoyment of those rights, opportunities and responsibilities. It means that differences in roles and biology that may impact equal enjoyment of these rights and responsibilities are evaluated ensuring that men and women's perceptions, interests, needs and priorities are equally considered. We do not conclude or assert that women's human rights principles and theories have the capacity to fully achieve this goal, but rather we contend it is an important first step in that process. As feminists we seek our own redundancy.

The book has examined women's human rights principles and theories in different discrete substantive areas of women's lives. Women live in a diversity of ways and in a range of different places across India. All areas of inequality are, however, interrelated. Improvement in a girl's educational levels increases her economic independence as an adult. Underage marriage decreases a girl's opportunity to further her education. Violence against women reduces their economic empowerment, endangers their health, leaves them vulnerable in the home and hinders them from having voice in the political arena. Lack of political representation and participation, in turn, reduces women's ability to change the institutions and policies which lead to discrimination and marginalisation. Lack of land and inheritance rights hinders women's ability to generate an independent income, to leave violent situations and to contest discrimination in the family.

The book aimed to introduce the reader to women's human rights principles and theories. In Chapter 2, we outlined the sources of women's human rights in India, and in Chapter 3, we outlined, chronologically, the development of women's human rights theories both to critique the human rights framework and to suggest different and varied ways of utilising women's human rights principles and theories to foster change. Throughout Chapters 3 through 8, we used women's human rights principles and theories to explore a range of topics, issues and situations of inequality.

The book aimed to link women's human rights theories with transformative practice. It aspired to show that theory, as an explanatory framework, has the capacity to foster reform in the Indian domestic legislative framework, to influence judicial decision-making so that it delivers positive outcomes for individual women and in some instances women as a class and to guide policy that reflects feminist strategies and perspectives. The book used examples from many areas of women's lives to illustrate how theory, by changing the way different people in different contexts approach sex and gender inequality and discrimination, can foster and support positive change. For example, in the area of violence against women, the most fundamental example of the discrimination and inequality faced by Indian women of all castes, classes and ages, the book used the *DV Act* as an example of how local feminists utilised theoretical research on family and domestic violence to draft legislation appropriate to the Indian context. Indian feminists utilised theoretical principles that linked violence against women to women's systematic exclusion from economic and political power structures; to the differing social roles, behaviours and attributes considered appropriate for men and women and to women's lack of power to resist violence in the home or escape an abusive situation. These theoretical understandings enabled feminist advocates to persuade the state to take some responsibility for violence against women, despite its historical exclusion from the human rights framework, through the enactment of innovative legislation. The legislation includes protection orders placing responsibility on the offender to cease the violent behavior, residence orders which recognise women's vulnerability in shared households by prohibiting the offender from entering the shared residence or parts of the shared residence and child and spousal maintenance orders giving women the economic capacity to exit violent situations.

The book aimed to use the language of women's human rights principles to advance understanding of how discriminatory structures embedded within law, society and culture perpetuate and entrench women's subordinate position throughout all layers of Indian society. For example, the language of *CEDAW* has been utilised in litigation in courts throughout India by advocates with positive outcomes. In the Andhra Pradesh High Court, for example, the judiciary held that, although the restitution of conjugal rights was an action that applied equally to women and men, in practice, it impacted women disproportionately because of their powerless position within the institution of marriage and because of their lack of economic independence. Although the language of *CEDAW*'s principle of substantive equality was not directly applied, it was, nevertheless, the basis of the arguments of the advocates and ultimately accepted by the court. Similarly, in the Supreme Court, advocates argued that electoral legislation that disqualifies any person from running for election as a member of a panchayat who does not have a toilet in their home, has unpaid electricity bills or has not met certain educational standards impacts disproportionately on women and, in particular, lower caste women. Although the court did not accept this argument, the arguments are now on the public record and in the public domain and can be drawn upon by a subsequent court, perhaps favourably.

The book aimed to provide a practical guide to applying women's human rights principles and theoretical perspectives to concrete problems. There are many examples throughout the book of the application of women's human rights theories and principles to concrete problems with a positive outcome. For example, in Gujarat, the removal of stamp duty for women when they purchase property recognises that, historically, women have not been placed on land titles, despite having a joint and shared responsibility with their husbands, fathers or brothers; in the panchayat system, the introduction of 33 percent reservations for women, a special measure recommended by *CEDAW*, has dramatically increased women's voices and participation in community decision-making throughout rural India and the introduction of the *Sexual Harassment of Women at Workplace (Prevention, Prohibition and Redressal) Act* 2013, to protect women from sexual harassment at their place of work, provides a mechanism for women to lodge complaints and receive redress. There are also many examples in the book of how women's human rights principles and theoretical perspectives could be applied to concrete problems of inequality and discrimination. For example, a substantive equality approach to political representation would favour reservations for women in the state and Union Parliament; a participative approach to achieving substantive equality would support women having equal roles in religious ceremonies, such as the annual pilgrimage from Alandi to Pandharpur in Maharashtra and a 'bottom-up' approach to underage marriage through educational programmes in villages might shift the patriarchal attitudes that support the marriage of young girls.

The book aimed to illustrate how women's human rights engage the state in a way that other approaches to claims cannot. Women's human rights create duties for states – legislative, administrative, policy and programmatic. Examples include the use of *CEDAW* and other international conventions by advocates and judges in their decision-making such as in *Vishaka* and other judicial decisions. Another example is the state response to the concluding observations of the *CEDAW* Committee such as the introduction of the *Protection of Children from*

Sexual Offences Act 2012, defining different forms of sexual abuse of children, shifting the focus to the victim and away from a morality based approach and the reform of the sexual offences framework through the *Criminal Law Amendment Act* 2013, which introduced standards more reflective of women's human rights principles that uphold the autonomy, dignity and physical integrity of women.

The book aimed to develop in the reader skills of analysis, critique and argument to equip her or him to use the law as a tool of change, rather than a mechanism of subordination. It aimed to stimulate the reader to question the tensions between different interpretations of women's rights. In Chapter 2, the theory chapter, we outlined a range of theoretical approaches to the human rights framework. Some theorists argue that the principles of equality and non-discrimination, central to the human rights framework, are unhelpful for women's empowerment, while others argue that we must continue to engage with them. Although we favour the latter, we do not discount the former and encourage readers to continue to question accepted approaches and to develop new and innovative approaches to understanding and ending the subordination of women. The book aimed to stimulate the reader to evaluate the international human rights framework and its applicability to the Indian context and the specific subcultures within Indian society in all areas of women's lives. Women's human rights are universal, but how they are realised depends on the different contexts in which women live. Ultimately, we hope to move beyond two discrete categories of human beings to accept multiple ways of being, all valued equally.

INDEX